ENDURE

ENDURE

How to Work Hard, Outlast, and Keep Hammering

Cameron Hanes

St. Martin's Press
New York

Athletic and recreational hunting activities pose some risk, and readers are advised to use their own discretion in using the information contained in this book. Neither the author nor the publisher accept any responsibility for any loss, injury or damages sustained by anyone resulting from the information contained in this book.

First published in the United States by St. Martin's Press, an imprint of St. Martin's Publishing Group

Produced by the Stonesong Press, LLC
Interior design by Peter Romeo, Wooly Head Design

www.stmartins.com

The Library of Congress Cataloging-in-Publication Data is available upon request.

ISBN 978-1-250-27929-3 (hardcover)
ISBN 978-1-250-27930-9 (ebook)

Our books may be purchased in bulk for promotional, educational, or business use. Please contact your local bookseller or the Macmillan Corporate and Premium Sales Department at 1-800-221-7945, extension 5442, or by email at MacmillanSpecialMarkets@macmillan.com.

First Edition: 2022

10 9 8 7 6 5 4 3

CONTENTS

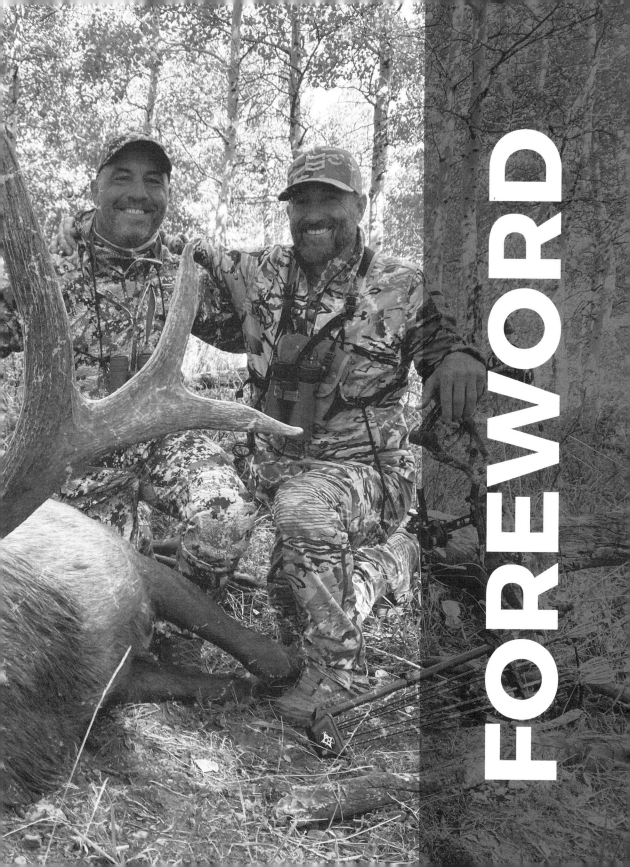

FOREWORD

Weakness haunts all men. All of them.

I'm not talking necessarily about physical weakness, like being too weak to lift heavy things. No, I'm talking about the real weakness: weakness of spirit.

Weakness of will.

The inability to take action.

That is what eats at a man. Some will tell you they don't care, and they'll make convincing arguments that they enjoy being lazy, but if you could be alone with them, offering them a pill that would give them an indomitable spirit and a tireless will to succeed, they would all take it.

All of them.

Every last fucking one of them.

Weakness haunts us all.

The times we could have done more eat at your self-esteem. They rob you of your self-respect and diminish your belief in your potential.

We've all had moments where we could have done more but didn't.

The true art of a full life is to minimize those moments when your inner bitch wins the battle and maximizes your ability to rise and grind.

There is an art to this.

Unfortunately, most of us don't treat our lives like a work of art.

The vast majority of us will leave this life like an unfinished canvas—a dim shadow of what we could have been if we had dedicated ourselves to mastering the mind, and consistently forcing the body into action.

We will apply some effort when the motivation is there, but more often than not, we find an excuse to nap and complain, rather than to push ourselves to perform past the threshold our comfort zone.

It is a very rare person who can lie down at the end of a day with full confidence that they have done their absolute best, and an even rarer person that can do that consistently, day after day, year after year, until the days of laziness and self-pity are but a distant memory, drowned out by the years and years of action and discipline.

There is an art to this, and one of the modern masters of this art is my good friend Cameron Hanes.

To the uninitiated, a quick glance into his Instagram page would reveal a bowhunter who enjoys lifting weights and running trails. But to truly understand Cam requires a much more careful and prolonged study. He is a master at one of the art forms that gets the least amount of attention—the art of the maximized life. In this work, layers upon layers of effort and discipline create a depth and texture to the life that's lost during a cursory examination by a person who doesn't know what they're seeing. It is an art form, with only the people who are also out there grinding truly understanding and appreciating how amazing this consistent effort is.

Look up the hashtag #keephammering on Instagram.

As of this writing, there're more than 449,000 posts, all of them inspired by the way Cameron Hanes lives his life.

In his world there are no days off. Days you are not getting better are days wasted.

The hammering never ends, and the inner bitch never has a chance.

Many people talk this kind of talk.

In fact, pretending you're a savage is disgustingly common.

Many of these posers will post motivational quotes on social media and even give out unsolicited advice on how to "chase your dreams" and "follow your goals," but my guess is that if you could randomly peer into their lives, you would probably catch most of these motherfuckers eating snacks and checking their posts for likes.

One of my favorite Cam Hanes quotes is "Nobody cares, work harder."

It's such a perfect statement for this day and age when grown men are using beauty filters on their Instagram pictures, and everyone is pretending they're exceptional. We live in a world today where it's never been easier to be full of shit. But on the flip side, the beauty of this time is that when you come across someone who's truly, undeniably smashing life, you appreciate it like a starving man being served up a juicy elk steak.

I'm going to describe some of the things he does, and the list is so preposterous that it seems like bullshit.

He regularly runs a marathon a day.

I read once that if you run a marathon it takes your body six months to fully recover. I don't know who wrote that, but someone needs to tell that silly bitch that there's a guy in Oregon with a full-time job with the department of water and power who runs multiple marathons every week. Sometimes he'll get up at 3:00 a.m. and run a full marathon before work. Then he'll come home from working eight hours, practice archery, lift weights, and do it all over again the next morning.

He's run multiple 100-mile races and several over 200 miles. These require days and days of running without rest. Tune into his Instagram a few days after he's back from one of these self-imposed, soul-crushing torture sessions and you'll see him with a big smile on his face running again or hitting the weights.

Now, if you told me ten years ago that there was a guy out there doing all this while holding down a full-time job and a family, I would have looked at you the way I'd look at someone who tells me their best friend is Bigfoot.

Maybe I would have believed there's someone out there who can do all this, but I would have assumed they're some science project being constantly fed performance-enhancing drugs by a team of doctors monitoring his body around the clock to make sure he doesn't drop dead from overexertion. But if you had told me that all this was being done by some smiling bowhunter with a forty-hour-a-week job, I would have told you to get the fuck outta here with that nonsense.

It doesn't seem possible, but yet it's a fact. What is perhaps even more impressive is that while he's doing all these things, he's also managed to become the best bowhunter on earth.

You see, that's where this whole Cameron Hanes story gets even more unusual. His obsession with physical performance is purely to ensure that he is at his best for his real passion: bowhunting elk in the mountains.

Hunting for wild elk in the mountains with a bow is an incredibly difficult thing to be successful at. The terrain is rugged, and the elk have senses honed to a razor's edge by millions of years of evolution.

It requires you to get inside of 100 yards undetected on an animal that has been avoiding mountain lions, bears, and wolves for its entire life, and then, under extreme pressure, to release a perfect arrow into the animal's vitals.

Because of all these factors, success rates for archery elk hunting are quite low. The average is somewhere below 10 percent.

Even elite hunters will often come home empty-handed.

Cameron Hanes, on the other hand, has been successful on every single archery hunt he's been on over the last ten years. It's almost impossible to overemphasize how extraordinary that is.

His insane dedication to fitness and his maniacal pursuit of perfection in the mountains have made him the boogeyman for mountain elk, and an incredible inspiration to fellow hunters like me. There is literally no one like him. A rare, freak of a man with a singular obsession: be the best bowhunter that he can be. Fueled by wild meat and superhuman discipline, he has turned his life into a masterpiece of dedication and focus, and long after he is gone, when men sit around the campfire and tell hunting stories, his name will be brought up with reverence and hushed tones.

I am proud and honored to call him one of my best friends.

—Joe Rogan
October 2020

LIFE IS NEVER MADE UNBEARABLE
BY CIRCUMSTANCES, BUT ONLY BY A
LACK OF MEANING AND PURPOSE.

— VIKTOR FRANKL

ANSWERING THE CALL

Every epic adventure begins with a call. Rocky Balboa gets the invitation to box Apollo Creed for the title. King Leonidas from *300* refuses to submit to the messenger from King Xerxes and kills him instead, guaranteeing a war. Will from *Good Will Hunting* gets to stay out of jail only if he answers the call to work with Professor Lambeau on math problems and attends therapy.

My call came from Roy Roth. He had been a grade above me at Mohawk High in Marcola, a small logging community at the edge of the Willamette Valley in Oregon, near the city of Eugene. We weren't super close in high school, but everybody knew each other since it was a small school. I called Roy "The Guru" because I knew he was a passionate hunter who was always out in the woods and ran a trapline, which meant he knew animals better than most. Trappers, if they have any success, are dialed in on wildlife. Back then when I hunted with a rifle, I'd tell my friends, "I'm going to call The Guru and see where he thinks we should go on opening day."

His invitation was simple.

"Dude, you need to bowhunt."

At the time, I was nineteen years old and going nowhere. I worked part-time at a warehouse earning $4.72 an hour and I attended a community college the other half of the time. I spent weekend mornings outside, trying to take photos of deer and elk, and the afternoons and evenings drinking beer and doing nothing but listening to Hank Williams Jr. I was basically a small-town loser.

After hearing all of Roy's stories about how great bowhunting was, I decided to buy a bow the following year. It was 1988 and I was twenty years old. My first bow was a $200 Golden Eagle Super Hawk Turbo Cam. Since it was shiny black instead of camo, I spray-painted it myself using ferns for the pattern in matte green and black paint. My bow was set at 90 pounds and I shot super-light arrows trying to get speed out of them. This combo made it very loud, so I tried to quiet it by duct-taping a 35mm film canister between the quiver and the riser to hold everything tighter as the quiver rattled. It came as no surprise that the bow eventually broke in half at the grip when I was at half draw shortly after that first bow season.

The first day I ever bowhunted, opening day of archery season in 1989, I went with Robbie Dunson, who lived down the road from me in Marcola, Oregon. He was nineteen years old when he bow-killed the world record Roosevelt bull, a species of elk on the West Coast. His dad, Dean Dunson, at the time had killed the number four biggest-ever Roosevelt bull. Bulls are very big and can weigh up to 1,200 pounds on the hoof (live weight).

I've always been attracted to people who are the best at whatever they do, knowing there's no one better to learn from, so I enjoyed hanging out with the Dunsons and asking them questions about bowhunting elk. The Dunsons knew archery hunting for Roosevelt elk as well as anyone on the earth at that time. I went to their house and shot my bow nearly every day.

That first morning I went out with Robbie. We were sitting by a thick section of *reprod* (a logging country term for young timber) when I heard the high-pitched bugle of a male elk. The fifteen-foot-tall trees shifted like the parting of the seas and a massive bull stepped out onto the logging road. I was leaning on my knees, trying to look invisible as the black-horned, six-by-seven bull bore holes through me with his eyes. He was in bow range and, when I decided that I should try to kill him, the thing I'd been practicing to do for months, I realized that it felt like my arms were asleep and my heart was beating out of my chest.

I don't know if I can even pull this bow back.

The bull stood there, only forty yards away from me. There was no question I should be able to kill him. I'd shot thousands of arrows at this distance all summer. I pulled back the bowstring and released.

The arrow missed the bull, shot behind his butt. That meant I was about seven feet off my mark, which was ridiculous. This was what I'd call "shitting the bed." My first bow shot of my life at an animal couldn't have been much worse.

I didn't get another opportunity that day, but something was ignited inside of me. I had never had any real ambitions or goals for myself. But something changed. Now all I knew was that I wanted to kill a bull. So right after that first-day hunting debacle, I became obsessed and hunted for the next eighteen days straight, determined to succeed.

That's right, eighteen days straight.

Finally, on September 13, 1989, I killed my first bull. The first animal that ever died from one of my arrows was a spike bull. Granted, it wasn't anything like the giant six-by-seven I blew it on, but it didn't matter. It was my first bow kill and my first bull elk. Truth is, I didn't deserve a big bull yet. I hadn't paid my bowhunting dues.

And, size aside, I didn't know many guys who had even killed a bull with their bow, so my spike bull accomplishment still felt special. It was an almost three-week grind, but it was worth it.

Some people live their whole lives never finding their true passion. I was twenty years old when I first tasted bowhunting success and that marked the time I discovered my purpose. Suddenly I had something in my life to focus my energy on. I quit college and quit about everything else just to be able to bowhunt more.

I'll never forget where this journey began and how long it's taken to hammer away at a dream. We all have to start somewhere.

Nobody is born great at bowhunting.

Bowhunting is not easy. Spending day after day in the unforgiving mountains to hunt is a feat on its own, but adding the extra challenge of doing it with a bow takes that challenge to another level. That's what drew me to the time-honored tradition of bowhunting. At times it feels nearly impossible to get within bow range of an animal and kill it with essentially a sharp stick.

The elk live in the mountains every day of the year, sleeping, eating, keeping a wary eye out for predators … surviving. Imagine sleeping under a tree one night; it would be absolutely miserable. But elk do it every single day, in rugged country. It's no wonder they are as tough as they are. So when you're bowhunting them, you have to be close, within forty yards ideally, in their "red zone," which means you have to outwit them.

The average success rate on hunting a bull elk with a bow is about 10 percent. So that's one kill every ten years or one guy out of ten who is going to have success. That's never going to be good enough for me. Never was, never will be. Average sucks.

Nowadays I earn success on virtually every hunt, in every state, every year. So I expect to be 100 percent when the average is 10 percent. That said, I didn't wake up one morning great at bowhunting. I have worked for more than thirty years to get to where I am today. It's not talent; it's drive. It's not raw ability; it's endurance. Hunting is my passion and being successful at it is what fuels me every day to get better than the day before. That's how I'm able to have a 100 percent success rate.

Regardless of how it may appear, this book isn't about bowhunting. It's not an advice book. I don't tell people what to do, nor do I try to speak for others. I just share what I do and what I'm passionate about, because life without passion is simply existence in my opinion.

We are all hunters in a sense, searching for a more meaningful life. Too many times the weight of this world becomes too heavy to carry through the mountains, so we turn back toward safer, more comfortable conditions. Too often we find ourselves waiting and wondering when success will find us. These pages provide the motivation to keep moving, to stay steadfast, and to be ready for that moment.

Rather than a book about hunting, these pages are about enduring. I love the word *endure*. That's what life is all about. There are hard times. It's a long race. Sometimes it can feel like a battle.

For those of us not born with it, greatness is easy to give up on.

There are countless excuses that keep people from going after an extraordinary life. But when we take on the challenge of pushing our limitations, we no longer see our limitations as barriers but as chances to work hard and buck the odds. In order to live a life marked by passion, tenacity, focus, and resilience, you have to simply keep hammering.

Keep hammering isn't some clever motto. It is a wake-up call to meaning. It's a reference that reminds us to pound away at the lie of impossible.

I get a lot of people who reach out to me feeling like they can't get started. For most of them, they can't get any momentum going. What I tell them is that you just need to get out the door and worry about today only. Don't worry about tomorrow. Don't worry about a week from now. You worry about today. Win the day. Do something positive. Worry about tomorrow tomorrow. To me, that is what enduring means. To get some positive direction going. To build up some momentum. What you're barely doing day one, you're doing easily on day twenty. That's how it works. You have to get started and then you have to endure.

A life well lived isn't a sprint down a smooth track but a steady jog up a rocky trail. Even if you're born a natural runner, the race of life involves preparation, perseverance, and a resistance to passivity.

This is your call to adventure. Let's take a journey together. Picture a place you haven't been, a road you've been longing to travel down, a destination you've dreamt of reaching. I don't know the directions you need to take, and I won't suggest you follow my path. God knows I've taken detours and wandered down a path twice as long as it needs to be. I'm not equipping you with all the necessary tools nor am I giving you the map.

All I'm asking is that you get up and go.

I don't give answers; I take action. I'm not trying to educate; I'm leading by example. I don't talk about tomorrow; I live out today.

I don't know the end result, but I promise you one thing. I know how to endure the race.

PART 1:

PREY

AVERAGE EFFORT YIELDS AVERAGE RESULTS.

CHAPTER 1

LIFE IS SUFFERING

Running has always made me feel free. Even though I was in my midthirties before I entered my first marathon, I've been running my whole life.

I started school a year earlier than most kids and I can still picture my five-year-old, first-grade self, running before school every day. A five-year-old grinding before school?

Apparently.

When I attended Dunn Elementary, they had a jogging contest where we had a month to run as far as we could on our own time and keep track of how many miles we accumulated. I arrived on the school property early every day to run back and forth, from fence to fence, which marked the school perimeter. Doing this thirty-one times represented one mile.

My first year of doing this, first-grade school year, I ran twenty miles in the jogging contest, and in second grade, when I was six years old, I ran twenty-seven miles. To break it down, there are about twenty school days per month, so my self-imposed goal as a five-year-old was one mile per day before school, the next year I wanted to do better. My mother kept the certificates the school awarded me for doing this extra work on my own time.

"This shows a willingness to exercise when you do not have to," the certificate reads.

Every day I came home saying how far I ran. I was striving toward a goal and receiving positive encouragement. Looking back, I realize that maybe I was running to try to cope with my parents' divorce. And to attempt to connect with a dad who was no longer in my life.

The biggest legend around Eugene, Oregon, when I was a kid was long-distance Olympic runner Steve Prefontaine, but for me, it was my dad. Bob Hanes was Superman in my eyes.

In a town known as Track Town, USA, my dad excelled at the sport. He earned a full-ride scholarship at the University of Oregon in gymnastics and, after flunking out there, earned a full ride at Oregon State for track, where they wanted him to pole-vault and high-jump. In high school, he was around six feet tall, and he could high-jump 6'4". My dad did what was called the Western roll, where the high jumper crosses the bar facing it with his stomach facing down as he passes over it. At the time he was friends with and, as stories indicated, competed against Dick Fosbury from Medford, Oregon, who won the gold medal in the high jump at the 1968 Olympics in Mexico City. During my dad's and Dick's high school years, Dick

I was lucky to be able to walk away with barely a scratch after crashing my truck while driving drunk. And thank God I didn't hit anyone. Unfortunately, I didn't learn my lesson for long. It would be years before I could accept how detrimental alcohol was to me.

invented a new method of jumping which would be named after him. The Fosbury Flop is what high jumpers do today, jumping back first and kicking their legs up to clear the bar as they glide over.

The track coaches came to my dad and said they felt he could potentially add a foot to his jump if he performed the Fosbury Flop. If they were right, theoretically that meant he'd jump 7'4". Fosbury's gold medal jump was 7'4¼", which also happened to be a new Olympic record. My dad never changed his jumping method and never competed for Oregon State, which is where Fosbury ended up and jumped for in college. Back then, my dad was more interested in partying than being a serious athlete. He'd been consumed by sport and being the best his whole life, so maybe he was burned out?

Axemen track coach dies at 62

Longtime South Eugene-High School assistant track and field coach Bob Hanes died of cancer Monday at age 62.

The 1966 South Eugene graduate, who still ranks seventh in school history in the pole vault at 15 feet, had coached the Axemen for 22 years, focusing on the pole vault and jumps. He was the inaugural inductee into the school's athletic hall of fame last year.

In recent years he had suc- cess coaching the Beard sib- lings in the pole vault. Lindsay Beard won the OSAA Class 6A girls pole vault title in 2007-08, and her brother, Charlie, ranks sixth in 6A history with a clearance of 16-5.

"He was an incredibly gen- erous, giving person who deeply cared about the kids he worked with," said Jeff Hess, South Eugene's cross country coach and former head track coach.

A memorial service will be scheduled at a later date.

My dad's obituary from The Register Guard.

Bob Hanes was a great athlete at South Eugene High School. In a school that saw all sorts of amazing athletes gracing its hallways, my dad was the first inductee into South Eugene's athletic Hall of Fame. Even years after he graduated, his fellow classmates still remembered him. When our daughter was practicing for the pole vault one day, a couple of her coaches came up to me to ask about Taryn.

"Is she Bob Hanes's granddaughter?"

I nodded. "Yeah. Bob was my dad."

"You know—your dad was a legend around here," one of the coaches said.

"Yeah, that's what I've heard."

When you grow up hearing more about your dad than seeing him, his legend only grows in your young mind.

He and my mom, Linda Brown, met at South Eugene. I never forgot something she told me when I was five years old. "Your dad's legs are so muscular, they're as hard as this wood table," she said as she pointed at our oak coffee table. Little comments like that made him seem larger than life.

Perhaps it was a blessing in disguise that my dad didn't get more of the individual glory in athletics, because he ultimately became known as an amazing track coach at South Eugene. He coached state champions in the long jump, triple jump, and pole vault. With a career lasting more than thirty years, my dad made an impact on thousands of kids' lives. I still get messages from students he coached and what a positive influence he was in their lives. Bob Hanes knew how hard it could be growing up and navigating life in general; his own dad died when he was only three years old, shot in an alley in Seattle. He cared so much for the kids he coached and always enjoyed helping them discover what they loved to do. And he believed in them.

Before my dad could become a legendary high school coach and teach kids to win, he first needed to overcome his own personal battle he was going through.

On May 30, 1975, Steve Prefontaine died in an automobile accident. Earlier that evening, Steve had won a 5,000-meter run at University of Oregon's Hayward Field. He was only twenty-four years old. The place where he crashed on the winding, narrow Skyline Boulevard is now known as Pre's Rock.

Four years earlier, another car accident happened only ten minutes from Pre's Rock. Nobody got killed, but it might have helped tear a family apart. It's one of my earliest memories of my parents when they were still married. In fact, it's one of my only memories. I was four years old and I woke up hearing my mother yelling. I went to find her standing by the door heading into the garage, talking loudly and frantically to my dad. When I stepped to her side and followed her eyes, I noticed the side of my dad's car was damaged as if he had just hit another vehicle.

I didn't know this at the time, but my dad was an alcoholic. Thankfully, Bob Hanes was able to walk away from this accident. Not long after that, my parents divorced. In a subsequent accident, my dad crashed near some train tracks and wound up in a coma for three days with head trauma. Another near-miss.

My mom had a job at the phone company, so she worked in downtown Eugene and was gone a lot. I wonder now if I started elementary school early because my mom needed a break from me, as I was oftentimes acting out after the divorce. She was probably thinking to herself, *I've got to work, so get this kid out of my hair. He can start school a year earlier than most.* My grade school was just up the hill from our house, so I walked to and from school every day.

After writing this section I asked my mom about those days, and she says starting me early wasn't to give her a break. She said I was a smart little boy and that I was ready for school.

Even though I enjoyed the jogging challenge I entered in first and second grade, I struggled with behavior problems. With my mom gone at work, I was what's known as a "latchkey kid." Coming home from school alone, letting

I'VE BECOME GOOD FRIENDS WITH PAIN OVER THE YEARS AS HE'S WITH ME ON ALL MY MOST MEMORABLE AND REWARDING CHALLENGES.

myself in, and looking out for myself until Mom got home from work later in the evening. To occupy myself, I'd usually cause damage. I once cut up the screen door screen with a knife, hit a neighbor kid in the head with a fist-size rock after I threw it across East 39th Street, stole candy from the local Safeway, and so on. One day in first grade while the teacher stepped out of the room, I went up to the chalkboard and wrote FUK in big, bold letters. This, and other issues, got me put on the "red light, green light" program. If I behaved well at school, they put me on the green light and gave me a green card to take home, but if I was bad in class, they put me on red and sent me home with a red card. I can't recall how often I got a red card compared to green, but it was a measurable thing. One thing has always stayed consistent from then to now: I love measurables.

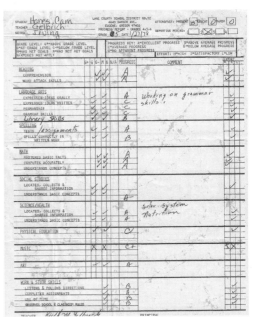

Green light might have meant a good day, but life didn't get better, however. Not long after the divorce, my mother began dating. I mean, who could blame her, she was a beautiful, green-eyed, twentysomething single mother of two boys. I hated when she'd leave on dates and I hated the guys she dated, because they weren't my dad. I couldn't believe she'd bring another man into our house. I remember saying, "Mom, I want it like the old times. Just us and Dad." Eventually, she remarried and my stepdad, Greg, entered the pic- ture. I didn't like him at all, mostly be-

I've never been accused of being a genius, but I'm not dumb either. I was smart enough to learn early on that if I was to succeed, I'd have to outwork other people.

cause he wasn't my dad. They had one thing in common, though. They both had drinking problems, so he brought with him the very same issues that had driven my dad away.

My childhood soon became some never-ending race I could never win as I bounced back and forth between my parents.

There's always gotta be a bad guy in every movie, and for me, it was my stepdad.

I believe it is our duty as men to help those in need. I helped carry an injured woman to a Flight for Life Colorado helicopter just off the summit of Mount Elbert, Colorado's highest peak at 14,443 feet.

Flight nurse Esther McIlvain said she normally has a partner on the search-and-rescue (SAR) flights, but altitude and weight required her to leave him and his gear at Leadville. Having help on the mountain to grab the injured climber in one go reduced the risk of an accident in a very accident-prone profession.

I wanted to spend time with my dad and to get his approval, but instead I got this stranger suddenly showing up and telling me how to live my life. He worked for a paving company and he drove a roller, so all day long he sat in the sun on hot asphalt smoking cigarettes. Then he would come home and drink, see me, and, in my mind, think of shit to do to screw with me.

Here's the thing about Greg, my stepdad: He's freaking tough as shit. He grew up in a small town in eastern Oregon, and his family owned a big ranch. Ranching is hard-ass work, so they were as tenacious as they come. Greg had two brothers and two sisters, all tough farm kids who grew up to become tough people. Even later in life after he got sober, he was one tough old bastard, running a 100-mile ultra at the age of seventy. I may not have liked him for years, but I have always respected his toughness. And, I wonder now if maybe, in his mind, being hard on me was an attempt to make me tough for life? I get tough love, but there was no love in this equation.

When I was a kid, my stepdad always seemed to be in a bad mood. He

I have been lucky enough to spend a decent amount of time with Courtney Dauwalter, one of the USA's greatest endurance athletes, training in the mountains and experiencing some grand "adventures." She took this photo as we descended Mount Massive, Colorado's second-highest peak at 14,421 feet.

was mean whenever he was drinking, which was often. Once I had to stack seven cords of wood, and after I finished my stepdad thought they weren't stacked well enough, so I am pretty sure he knocked a bunch of it over and told me to do it again. He didn't work in the winter as the guys who work for paving companies usually get laid off and collect unemployment, so my stepdad was around more than either of us liked. One time we had a terrible confrontation in the kitchen that turned physical.

"Take the chicken scraps out," he told me one morning before school.

"You take them out," I said. "You're going to be sitting here all day not doing anything."

We wound up on the floor of the kitchen with his veiny, dark tanned arm around my neck. I probably deserved it. I didn't like him, so I didn't show him any respect during those years. My stepdad was not a bad person, but when you did these sorts of things, you weren't going to get a good review from your stepkid.

When things got really bad, I would go live with my dad, but that meant leaving my mother and younger brother. Pete is two and a half years younger than me, so he was very young when my parents divorced, and he didn't really know our dad. He knew our stepdad better, so when he started calling Greg "Dad," it felt like a knife in my gut. "You're not doing that," I told him. I very much regret doing it now, but I would beat Pete up just to make him go see our dad. I was always worried how my dad felt. Pete never had a connection with our dad, so it made sense for him to accept our stepdad, but I wasn't about to. *No, I'm never accepting this guy*, I told myself. All because I felt like I needed to have allegiance to my dad.

Looking back on it now, I would hate to put my kids through something like this. Kids shouldn't have to deal with that kind of shit. My childhood sucked, and it was something hard that I had to endure. But, honestly, I don't wish I had a better childhood, because it made me who I am today. We all have struggles, and those struggles can define who you are. It's all part of the journey.

Some of those struggles come from unexpected places and unpredictable situations. In the same way you can't control the weather, your life will be filled with unexpected storms that can hit hard and either break you, toughen you up, or simply teach you about the darker parts of life that don't get featured in Hallmark movies.

When I was in third and fourth grades, my mom worked with and became friends with this lady at the phone company. I remember her being very nice and pretty. They went out on the weekends, leaving Pete and me with the woman's teenage sons to babysit. My stepdad had a Harley and so did the husband of my mom's friend, so I think they would go on road trips or maybe just out for the night. While it was a long time ago and I don't remember all the details, there are a few things I do remember that might always haunt me.

The teenage brothers weren't the greatest babysitters. They used drugs and made me and my brother fight in front of their friends. They'd yell and scream and treat it like entertainment, coaching us on how to hit each other hard. Whenever there was blood, the boys yelled louder and got more fired up. Pete and I didn't like it, but I don't remember having a choice or maybe it was a way for us young boys to try to earn the approval of older boys.

The brothers watched us at our house as we had a pool table and they and their friends had something to do as they acted crazy and got drunk and high during those stressful nights. They made me smoke pot so I couldn't tell on them. We'd do whatever they said, so I smoked pot and then they'd put shaving cream in my mouth as they said it'd mask the scent of pot. The younger brother did most of the communicating with us and said if we told on them, they would tell my mom that I smoked pot too. If I hadn't already learned that life wasn't always going to be fun and loving, I did then. My young eyes were opened to the fact that there were people in this world that you could never trust and would hurt you for entertainment.

Teenage boys have zero compassion as it is, but these two brothers were beyond bullies. Once they got me going so fast on a steel merry-go-round at the park that I got scared and jumped off, cracking my head open on the pavement. The back of my head was split open and there was lots of blood, but they made me tell my mom that I fell on my own. I think I ended up telling her the truth. I still remember that blood-soaked, blue-and-white-striped shirt and them laughing, "Oh shit, your head is fucked up."

My mom didn't know it at the time and probably their mom didn't know it either, but in my eyes the babysitting brothers were evil. I didn't tell my mom all they did to us until many years later. Ultimately, the older brother overdosed on heroin and died in a park in Eugene, while the younger one took some hallucinogenic mushrooms and killed his best friend with a knife when he was only fifteen. Since he was a juvenile, he got out for that murder

in his twenties but then he was involved in another murder, so went back to prison for many years. He's out again now.

In middle school, I lived with my dad in Eugene while my brother lived with our mother and stepdad in Marcola. I missed Pete like crazy. I'd often cry just thinking about my brother and how much I missed him. I had a paper route, so I woke up at four in the morning to deliver papers. Sometimes I would be outside riding my bike in the cold rain, and I had a lot of time to think. Every day in the summer during this stretch I would also pick strawberries and beans later in the morning for Evonuk's after I delivered papers. My goal was to earn ten dollars a day for BMX stuff. During this period of my life, with all the time to be in my own head, one constant thought came to mind.

This sucks.

Happiness seemed like a foreign concept. Pain was a constant.

Nothing about my life in middle school stood out. I was pretty miserable. Even when it came to sports. Despite the competitive spirit inside of me, I wasn't a natural athlete. Nothing ever came easy. My dad's genes hadn't passed down to me, it seemed, so I realized that I had to work hard at everything if I hoped to compete.

Since my dad was some legendary track guy, I decided to attempt to follow in his footsteps. During one particular track meet, I was excited to see

The age of innocence

my stepmom, Kandy, come watch me, knowing that she was going to tell my dad how I did. He wasn't there himself, but his spirit loomed large like it always did. It was really hard to get his attention in athletics since he was gone, traveling around with junior national teams. You couldn't do regular shit and be celebrated. I knew I had to make my mark, so I decided I would do it in the 800-meter race at that meet.

Our middle school district track meet was held at Springfield High School, which was a big deal as they had a nice rubber track and grandstands. I was wearing all green, which was the color of my middle school, the Hamlin Loggers. When the gun went off, I took off as if it were a 200-meter dash. I ran like Steve Prefontaine, going out hard and refusing to let go of the lead. For a short while, a very short while, I raced at the front, but by the end of the first lap, I was dying.

I still remember the guy who won the race. Greg Suiter. He was a natural track guy who won all the time. He looked like a runner, tall and lean. I was this short-legged kid gasping at the end of the race and finishing last. I was thankful my dad hadn't accompanied my stepmom to this meet.

This was my normal. I just didn't have it. That's what I grew up with.

Life has always been a grind.

Life has always been a grind, but maybe at this point is was more than a "grind." Maybe it was plain painful? Obviously, for kids, a parents' divorce is always hard. What kid doesn't want a mom and dad around to love them, ask them how their day went, give them guidance and help them grow? That wasn't my life. And when I was living with my dad, he was never around because he was working at his record store, Vintage Vinyl in Portland, trying to keep it afloat, and I was now separated from my brother. All I remember feeling was alone. Sad and in pain. So, yeah . . . it was a grind.

"'Why run?' is a question often asked," Steve Prefontaine once penned in a high school essay. "Why go out there every afternoon and beat out your brains? . . . What is the logic of punishing yourself each day, of striving to become better, more efficient, tougher?"

This was a question that I would come to ask myself—and come to be asked quite frequently—the older I became. Prefontaine's answer sums up his legendary mindset.

"The value in it is what you learn about yourself. In this sort of situation all kinds of qualities come out—things that you may not have seen in yourself before."

This can refer to running a tough race, or it can relate to enduring a terrible childhood. What do you learn about yourself, even in dire situations?

I have to acknowledge and thank my stepdad. He was the one who initially got me started in hunting.

There is an irony in the fact that my biggest hero growing up never hunted. He had no use for hunting. My dad used to sarcastically make fun of me and say, "Every time you kill an animal, you lose a brain cell." Of course, I know he was proud of my accomplishments as a hunter. After my first book on hunting, *Bowhunting Trophy Blacktail*, came out, my dad went to bookstores and got them to buy half a dozen copies. He supported and loved me, but he still never hunted.

My stepdad was the one who took my brother and me hunting with him. Perhaps my mother urged him to "do something with the boys." Hunting was something most rural people did. For some, it was more of a casual hobby, and they definitely didn't train for it like an athletic event back in those days. I was not a good hunting partner at that time, because I wore big-legged jeans that made lots of noise when I walked. I was never quiet. My stepdad would be smoking a cigarette as we crept along and he would mostly just get mad because we were making too much noise. As a result, I never really enjoyed hunting with him, but he did get me started when I was fifteen years old and my brother was twelve.

I have to hand it to my stepdad. Not only did he take my brother and me hunting, but he took us out to this big deer hunting camp over in eastern Oregon that his brothers went to. I know now how big of a deal this happened to be. These grown men likely didn't want kids around. I know I wouldn't have if I had been them. I guarantee when Pete and I showed up, they were looking at themselves going, "What is this? Freakin' daycare?" They wanted to get together to hunt, drink, and play poker at night in the camp tent. But my stepdad bit the bullet and took us. I killed my first deer thanks to him.

My brother and I were on our own when I killed a young spike. I had a beat up .300 Savage with a cheap 4x scope, and I thought I saw horns, so I put the crosshairs behind the deer's shoulder and hammered the shot off from 150 yards. After I fired the shot, my brother looked at me with surprise.

"You shot a doe?"

"That wasn't a doe," I told him, but I suddenly had doubts.

Oh, shit, did I kill a doe during buck season?

When we got to the deer, thank God there was an antler spike growing out of its head. It was legal, but only barely.

My stepdad didn't see me make my first kill, and we never went hunting together again that I remember. But he got me started on that path as a hunter. His taking us to that hunting camp was probably a disaster for him, but it was life-changing for me.

Don't ever prejudge who can and cannot make an impact in your life. Even the most unlikely of people can turn out to be instrumental in your journey.

Maybe the villain in your story is actually just an antihero in disguise.

It's easy to use your childhood as a crutch instead of seeing it as a chisel.

There are a lot of divorces out there, so that means a lot of kids come from broken homes. I always hear people say, "My family is so dysfunctional," using it as an excuse for something. But it's not really a valid excuse, because everybody's family is dysfunctional in some way. There are so many crutches people want to use to justify themselves, but for me, you

What are you passionate about? What is the one thing you could never give up? How much would you endure to never let it go? All you need to have is a passion and a will to sacrifice greatly. That's enough. That's all I've ever had.

have to eliminate every single one of them. Get rid of all of them. Then tell yourself it's up to you. What are you going to do now that you've let go of those crutches?

I could blame alcoholism on a shitty childhood, but I don't. Blaming others is an easy way out. It was too easy to look at my stepdad's drinking and become indignant. But I could have easily had the same sort of problem. Everything I do is to the extreme, so when I did finally start drinking when I got older, I was all in. I would get drunk as hell. If I hadn't straightened my life out, I couldn't have blamed anybody except myself. I know my dad was an alcoholic too, and it greatly impacted my life. But I'm not perfect either, so I can't judge him. He had a lot of potential that he never got to take advantage of because of drinking in the prime of his athletic life. Cancer took him in 2010 at the age of sixty-three, which seems pretty young to die from cancer. He had been sober and had lived a clean life for more than thirty years, so who knows why he got cancer? I think he had a lot of regret, but sometimes that's just life and how it plays out. He's the reason why I am the way I am today. Even though I didn't get to be around him as much when I was a kid because of the divorce and because he stayed busy with his record store Vintage Vinyl, we got very close before he died, and I saw the impact he had on people. He was always who I wanted to make proud.

My dad never lived up to his full athletic potential, but he put me on a path so I could live up to mine.

I recently told my mom that I'm so glad I went through what I went through: all that shit, being miserable, and hating my stepdad and hating my life. Feeling like I was never happy. I'm glad I was forced to weather those storms. In some ways, that's why I'm good at what I do now.

We all grow up having to rely on people. Our parents, family, friends, neighbors, teachers. I didn't have anybody to rely on, so that meant I had to do things for myself. If I didn't push myself—and there was a time I was quite happy *not* pushing myself—there was nobody else there to push me.

I found a true passion and calling in bowhunting, and I found the perfect person to push me with it. But when Roy ended up moving to Alaska, I had to make a choice to either go hunt by myself or not go, because I couldn't get anybody who wanted to do it with me. Of course, I went hunting by myself, and I was comfortable doing this because I had grown up being independent and being on my own. Not by choice but just because that's how life can work out.

Sometimes I hear someone give a familiar excuse when it comes to working out. "Yeah, I was lifting good, hard, in a groove, but then my partner's

The divorce of parents can be hard on the kids involved obviously, but some good can come of it. My brother Taylor has always been there for me in tough endurance races. I took him to kill his first buck when he was a young man, actually his first three bucks, and he helped me get to the finish line of my first 200-mile run. I'm so thankful for him, and my half-sister Megan, for that matter. The fact that these two amazing humans are a result of my mom and dad getting a divorce is proof of a silver lining in what, for the kid involved, seemed like the end of the world.

work schedule changed, so he couldn't make it." What does that have to do with anything? Who cares? It's not about somebody else. It's about you.

Being on my own made me tougher. It made me independent and allowed me not to have to rely on others, to become a good problem solver. I had to use my imagination, because nobody else was there to use it for me and I became creative and resilient. My dad's absence and my stepdad's antipathy helped me overcome my averageness.

Of course, I first needed to go through high school to discover how truly average I happened to be.

LOVE THE STRUGGLE

Life gives perspective.

Suffering grants power.

The experiences of my life, mostly from the adversity, have given me perspective I haven't always had. I've come to love the struggle.

How much pain and suffering will you go through for success?

On most of my hunts, this is what has probably made the biggest difference—the ability to suffer more. To battle through the burdens. To fight my fears and self-doubts.

Fighting is part of me. It's one reason I'm very thankful for my upbringing despite the pain.

Suffering in silence for hours, working toward that finish line . . .

It's what I love about the journey that is mountain endurance running.

I write and talk about the work required to succeed in the grand tradition of bowhunting. It's a special journey that is humbling.

It takes pain.

It requires devotion.

It supplies anguish.

It rewards achievements beyond belief.

It creates seasoned veterans.

The journey is long. So long.

Running miles in the early morning and during lunch and the afternoon.

I want to sweat and be miserable. That is always my goal.

Train for misery and embrace the pain. This is my approach, because you know you'll experience it in the mountains.

I want to find my limits.

I want to find out what happens when I push myself too far. Haven't been there yet, but I can't wait.

There are many days I hurt when I run. Ankles, knees, hips, the list goes on. I have put in many, many miles, and after doing so for years, you are going to be nicked up.

Either you quit or you push through the aches.

I push.

I ignore it.

I'm pretty sure no one has ever died from a blister.

I love training and working *hard* toward my goals, be it bowhunting, running, lifting, or otherwise.

My past pain serves as a life preserver in the wilderness. My painful history helps carry the heavy load in the mountains.

When my shoulders ache, my back tightens, and my quads engage, I feel the hunt has finally given the one thing I long for. Obviously, the suffering endured while packing meat out means success, but it represents more than that. The dripping sweat and fight for solid footing gives me what I need.

I've come to long for and embrace the struggle. Without it, I am not me.

CHAPTER 2

PUSHING ABOVE AVERAGE

My first out-of-state hunt was to California where Roy Roth and I and our friends pursued wild boar.

Success starts with confidence. As I look back over my life, for most of it, I see an up-and-down journey, a never-ending battle to earn "above average." The passion has been there since my first bowhunt, but there have always been whispers of wondering whether it's all worth it. There has been a target on my back, being judged by everything I say and do or maybe it's just been my own doubt that magnifies the negative energy others put out there? Confidence is so tough to earn and so easy to lose. It almost doesn't seem fair, but once you have confidence, you begin to work hard, and that's when you begin to find success.

As a freshman entering a new high school, I had no confidence and zero success to point to or build momentum off of. Life got worse after I decided to live with my dad when he moved to Portland. Suddenly I found myself at this big school I didn't want to attend where I didn't know anybody. I struggled in my classes. I mostly earned Ds as a freshman. I ate like shit and wasn't active, so I started gaining weight and to make matters worse, acne became an issue. When I was out of school, I would walk around Portland, near Burnside Street, with no money to spend, just to burn time. Some people go watch movies; I watched drunks stagger around downtown, and saw people get assaulted and, one day, robbed at the bus stop.

The worst part of that year was how much I missed

I don't remember much else taking precedence over high school football when I was a senior. We were pretty good because we had a great athlete in Don Mannila as quarterback. He and I were close friends, so he looked for me a lot as I played wide receiver. That resulted in me leading the team in touchdowns. The photo here is of the players who earned league all-star honors.
Top row: *Glen Roberson, Tim Benson, me.*
Bottom row: *Tim Thompson, Jack Deveraux, Jeff Moss, Don Mannila.*

my mom and my brother. I wanted to move back with them, but I didn't want to hurt my dad and I hated my stepdad. On weekends I rode the Greyhound bus to Eugene to see my mom, and after the weekend was over, I hopped back on the bus and stared out the window, many times with tears streaming down my face on the ride back to my dad's. I wasn't truly happy in either place for different reasons.

Soon I realized things had to change, that the situation in Portland was dire. Feeling alone and isolated caused me to not give any effort to school or make friends. My grades were all Ds and I was overweight and insecure. So I moved back in with my mom for my sophomore, junior, and senior years. I knew it hurt my dad, but I was miserable and felt desperate.

I then attended Mohawk High School in Marcola. It was a small school in a small town. Marcola was a logging community, with a lot of the guys working in the woods. I loved growing up in a small town, but like so many others from humble beginnings, I carried low expectations and no dreams. I wasn't looking down the road. The change of schools did help me, because even though I never did my homework and wasn't considered "smart," I also wasn't dumb. I began to get good grades. I ended up getting straight As when I was a senior.

Sports not only provided an outlet for me, but I found direction in it. I played everything, and once I got back in shape and my feet under me, always was in the starting lineup on my teams. I was a wide receiver on our football team, and we were pretty good by my senior year. I became the leading scorer on the team, but that was mostly due to the fact that we had a great quarterback. Donnie Mannila and I were pretty much best friends at the time, and we lived three miles apart on Wendling Road, the same road our high school was on. Every day in the summer, I rode my bike to his house, where I would run routes, catch ball after ball, lift weights, and go to the swimming hole where we'd cuss the "flatlanders" (people from town). Donnie was one of Mohawk's best athletes of all time. All those days of him throwing me balls helped us develop a good connection, so he looked for me a lot during the games.

Donnie and mostly his dad, Don, planted seeds inside of me for when I began to start running. His dad was a dang good runner; he broke forty minutes in the 10K (6.2 miles), which isn't easy. Donnie and I ran together and raced each other. We began to call this the Wendling Road Track Club. It wasn't long-distance running, nothing compared to what I do now. It was something we did simply to get in shape for football.

I discovered that I wanted to work hard to become the best athlete I could be. I like being part of a successful team, I like scoring touchdowns, and it was fun to see the work Donnie and I put in during the summer pay off. I also wanted to be a good student but, just like athletics, was never as good as Donnie, as he was in the Honor Society. Nobody was there pushing me or encouraging me. Nobody was in my face telling me I needed to do better. I don't ever remember being asked about my grades. I just wanted to do better on my own.

Because of my up-and-down life, I learned to be self-sufficient. Now I was learning how to push myself. My mom was doing the best she could. I never for a moment doubted that she loved me. She always loved me, but there was a lot going on for her. She had remarried, was working, and had to care for two other little kids, my half brother and half sister, Taylor and Megan.

She had Pete and me as well, of course, to try to corral. I was used to being on my own, so I didn't care as long I was around my brother, even though we fought a lot over sports because we were so competitive. It was during this time frame I discovered I could motivate myself in sports.

When I wasn't playing sports what I remember most is trying to stay as far away from my home as I could, because there was always a lot of tension if my stepdad was around.

In the summer after my sophomore year, I found a safe haven at Grandma Heloise's house. In between playing catch, haying, or swimming, on most days I would ride my ten-speed bike twenty miles to my grandma's green house on 24th and Emerald in Eugene. Grandma Heloise was my dad's mom. His dad died when he was three years old, so my dad grew up without a father, since my grandma never remarried. She was a schoolteacher who was kind and gentle, and she always cared for me.

Grandma Heloise was always happy to see me. She would make me a plate full of saltine crackers with peanut butter and I'd read a Stephen King book while she played either Mozart or Beethoven and read her book of choice as the grandfather clock audibly ticked the seconds off. I hung out there a lot, watched MTV, then rode the twenty miles back home only to do it all again the next day.

I have good memories of being with my Grandma Heloise. Sure, I wasn't very productive at her house, but I still biked forty miles a day. That was worth something because it helped me get in shape. A few times I remember my dad would come by. Back then he was still drinking, so I would rarely go to his house, only Grandma's.

Just a short way down from my grandma's house was Hayward Field, the famous track-and-field stadium for the University of Oregon. What was once a cow pasture has became the site of more US Olympic Trials and NCAA Championships than any other venue in the country. Whenever there were track meets, I'd go over to Hayward Field and watch them through the fence that surrounded the field at the time, since I couldn't get in. There was also University Park that I would wander over to. They had this outdoor basketball hoop where I'd play ball with others. We got some really good games going.

After my junior year of high school, I went to work at my grandfather's ranch in eastern Oregon during the summer. Grandpa Bob, my mother's

One of the last animals I killed with a rifle hung in the Osburns' barn. I met up with the guys in mid-morning after the morning hunt on the 3,000 line, which was a logging road in the timber country. As we were hanging out BSing, I saw this buck moving along the timber edge over 300 yards away. I took a rest and squeezed off one shot, putting the buck down. And by the way, I still cut the sleeves off my shirts at times, just as I did in this photo.

dad, was a trainer of racehorses and he was super tough. This was a guy who moved out on his own when he was fifteen years old, then joined the Army and served in Korea. Believe me when I say there was no babying going on when I worked for him. Papa taught me a lot about being super tough, as well as a lot about horses. I warmed up his racehorses at the track before I gave them to the jockey to race, so I was what they called a jockey boy. Holding a racehorse back is hard. You can't be too big because you don't want too much weight on a racehorse. I wasn't big, but I had to be pretty strong to hold those horses. Papa knew what he was doing; his talent as a trainer was matched only by his big personality and aggressiveness. He was once picked as the quarter-horse trainer of the year in Oregon. He had a really good thing going, but it was mostly due to his hard work and never-ending drive to win.

I learned something else from Grandpa Bob. I was taught that tomorrow is not guaranteed.

My Nana, my mom's mother, drove over from their ranch in eastern Oregon to visit and go to my homecoming football game on a Friday. Late Thursday night, the Umatilla sheriff's department called and told us that Papa had died in an automobile accident. It was very painful to hear this, since Grandpa Bob was a big part of my teenage years. The following night, the homecoming game was tough to get through, but I had a good game and made some difficult catches.

Papa taught me to give everything you have each day and the only thing that mattered was winning. When a horse wins, the trainer, the jockey, and the family get to take a photo in the winner's circle. Anything less than that is a failure.

By my senior year, I loved joking around with Mannila. I'd stare at my hands and say, "These are the hands that are going to take us to state." Donnie and I had a good rapport. But even back then, I could see some of the traits that have led to my mindset behind hunting and training, because I don't remember the catches the most. What I remember the most about playing with Mannila is one momentous drop.

"I'll never drop a pass." Famous last words I loved to always say to my quarterback. I will never forget my last game during my senior year. We were playing the Lowell Red Devils at Lowell in a game we would win 19–0, and I even scored a touchdown in that game. But I also dropped a two-point conversion, and it was the first pass I dropped all season. I was the biggest baby, pouting on the sidelines simply because I dropped a pass. That was my competitive nature rearing its ugly head.

Even back then I wanted to be the best. With football, I would learn very quickly after high school that I was, at best, an *average* player.

In the Cam Hanes dictionary, the word average has no meaning. My best wouldn't come from something that involved a ball.

Are you good enough?

This is the question every sport asks. As players go from high school to college to professional athletics, the answer most eventually come to is that dreaded two-letter word:

No.

I graduated high school younger than most at seventeen. I decided to work for a year at Safeway, where I ordered bread and dairy for the grocery store. Mannila was a year behind me, so after he graduated the following year, we both went down to Southern Oregon State where we tried to play college ball. Donnie managed to do it for four years and ultimately was a starter. I managed to drink a lot of alcohol.

High school graduation, 1985

Along with Donnie, my college friends who were also on the team, consisted of two guys from Portland, Keith and Joe, as well as Jeff Beathard. Jeff's dad, Bobby Beathard, was the general manager of the Washington Redskins, and he arrived with some East Coast crazy in him. I thought I was good at playing wide receiver, but Jeff had the best hands I had ever seen catching a football. He was the last pick in the 1988 NFL draft, chosen by the Los Angeles Rams.

Early on in life, I was trying to figure out what married life and being a young dad was all about. I worked for Roth Construction pouring foundations and finishing concrete while also working at a hardware warehouse. Life wasn't that fulfilling. What was my purpose?, I wondered. Is this it?

After trying to make the team, I redshirted for Southern Oregon State, meaning every day I practiced against the starting defense. There were definitely some beasts out there on the field. I definitely wasn't one of them. It was fun, especially since there were some elite athletes on the field who eventually made it to the NFL.

The irony of college was that throughout my high school years, I never drank even one beer. All I cared about was sports and grades. I knew I wasn't an elite athlete, but I still tried my hardest, especially because I wanted to impress my dad. What I learned at Southern Oregon was that even though I wasn't good enough to play college football, I knew how to party. I drank a lot of beer and eventually went back to Eugene with this new "skill" mastered.

I began to go to Lane Community College, but mostly I just screwed around, drinking beer and not doing much of anything. I got a job at a warehouse, crushing cardboard boxes and making them into bales, all for $4.72 an hour. A job a monkey might very well be able to do. After I created big bales of cardboard, I stacked them up with a forklift so people could come and recycle them. The best part about this job (maybe the only good part) was that this was the place where I met Tracey, my wife. Nothing about my life back then seemed unusual or extraordinary. I didn't feel like I was wasting any talents or opportunities, because I honestly didn't feel like I had any. It wasn't like I was letting anybody down. Nobody expected anything from Cameron Hanes, so I didn't expect anything out of myself.

My one and only direction in life—athletics—was suddenly gone, so I found

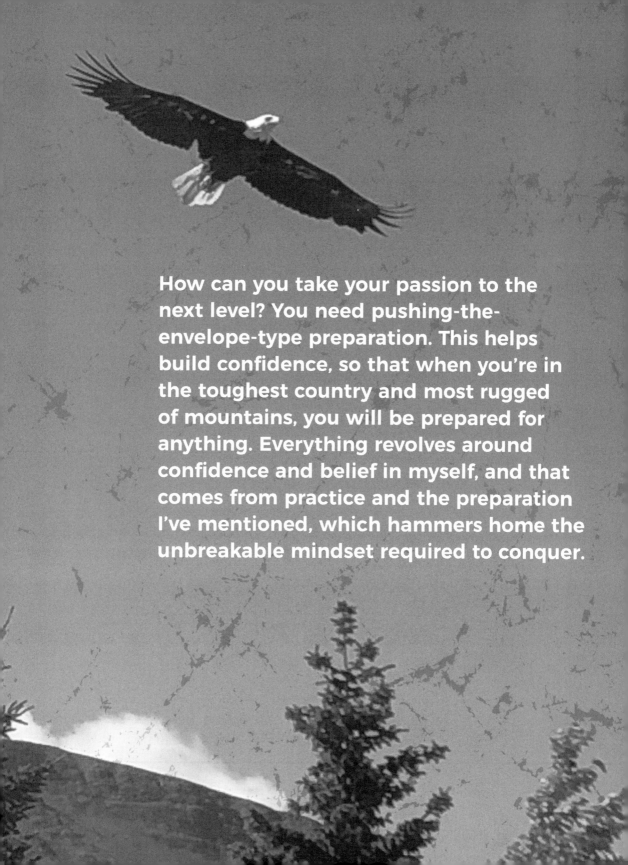

How can you take your passion to the next level? You need pushing-the-envelope-type preparation. This helps build confidence, so that when you're in the toughest country and most rugged of mountains, you will be prepared for anything. Everything revolves around confidence and belief in myself, and that comes from practice and the preparation I've mentioned, which hammers home the unbreakable mindset required to conquer.

myself pretty much lost. Nothing was challenging me. There was nothing I could point to that I was good at except being a smart-ass, I guess. My mouth got me in a lot of trouble.

There are people who mold you during your childhood, both in good and bad ways. They care for you like Grandma Heloise or they teach you like Grandpa Bob did. They help challenge and motivate you like Donnie did. Family might provide an outlet and friends may prove to be motivators, but ultimately you have to decide to dream. You are the only person to push yourself.

Confidence can come from others, but it still needs to be built inside of yourself. That takes time.

After the Southern Oregon State experience, knowing I didn't have organized sports to do anymore and realizing this meant I had no real focus in life, I was left wandering for a while. Thankfully, Roy kept on me and kept encouraging me to bowhunt, telling me it's way better than hunting with a gun, that there were fewer people and that I would enjoy it. Roy got me started, but the only way I could build confidence in anything was to go out and do it. Soon I focused my energy on bowhunting. Like athletics, it provided a challenge.

This time, however, I had a different answer to that age-old question of whether I was good enough.

Yeah, I'm good enough. In fact, I'm a lot more than that.

I found the perfect thing to work hard at, something that challenged me and that not everybody was good at. When I was successful at bowhunting, it gave me a lot of confidence, and for a young man, having confidence and getting positive reinforcement in anything was a powerful spark for change in my life.

Here's the truth: I'm an average guy who has experienced above-average bowhunting success over the past three decades. One thing is for sure—if I can do it, anyone can. I came from nothing and had no one pushing me or even believing in me. For this reason, my story proves that, in bowhunting, the most average person can achieve the grandest of dreams.

Confidence is everything in bowhunting. The bowhunter's arena is God's country, and the only witnesses are the hunter and the hunted. There are no crowds to push you on. You must be self-motivated. To experience victory, you have to be tough, and you don't get tough by thinking about it or delaying it. You must train for tough.

You must believe that you *can* be tough.

START DREAMING AND START LIVING

Be the exception. Break the chain. Burst through the bonds of low expectations.

There doesn't have to be a huge plan to be exceptional.

There are no designated ten steps to get there.

It doesn't require resources or people.

It can start with passion and build from there brick by brick. That's all I've ever had and done.

I'm flawed in many ways; blessed more than I deserve and yes still have that chip on my shoulder. A dichotomy? Affirmative.

In that same vein . . .

I love many, but trust few.

I feel pain but try to convince myself I'm bulletproof while being weak and lacking confidence.

Life is messy and beautiful. Our childhood can be miserable and black, but any child can dream. Any kid can work hard and see that dreams can come true. If they realize that, even if no one believes in them and their heroes are gone, all hope is not lost. If they believe in themselves . . . that's all it takes.

This doesn't just apply to kids, either. A lot of adults need to start dreaming and start living again.

I didn't have a big plan. All I had was a deep passion for bowhunting and a burning desire to prove people wrong. And that's enough if you believe it is enough.

All I am is a bowhunter who is trying to raise my game to the highest level I can. In that regard, I believe the only limits we have, both physically and mentally, are those we place on ourselves.

The dreamers say believe and you will achieve.

The rare people who do become truly exceptional at something do so not because they believe they're exceptional. On the contrary, they become amazing because they're obsessed with improvement. And that obsession with improvement stems from an unerring belief that they are, in fact, not that great at all. It's anti-entitlement. People who become great at something become great because they understand that they're not already great—they are mediocre, they are average—and that they could be so much better.

How lucky are you that you don't need anyone to believe in you or your dream, and yet you can still make it a reality?

You can become exceptional!

CHAPTER 3

DIVING INTO A DEEP HOLE

Two of the most haunting words in life come in a question.

What if?

The older we become, the easier it might be to find ourselves saying these words. They can be uttered in regret and disappointment. They can be wishful and wanting. In my case, they can also be filled with gratitude and relief.

When I think back to those days after coming back home from Southern Oregon State, I remember a young man aimless and adrift, feeling lost without athletics and figuring this was how the rest of life would be. I didn't see the warning signs on the side of the road telling me to proceed with caution, warning me that I was headed toward a dead end, insisting that there was road work ahead. I ignored them all.

It's hard to see those signs when you're behind the wheel guzzling a beer.

What if I hadn't gotten lucky? I could have died.

Not everybody gets so lucky. I'm thankful now that I got a second chance. It just took me a while to realize that it was indeed a second chance.

After turning twenty-one, I thought it was really cool that I could buy beer. On my way home from work, I'd swing by the Riverview Market and buy a six pack of tallboys. *This is the life*, I thought. *I can pound some Coors Light. I'm a stud now.*

A stud who started getting fat. But nobody cared. I wasn't living up to any expectations. In fact, I was living down to them.

I would oftentimes drive to a swimming hole north of my hometown called the Powerhouse. I liked to pull my truck up to the side of the bridge, then climb to the roof of my vehicle and do a backflip or a handspring or swan dive into the water below. The Powerhouse was narrow and deep and flanked by boulders. If I had been off too far either way, just a few feet, that wouldn't have been good. Hitting those rocks would've killed anybody in an instant.

When Tracey and I got married, we didn't have enough money for a tropical honeymoon. However, we were gifted enough money as wedding presents to be able to go to San Diego, where her sister lived, then up to Los Angeles to stay with her brother. This was one of the very few days in life that I spent on a beach. Truth is, I'd rather be miserable and running than lounging on a beach. I don't feel worthy of rest most days.

My friends and I came up to the swimming hole to drink and accomplish nothing. That was my life. Nothing great was happening. This was small-town living. Nobody was thinking they were ever going to change the world. We were just getting by. There was no looking down the road and planning ahead. Nobody ever talked about what they might be doing in six months. We only asked what we were going to be doing tomorrow. Chances were high that we would be back at the Powerhouse, drinking and hanging out.

We all have routines. They can be productive or they can be poisonous.

Roy helped to break that routine when he introduced me to bowhunting in 1989. Bending my first bow back and loosing one arrow after another was a start, a crack in my mediocrity. Killing my first bull after eighteen straight days of elk hunting was like a drug, and I couldn't get enough. The challenge of the bowhunting woods stirred my soul. I found myself drawn to it. My life had purpose in the pursuit, and I had a dream. My goal became to be a backcountry bowhunter and eventually hunt more wild country than I ever had. But just like hunting, it took time for me to break all those habits and to believe there was a better way to live.

I had found my passion and purpose. I just had to find the strength and persistence to pursue it.

The easiest thing to do in life is to give up on a goal and to stop pursuing a passion. I get it.

I run into a lot of people who are new to bowhunting. They get a bow, go on a hunt, and discover it's just too difficult, so they quit. I understand.

I missed sixteen deer the first year I went bowhunting. So I've been there.

What if I had given up after that first year?

Roy Roth and I didn't have much in common growing up; but once we formed a bond through bowhunting, we became like brothers.

There's that question once again. What if?

Here's one reason why bowhunting is both exciting and excruciating: It's difficult and frustrating as hell. Especially when you're used to hunting with a rifle. People become accustomed to the ritual of seeing an animal in rifle range and then boom . . . it's over. It's done, you've made the shot. The animal is dead. With a bow, being in bow range doesn't mean anything. Even if the animal is in rifle range, when you're bowhunting, the hunt has just started. Moving from rifle range and into bow range means you're moving into the animal's "red zone," and that ups the challenge immensely. In bowhunting there's no guarantee it's going to work out.

Nothing great comes without obstacles and hardship. Whenever new hunters decide that bowhunting is not for them, I encourage them to stick with it. Try a little harder, be a little more patient, stay in the hunt a little while longer.

For me, I never liked to fail. I didn't want to be a failure with the bow. So after that first year of killing the spike bull elk, my second season behind the bow I killed a Pope & Young three-by-three blacktail, a raghorn five-by-five bull, and a bear with a $200 bow and using $30 binoculars. I could only afford to hunt in Oregon instead of traveling anywhere out of state. I bought three tags and filled three tags.

That second year of bowhunting wasn't just memorable for me. It was monumental.

I had some success on elk and lots of failure on deer in year one, so I put in more work and decided to go back and try again.

Failure is humbling, and in bowhunting, it is an important part of the journey.

If you keep navigating through it, failure will become the exception. But it takes dedication and time and experience.

When the expectation bar is set low, or when it's not set at all, then you easily accept the average things in life. For instance, I remember back in those days when I'd get past my straight eight hours on the shift and was making time and a half, over ten dollars an hour, I thought I was rolling in the dough. This guy, Vikas Sharma, and I would compete to see who could work the most each day. We started work at 5:00 a.m., cleaning truck trailers and working sometimes sixteen straight hours, ending the shift at night, loading those same trailers with hardware products for Coast-to-Coast hardware distribution center. It might sound like awful, manual labor for little money, but the funny thing is I remember loving it. We worked hard and it felt fun most days.

The motto of this story: A good work ethic can only get you so far.

I needed to want more out of my life.

Bowhunting was the thing that spurred me to expect more of life.

I remember this hunt like it was yesterday.

I was in my early twenties and it was my third season of bowhunting. I loved the sport and had killed a few decent animals in three years, but I was still not completely committed and focused like I am now. I drank on the weekends and wasn't 100 percent dedicated to the art of bowhunting.

I was invited by Wayne Endicott to join him in the country he had hunted since he was a young boy. Wayne owned the Bow Rack, the archery pro shop in Springfield, Oregon, that opened in 1971. Wayne was a not only a passionate archer, but he was a friend who in the end became one of my

The result of my first true backcountry bowhunt in 1991 with Duane Leavitt, Wayne Endicott, and Roy Roth. Still one of my best ever mule deer and this was my third season of bowhunting.

biggest supporters. Over all these decades he has remained the same . . . a passionate hunter still taking those who are willing and able into the mountains to enjoy the chase of bowhunting dreams.

One week of bow season in 1991, Wayne, Roy Roth, Dwayne Leavitt, Jeff Brooks, and I ventured toward the legendary Steens Mountain. We all piled into a couple trucks loaded with gear, pulling a trailer of llamas ready to take on the Steens Mountain backcountry in rugged and scenic southeast Oregon. The mountain sat in Oregon's high desert and reaches up to more than 9,700 feet. Its name came from US Army Major Enoch Steen, who fought and removed the members of the Paiute tribe from the mountain.

The country was rugged and big, but the bowhunting gods smiled on me on opening day. After missing the biggest buck I'd ever seen with my first arrow, I connected on my second frantically released but well-placed arrow.

Being that it was the biggest buck I'd ever seen on the hoof, obviously it was the biggest buck I'd ever killed. It happened not because of me or my skill but more because of my bowhunting brothers, namely Wayne, who invited me on that trip.

Not long after my Steens success on a true signature bow kill, on another hunt in the reprod of western Oregon, I killed my biggest bull. Picture the young hunter I was with my thirty-dollar Jason PermaFocus binos, the Fine Line sights, the fresh double-dipped orange and white XX75s, and the Oregon Valiant Crusader III DX bow. On the hood of my quiver I had glued two bear claws from the first bear I'd ever arrowed. In between those bear claws was a metal six-by-six bull elk head silhouette I rubber-cemented on as well.

My shot was perfect, a thirty-five-yard quartering-away shot. The arrow went in at the last rib and stopped on the far side shoulder, meaning I had only one hole (the entrance) from which to leave blood. I was using Thunderhead 125s, which are good, tough heads that did the job. That one perfect arrow put the bull down quickly even though I had a scant blood trail to follow. The Roosevelt bull was a big-bodied beast though, and his heavy hooves scarred the soft soil deeply. I followed his fresh, deep-cutting tracks for fifty yards down the hill before pulling back a wet fir bough revealing the fallen beast in a tangle of fireweed.

This dark-antlered five-by-five was my best bull to date.

I remember every detail of these hunts like they were yesterday. Hence the saying, "The beast is dead. Long live the mighty beast."

Bowhunting had gotten in my soul. At that time I had no idea how it would end up directing my every step through the journey of life.

Despite my growth and successes in bowhunting, I was still going nowhere with my life. I was twenty-two or twenty-three years old, living with four guys, and we drank beer all the time. One of my roommates got two DUIs in three weeks, both while driving my truck. I'm glad I wasn't driving those times, but it was more a matter of luck than good decision-making. I just never got caught. I wasn't living healthfully and still didn't have a real sense of purpose. I wasn't accountable for anything or to anybody. I felt shitty all the time.

A wake-up call arrived when I crashed my truck one night while drunk. I was driving too fast and flipped the vehicle, rolling it. The roof was crushed all the way down to the top of the seat. The truck was totaled. Of course, I didn't remember a thing.

I could have easily died or killed someone. There was no police report since this was a rural area and the law were seldom around. Wrecked cars were left in the ditch all the time. We simply called a tow truck and they took it to a wrecking yard.

Did I wake up? No. Not yet.

Did I see some sort of connection between me walking away from the crash and my dad walking away from his? Was I following in his alcoholic footsteps?

My life had become living with a bunch of guys, just partying. Basically working during the week, going to the clubs on weekends, just drinking at the apartment or at the lake.

In my early twenties I liked to work as little as possible, get drunk on the weekends, and be a smart-ass pretty much all the time. I remember at a party once I said something to some guy who had just gotten out of jail and ended up with cut above my eye.

It wasn't a great life.

I thought I was one lucky bastard to be walking away from that crash, but no . . .

You're a complete fuck-up and this time you got lucky, Cam.

You haven't gotten a DUI. Yet.

You haven't hurt yourself or anybody else. Not yet. Sure, you've gotten punched from being a smart-ass and drunk. You've gotten into fights, even with friends.

You're an idiot.

You're a loser.

What if I would have died that night? A wannabe athlete, young and dumb, putting alcohol over life would have meant giving up bringing three amazing souls into this world. It would have discarded a wonderful wife and deep brotherhoods and incredible memories and amazing experiences. There would have never been a *Keep Hammering* lifestyle, because I would have died as a result of being hammered. I would have never endured the devastating loss of my dad and my best friend which, through heartache, has made clear my own existence and purpose.

When I crashed my truck while driving drunk, no one believed in me nor was surprised that it happened. I walked away with nothing more than scratches and, of course, another chance to turn my life around. Thank God I eventually did.

I decided to quit college after becoming obsessed with bowhunting.

Was that smart? No.

Would you do that? Probably not.

People said I got lucky. In my second year of hunting, after I killed a raghorn five-point elk, people said they heard I shot it with a crossbow or a rifle, which would have been illegal. People like this started making up stories to discredit my accomplishments. My first taste of hater envy. I didn't like it but couldn't do anything about it.

After I killed the nice five-by-five Roosie and the big mule deer, this really stirred up hate. My photos at the Bow Rack got messed with as someone poked my eyes out with a tack. It didn't matter.

Weak people hate success. I just kept hammering.

From the beginning of it all, Roy Roth was there. He always believed in me even when I was a part-time college student and a full-time loser. Once he even vouched for me when we were going on a hunt with some other guys. Because of the reckless lifestyle I was living, someone mentioned to Roy that they didn't want me to come, but Roy told them he wanted me there. When they tried to rationalize, saying I wasn't practicing and that I was drinking all the time, Roy didn't budge. He wanted me on the hunt with him.

Roy always had my back, even from the very beginning.

Roy Roth and I biked in ten miles on logging roads to where he killed a nice five-point bull. It was a long day getting it out of the woods, but we loved it. For us, the bigger the challenge the better the experience was.

I was the only one who ended up killing on that hunt. I got it done somehow, for whatever reason. At the time I was still practicing and shooting my bow, but I was simply giving an average effort just like a lot of other guys. I've always been a good shot, even at the very beginning, but I wasn't putting in the time.

My early success in bowhunting was like a launching pad for me. Now I had material to write about and my big mule deer ended up landing me on a magazine cover, and that buck also got me in advertisements for Oregon Bow.

The same year I killed my first bull, in 1989, I also wrote my first hunting article, "Bulls, Bugles and Botches" for *Western Bowhunter* magazine. I was short on writing talent but long on desire, the story of my life. At the time, I wanted to be a hunting writer more than anything in life. I told my buddies, "I'm pretty sure I could write just as well as some of the guys getting published in the big hunting magazines. And I'll bet, all things being equal, I could hunt just as well, too."

Nobody believed those words except Roy. I can see why others wouldn't believe them. I was drinking and doing all sorts of other stupid shit at the time. Even though writing was kind of in my heart and something that I did all the time, it wasn't in my heart enough to inspire me to give up my unhealthy lifestyle. Bowhunting was the thing that got me on the right path.

Roy Roth was the one who helped keep me on the path.

Being a loser isn't cool. But you know what's worse than that?

Being a loser dad.

Tanner, our first son, was born in 1993, and something inside of me switched. They say parenthood changes everything, and it did for me. Suddenly I wasn't just on my own. Now I was affecting other people's lives.

I gotta be an example.

Every parent wants their kids to have more than they had. To have a better life than they had. My dad wasn't around, and I remembered all the moments desperately wishing for him and wanting to see him. I wanted to be there for my children.

I didn't want to die in a DUI crash, nor did I want to destroy a family by drinking.

Every man and woman has chinks in their armor. Over the years, I have discovered my weaknesses and know what goes on in my head and my heart. Even back then, I knew the truth. I couldn't lie to myself.

Alcohol was poison.

Hunting partner Chad Montgomery with first record book buck

Staring at my arrow stuck in the ground a mere twenty-five yards away, I strained to see the color and consistency of the blood that was covering it. I was able to sit and stare at my arrow for a long twenty minutes before getting down from my tree, and trailing my buck. What the arrow revealed was disappointing. From near as I could tell, the blood on my arrow came from little more than a flesh wound of the neck. However, as I progressed on the trail,

the blood sign got heavier with each step. I then concluded that I lucked out, and caught the jugular and would find my buck shortly.

Searching for the protruding tine of an antler, or the form of the buck's body, my eyes were up more than they were following blood. It is hard to describe the sinking feeling I experienced as I watched my buck explode from his bed. The buck ran off through the timber for only about fifty yards before walking out of sight. Knowing he was hurt and that animals have an incredible 'will to survive' I decided to back off and give him some more time. I let about thirty minutes pass before picking up on the blood trail where I had last seen him.

I was disappointed, to say the least, when the blood sign got progressively weaker. It was a little after 10:00 a.m. when I grudgingly resigned to going to meet Chad, bringing him back for additional tracking help. Giving a last ditch effort, I checked trails that cut through a grassy meadow, for fresh tracks. I was elated to find a speck of blood, and with renewed optimism I continued forth.

As the blood trail picked up substantially, I figured I had jumped him. Deciding to nock an arrow, I was ready for anything. As my eyes scanned ahead for blood, I spotted a deer lying behind some blackberries. With my heart pounding I eased around to get a clearer look at the deer and noting there was no movement or signs of life, I went to examine my trophy. I gave thanks for the patience and persistence required to recover this buck, then I sat back and stared at my magnificent and most rewarding blacktail to date!

Let me give credit where credit is due. I owe that buck to good

From one of the first articles I ever wrote in **Western Bowhunter** *magazine.*

It's one thing to find your true passion in life, but what about your poison? What is the one thing or multiple things that hinder your ability to achieve the type of success you desire? Who or what is preventing you from fulfilling your potential? For me it was a number of things: alcohol, toxic people, lack of confidence, average physical ability, and so on.

Recognize this in your life and you're in control regardless of what others might lead you to believe.

Remove the obstacles and distractions and watch your dreams become reality.

I had seen what alcohol did to my dad, ruining what could have been something incredible, and I was seeing it do the same thing to me. So I stopped drinking. Who knows what would have happened if I had kept that lifestyle?

What if . . .

I know one thing. There would be nobody wanting to read a book about some drunk who lives in Marcola. I could easily still be there, drinking the days away and spending the nights sleeping without a single dream.

Alcohol wasn't going to help me in any area of my life, especially with my hunting. I'm not judging anybody else, but for me, I had to quit drinking.

You have to know what your strengths and weaknesses are. You have to be honest with yourself, sometimes brutally honest. Then you have to put in the work.

Failures don't necessarily mean your fate is written in stone.

When I came back from the one year of redshirting at Southern Oregon State, I found myself lost without sports. But what if I would have stuck with my dreams of playing college ball? What if I could have afforded to stay at the university and keep trying? What if someone was there supporting my hopes and dreams, either with encouragement or finances?

We wake up with a hundred what-ifs every day. They might be interesting to think about, but they are in the past. It's more important to ask yourself future what-ifs.

Becoming a dad changed my life. Was I going to be a "loser dad," or was I going to show my kids how to pave a path to success? I made a lot of mistakes, but I've tried to show them that through hard work, you can achieve some pretty crazy goals. It worked. They are more successful than I ever was.

As I began to get more involved with bowhunting, I began to ask myself new questions.

What if we threw out what people think about hunters?

What if we tossed away the stereotypes and semantics about them?

What if we invented the ultimate predator? What would that look like?

To me it resembled a professional athlete, someone who focused on nutrition and who trained hard. Someone who wanted to break down their mental barriers so they could be stronger than they've ever been.

I'm grateful for second chances and for slowly making the change from that guy jumping off the hood of his truck into some deep, boulder-lined swimming hole half buzzed. Thank God I made those changes. I'm grateful every day for my children—Tanner, Truett, and Taryn. I believe they will make a positive impact on the world.

Take it from me. Don't have your friends and family one day reminiscing on your life's potential, wondering . . . what if?

Learning from giants: The Dunsons, who helped me when I started bowhunting, set the Pope & Young world record for one bull and also had the #4 Roosevelt bull ever killed, but this bull I killed in 2021 is much larger.

DREAM BIGGER, ACHIEVE MORE

To build momentum, you have to get started.

To get started on your journey, you don't need new shoes, a new bow, protein, pre-workout, etc.

You just need to get out the door.

You just need to take that first step.

You just need to shoot that first arrow.

My first bow cost $189, but starting with it led me to hunting in places I never thought I'd see and barely knew existed.

My first race was a 5K, which has evolved into epic mountain races hundreds of miles in distance.

With hard work, dedication, and focus, you can be whatever you want to be. The key is to find something you're passionate about.

After my stepdad took me and my brother to our first "deer camp," I killed a spike buck at about 150 yards with a .300 savage mag. It didn't matter how unimpressive the antlers were; I was very proud. This experience ignited a passion for the mountains and the challenge of the hunt.

I got positive attention for killing that very small buck.

For a fifteen-year-old with braces and acne, that was empowering.

That experience in the clean mountain air inspired me to write a story for English class in school. My teacher, Mr. Haller, said I was a great writer. He may have been lying, but I believed him and built on that one random comment. I've continued writing, penning books, being a magazine editor, and so on.

A life-changing journey really all started with a whimper . . . a small buck and an English paper from an awkward teenager.

You don't need a big break to "make it." You need to just take one small step. Then another. And another.

A successful journey might start with a simple compliment, a pat on the back, or sharing a hunting camp with a kid. It doesn't matter where you're starting from.

Find that passion and you'll find your purpose.

Figure out what gives you joy.

Follow the road that brings you fulfilment.

Here's all I need to be happy: wild mountains, a good bow, a sharp knife, sturdy boots, a strong spirit, and the wind in my face. With these, I can do what I was born to do.

Bowhunt.

PART 2

IF YOU'RE NOT
OBSESSED,
YOU'RE GOING
TO BE
MEDIOCRE.

PREDATOR

CHAPTER 4

STRANGE AND
UNEXPLORED
TERRITORY

I've always loved the feeling of going into the mountains with bow in hand and coming out loaded down with a buck. To me, that's classic bowhunting and perfectly encapsulates one of my mantras: Train, Hunt, Provide and Honor.

It has been said that life offers two paths, one easy and one hard. As Roy and I entered the unforgiving sanctuary of the Eagle Cap Wilderness for the first time and witnessed the awe-inspiring Wallowa Mountains in northeastern Oregon, it was obvious that we had chosen the latter. We were always drawn toward the more difficult path. To us, harder was *always* better.

On my first elk hunt in the Eagle Cap Wilderness, which is Oregon's largest designated wilderness area, spanning 1,800 square miles, I became hooked on this form of bowhunting. With its granite crags and bottomless canyons, this rugged land was no doubt the roughest in Oregon. It was home to a bevy of big-game animals, including bighorn sheep, mountain goats, mule deer, bear, cougars, and Rocky Mountain elk, to list a few. Many bull elk roamed this wilderness without ever being bothered by a human. There is something magical about wild and rugged country, but it's not something that can be explained. I've tried for decades. If the unyielding characteristics of the wild are in your soul, then you know. If they're not, no words will make them so.

Roy and I were 400 miles from home when we arrived at the trailhead. This was a big deal, because prior to this trip, Roy and I had done 99 percent of our hunting within twenty minutes of our western Oregon homes. Suffice it to say, we were in way over our heads.

Arriving at this point was a journey itself. Normally we

bought gas for our trucks five dollars at a time, but we didn't have enough money to make it to "The Caps," in the far northeast corner of the state. Roy ended up selling a collector's edition .30-30 rifle his grandpa had given him for $300 to use for gas money. We could ill afford to hire a horse packer, so we convinced Roy's dad to buy two pack llamas to carry some of our gear, which we led into the Eagle Caps.

We had to sacrifice to make it to the wilderness, and the path ahead looked daunting and dangerous. Regardless, where the heart goes, the body will follow, so Roy and I figured out a way to get into the backcountry.

Did we know if there was going to be a payoff or a payout or anything accomplished on this trip? Of course not, but we were there anyway. If you want something badly enough, you will find a way to make it happen.

Roy and I wanted to live life on the edge. We were in this huge wilderness in order to be wild and free and chase adventure. This was our only goal.

This would be the place where Roy and I learned the most valuable lessons about bowhunting. And, ultimately, about life.

Bowhunting in general is hard. There are lots of tough men who do it. But it's not easy. The mountains can break even the toughest man. Roy Roth was the toughest human I'd ever met and ever seen out in the mountains. Hands down. Roy was the toughest bowhunter I'd ever seen, and he always carried the best attitude. I learned so much from him. He is a big reason I am the person I am today.

As a kid, I always knew Roy was good in the woods. He could always get to the best fishing holes before the rest of us. We nicknamed him "Gazelle Roy" because he was big but he moved like a gazelle. He was a great athlete; he played football and he was really good at baseball, specifically,

Roy Roth and I during a successful moose hunt in the backcountry of Alaska. He used my bow to kill this bull with one perfect arrow at sixteen yards.

third base. From the moment Roy told me I should start bowhunting, we connected and hit it off. We started hunting together and we just clicked because we both had no limits on how much misery we would suffer to chase success.

Roy's dad owned a construction company, so Roy worked for Roth Construction, and for a while after graduating high school, I worked for them, too. Most of the time we would work really hard in the morning and then get off early to go shoot something—carp in the summer, which we would then use for bear baiting. We both became quickly became obsessed with archery and bowhunting and pushed each other to achieve more.

"Has a man ever done it?" This was what Roy and I talked about. If a man had done it before—any man, ever—then we thought we could do it too. If a man had never done it, then there might be a chance we'd fail, but we'd give it our best anyway. We wanted to find the limit of what was possible. That was why we drove eight hours to this wilderness in eastern Oregon. We knew it was better hunting, that the land was wilder, that there were fewer people out there simply because it was so difficult, which, all considered, made the wilderness with all its unknowns seem like a big piece of candy and we were kids with an insatiable sweet tooth.

This hunt was one I will never forget as it was my and Roy Roth's last hunt together. I arrowed a great bull in the snow and it was an incredible bookend to the hunting journey we shared together for nearly 30 years.

Here's one of the endless examples of Roy's toughness.

Shortly after Roy's dad bought some llamas, we trained them to haul our gear. During one scouting trip deep into Oregon's Three Sisters Wilderness with the llamas, Roy was heating some dinner on a single-burner propane stove, using a pot with a handle that hung down on the bottom side of the pot, essentially right in the propane flame. We were heating water to make a little mac and cheese, so once it came to a boil, Roy gingerly lifted the handle and grabbed it to lift the pot off the burner. Since the handle was branding-iron hot, as Roy began to lift the pot, the handle melted the skin on his fingers.

Most people would have immediately dropped the pot, but Roy couldn't because boiling water is a precious commodity in the backcountry. So he set it down as fast as possible while exclaiming, "Jimmity Christmas that is hot." Roy didn't cuss then, and in all the years of knowing him, I never heard him utter even one cuss word.

Roy had deep burns, seemingly to the bone, on the bend of the second knuckles of a few fingers where the pot handle had rested as he lifted the pot. We stayed in the wilderness for a couple days after that, and he never mentioned it again. He just wrapped his fingers in duct tape and kept on keeping on.

That was Roy. We both loved bowhunting because it came with more adventure. The seasons were longer, so there were more opportunities. There were fewer people to deal with as well since it was so difficult.

Mountains are the great equalizer in life. Roy and I believed this, so we sought out more rugged country than anybody else, knowing that would give us an advantage because in the regular world, the people with money or connections had an advantage over regular guys like us. But material success, money, and reputation don't mean anything in the mountains.

The mountains don't give a damn.

How tough you are and how good of shape you're in gives you currency on the mountain. We came to realize that the tougher we were, the more success we had.

The mountain still always had the upper hand though.

I've long ago realized that those I most look up to are those who are at home in the mountains. Their resolve, confidence, and spirit are honorable in my eyes. One such individual is a man most won't know or have even heard of: Billy Cruise. The legendary Billy Cruise motivated me for years.

Five miles from our chosen Eagle Cap Wilderness entry-point trailhead, Roy and I came upon a big outfitter's camp. Since we had come here solely to get away from other hunters, we kept going and eventually ended up fifteen miles from the trailhead, at the bottom of a huge canyon. This was where we crossed paths with a long-time wilderness bowhunter, a dentist from Eugene, Oregon.

"Do you guys need some help?" the man asked as he eyed us and our ragged packstring.

"We've been walking all day and are just looking for some good elk country away from other hunters," I said.

The dentist proceeded to tell us a life-changing story about a man named

Billy Cruise, an Oregon elk-hunting legend and founder of the Oregon Bow Company, the same brand of bow I held in my hand. Billy had died in a plane crash while scouting for elk a few years earlier, but his legend lived on, especially for a couple of young, hungry bowhunters like Roy and me. The dentist had shared many camps with Billy.

"Most of the guys in our party hunted within a few miles of camp, but Billy would head to the deepest and nastiest country in the Eagle Cap," the dentist said. "Every year, without fail, we would all be sitting around camp, eating dinner or playing cards long after dark, when Billy would burst into the tent and roll a couple of bloody elk ivories onto the table. He would then launch into a story of how he arrowed another big wilderness bull and packed it out of a hell hole.

"I could tell you guys where Billy hunted," the dentist continued. "No one ever goes there. It is too rough for horses, and too steep to hike. You boys are more than welcome to give it a try."

"Perfect!" we responded. "We just want to get away from people."

"You won't see a soul," the dentist assured us.

Lining out down the trail, Roy and I tried not to look back. We wanted to play it cool and hide the big grins tattooed across our dirty faces. That dentist had just given us the secret to happiness. We had never met Billy Cruise personally, but walking in his bootprints had put a new bounce in our steps.

Making one last 4,000-foot vertical climb, we ended up twenty-one miles from the trailhead and our truck. We didn't care. We were living for the moment. We were heading down the hard path toward the unknown.

After a race in his freshman year at the University of Oregon, Steve Prefontaine once said, "I've never been here before. It was unexplored territory. It's strange. You find yourself in a spot in time you've never hit before and you don't know if you can finish. But I'm always exploring myself. I haven't reached the threshold of unconsciousness yet. Maybe I never will."

This was strange, unexplored, and exhilarating territory Roy and I were exploring. After many days and a number of close calls with some really big bulls, in terrain every bit as nasty as the dentist had promised, I arrowed a lonely spike, my first wilderness bull. The crazy-long pack out did little to deter our enthusiasm. Backcountry hunting was in our blood.

The dentist was right. We did not see another soul. And even now, many years and hunts and bulls later, I still have not seen another person back there.

Why am I drawn to do things like this?

Many years after first hunting in the Eagle Cap Wilderness, I completed the Western States Endurance Run, 100 miles through California's Sierra Nevada mountains. I clocked in at 22 hours, 41 minutes. Several times during the race, I found myself wondering why I was attracted to things like running a 100-mile race.

I believe it goes back to the intimidation I felt when I hunted Eagle Cap as a young, solo adventurer. To me, an inexperienced young bowhunter, it seemed immense and overwhelming. Scary, if the truth were known.

Since running my first marathon some years ago, I've had a crazy thought.

What if I could run across the entire Eagle Cap? Through the rivers and creeks, up the drainages, and over the mountains.

If I could do that, I could do anything.

When the day came when I actually could do that, it gave me confidence to face all my doubts and fears and beat them regardless of the obstacles that stood in my way. But being able to accomplish that took time.

One of my favorite books of all time is *Hunting with the Bow and Arrow* by Dr. Saxton

As young fathers, Roy and I wanted to share the wild with our kids. This photo was taken in Alaska on Tanner's first bear hunt. He was seven. Roy's son, Taylor, was also seven at this time. I think it was experiences like this that helped prepare these boys to weather tough situations.

Pope. Written in 1923, it details the adventures of Pope and his friend Art Young. On page 181, it reads, "We also began preparing ourselves for the contest. Although habitually in good physical condition, we undertook special training for the big event." In this case, he and Young were preparing for a grizzly bowhunt. Pope continues, "By running, the use of dumbbells and other gymnastic practices, we strengthened our muscles and increased

> ## "The love of the chase nonetheless thrills us and all the misty beyond echoes with the hunter's name."
>
> **—Saxton Pope,** *Hunting with the Bow and Arrow*

our endurance." On page 206, regarding the tough backcountry hunt, he writes, "We were there to win and nothing else mattered," adding later, "We were trained down to rawhide and sinew, keyed to alertness and ready for any emergency."

Back in those early days when I was a young up-and-comer, I quickly dismissed those few sentences. Over time, however, lines like "trained down to rawhide and sinew" resonated with me. That was some hardcore stuff. If Pope and Young realized the benefits of being fit back in the 1920s, then I bet the same held true for me and many other bowhunters. Starting way back when, the better shape I got in, the smaller the Eagle Cap Wilderness seemed to me. And now it seems quite manageable. In fact, I now feel at home in even the most rugged of mountains. It's where I'm most at peace.

Roy and I were both drawn to the mountains, pulled in by the danger and delight of the hunt. I never feel more capable or stronger than when hunting or running in the mountains. It's like I'm invincible. I can do anything. Roy felt the same way with regard to hunting in wild country.

To those who are drawn to the wild, the intensity and purity of life in high altitudes comes with unspoken risk. Because men—all men—are mortal. The mountains can be as ruthless as they are majestic, and this was what drew Roy and me like moths to a flame. To us, this dichotomy was everything. Without it, what's the point?

From the very beginning I knew that there was a lot of risk to what we do. That was part of the deal. Maybe the grandest part?

What is the most difficult challenge you must overcome to achieve your goals? Are you afraid of the hard work, or do you fear failing in other areas of your life? What "wilderness" awaits you on your journey? How can you be mentally and spiritually tough enough to battle the isolation, the doubt, and the questions? As my friend Michael Chandler said, "Life is all about the ups and the downs, the peaks and the valleys. How much mental toughness we store up on the peaks will determine how triumphant we are in the valleys."

FIND YOUR EDGE

I go where others won't go or can't go because it's too far and too difficult.

This is what I've relied on over the years.

If I can, I eliminate the competition. I make the hunt where it's just me against the animal. That's always better odds than trying to outwit my quarry and beat every other Tom, Dick, and Harry while doing so.

There are places I can drive to, park, and easily walk into hunting country.

Places anybody can go.

If it's easy for me to get there, then it's easy for everybody to get there.

That makes it a no-go for me.

I want to find the places that are almost impossible to reach. I want to walk paths where people have to give more to make it happen. I want an untamed wilderness with rocky crags and miles of unyielding country fending off intruders.

Places like this are different. There are people in the civilized world with more money and more connections. There are smarter individuals with more friends and more resources than I have. They all have an advantage over me in the regular world. I can't do anything to compete with them in their arena. I'm not going to have more money and I'm not going to be more influential on their home turf.

In the wilderness, all that changes.

In the mountains, all that is different.

You can have all the money in the world, but in the mountains, you're just another mere mortal.

If I'm better than my competition in the mountains, then all of a sudden I'm the guy calling the shots.

I can't control the wilderness with its weather and the toll the terrain takes on a person's body and soul. Nobody can control that. No, but I focus on what I *can* control in order to be the best I can be when I enter the wild.

Where do I have an edge? That's the question I answer.

I figure it out and then I exploit it.

Years ago, I accepted the fact that having success in the bowhunting woods was going to be one of the toughest challenges I ever faced. So what did I do?

I began a regimen to try to hone an edge in the mountains, both mentally and physically.

I run.

I lift weights.

I shoot my bow.

I obsess about bowhunting every day.

I do all these things because I must if I'm to achieve my dreams.

So what's your edge and what are you doing to keep it?

CHAPTER 5

DON'T LET THEM OUTWORK YOU

My success isn't all about what I do. It's also about what I don't do. I don't drink, fish, golf, play poker. We haven't taken any family vacations. Nothing distracts me from being disciplined. Most people won't give up all I will. It's as much about what I don't do as opposed to the daily work I put in. All part of being tunnel-visioned.

I looked over the lonely wilderness and, holding my bow firmly and feeling the weight from my pack, loaded down next to me was the trophy of a lifetime. Some people dream of being wealthy or famous or maybe playing in the Super Bowl as millions of viewers tune in and cheer their every move. Conversely, this was what I dreamt of.

There was no cheering crowd. The only sounds I could hear were the wind or sliding shale or a rolling rock.

The only thing missing on this hunt was Roy.

After our first adventures in Eagle Cap, I thought about that hunt every single day of the year. Now I was back, and once again I was victorious. The only problem was that my partner had moved to Alaska. I was starting what eventually became an annual solo adventure for me.

Roy had helped the pastor of his church move up to Alaska. After driving all the way through Canada and back, Roy knew he had to move north. It felt like a calling. He ended up being hired by a big construction company up there, so he moved his family to Alaska. Roy was very smart when it came to the construction business, and he eventually started his own company and became very successful as a general contractor. Roy essentially took over his Dad's business, Roth Construction. They worked together, but Roy went from an understudy to running the show.

The only problem was that now, back in Oregon, I had lost a kindred spirit.

I tried to talk other people into going hunting with me, but the few I persuaded only went one time. One and done. The solitude, the big country. It was too much for others. Nobody else wanted it the way I wanted it. The way Roy wanted it. I tried desperately to find another partner who shared my backcountry passion, but I couldn't find a single soul.

You can't talk someone into loving backcountry bowhunting. You either love it or you don't. There is no middle ground.

When I realized I was just wasting energy trying to talk people into feeling the way I did about the backcountry, I was left with a decision. My choice was either to go by myself or not go at all, simply because I couldn't get anybody who wanted to join me. Of course, I chose to keep going. I decided I couldn't rely on anyone but myself. Once again, I was forced to push myself and go alone. That wasn't my first choice, but that's how life works sometimes.

For the next twelve years, I ended up hunting in the sprawling and unforgiving Eagle Cap Wilderness, most of the time on my own. My entire existence seemingly revolved around preparing for just one crack at the wilderness bulls and bucks where Billy Cruise had walked.

The wilderness is hard. It will test you and have

Born to bowhunt

you questioning how much you actually want to be back there. This started a good journey in the wilderness for me. I learned more about myself on those solo hunts than I could have in a lifetime in the everyday world. Maybe that's because those hunts have taught me to bleed.

Bowhunting is not like other sports that demand super running speed, agility, strength, and coordination. In bowhunting, anyone committed to doing their best and to respecting their quarry, the country, and the time-honored pursuit can reach great heights. From personal experience I can

It took me eight years of bowhunting before I killed a 6x6 bull on my own in the wilderness. I had killed bulls every year, but they weren't considered "wall-hangers" or trophies. This one was, and it fell to my arrow twelve miles from the nearest road. Wilderness hunting, solo, helped make me tough.

tell you it boils down to how bad you want it. Are you willing to bleed? In most cases, it takes some blood to achieve your goals.

The truth is, many bowhunters aren't willing to bleed. Bowhunting is just a fun hobby, right? A great way to pass the time. A way to get fresh air, take a vacation, and maybe even put meat on the table. I agree with all of that, but that doesn't motivate me. What compels me most is the test.

From the very start of my backcountry bowhunting journey, I was drawn deep into the most wild and remote country I could find. I always wanted to be farther in than anyone else so I could hunt undisturbed animals. Perhaps there was a hidden desire inside of me, however: a desire to push against the barriers of my own psyche and self-imposed limits of what's possible?

What I learned quickly was, the harder you push, the more people you leave behind.

The farther you go, the fewer who will be willing to go with you. The reasons why they quit are simple: They can't handle it, or they don't want to.

Will you continue on, even if alone?

Most won't.

I knew that if I could get back farther into the wilderness, I could find better hunting. I could get away from other hunters if I was in better shape. And if I was mentally stronger, I could outlast anyone.

After Roy moved his family to Alaska, convincing anybody to hunt the wilderness with me was a losing battle. I couldn't figure out why no one wanted to leave town Friday after work, drive all night, hike all day in the wilderness for what amounted to a one-day weekend hunt and do the same thing in reverse to get back to town late Sunday night or early Monday morning just before work. To me, it seemed like the greatest weekend ever. But everyone is different, and has different wants, needs, and priorities. My goals and objectives were crystal clear.

So, I often made the drive alone and hunted alone. The choice was either go alone or don't go at all.

The wilderness tested me, mentally more than anything. The mind is powerful and can actually create issues that aren't even really there, as we can obsess about things in distractionless country. Sleeping deep in the mountains alone is not natural for humans these days. We are taught to fear

The first magazine advertisement I was ever featured in.

the dark, taught that there is strength in numbers, and we are conditioned to greatly enjoy and become softened by the comforts of home.

I learned to overcome my own self-doubt in the wild, unforgiving country. I discovered how to confront my common fears. Facing them changed me forever.

Since, in the early days, I couldn't afford premium hunts and never drew any highly regarded tags, I learned that the remote setting of the wilderness offered some amazing opportunities while at the same time weeded out 99 percent of other hunters, as it is tough hunting and tough living. It was hard for me too, but walking in prime mountain elk country with not a single boot track in the dusty pack trail helped ease the pain for me and kept me focused. Backcountry hunting opened up a whole new world of possibilities.

Being "in deep" seemed like the great equalizer to me. It was one of the few places I knew of where money and status didn't make the hunting any easier. I was a warehouse worker back home, but putting good bulls and bucks on the ground in the mountains made me feel like I was capable of great things. As a young guy searching for direction in life, the wilderness had a big impact on me. However, initially, learning the ropes in the wilderness, trying to kill an elk with my bow gave me that old familiar feeling of trying to achieve the impossible. The elk hunting back there was intense . . . wild country, highly strung elk, on edge from living in an extremely harsh environment while trying to steer clear of the natural born killers of the mountains, cougars, were real tough to get in bow range of. And the intimidating expanse of Oregon's largest wilderness area, as a solo hunter, shook my confidence. I wondered many times if I had what it took to get it done "in deep"?

I did.

And becoming aware of this changed me forever.

Life is a test. There are times when you realize you're not passing the class and you need to change your study habits. Kinda like what happened after our first son was born. Once I held Tanner in my arms, I wondered what I was doing with my life. I knew I needed to do better. Suddenly it wasn't just myself I was letting down. Now I had a life that depended on me, and there was a legacy attached to it.

What was going to be my legacy?

I didn't really know. I didn't really have a path or an answer. I didn't have a degree, and I didn't have anybody coming alongside of me sharing wise counsel or even just solid advice for a young dad. I didn't have any insight, so I gradually learned through a lot of trial and error. Like all things in my life. There has never been a grand plan, or frankly, any plan at all. It's just been about doing what I can day by day.

When I realized things needed to change, I thought to myself, *Well, all I really know how to do is work.* So I figured I would work as many hours as I could. That was all I really had to offer: hard work. I began putting in a lot of hours, and then I discovered that guys would listen to me. Somehow I could convince them to do things when other guys couldn't. I don't know why it's like this, but when some guys talk, people blow them off, and when other guys talk, people pay attention and say to themselves, "Okay, that makes sense." I knew I had some leadership qualities, so that plus being willing to work my butt off led to more opportunities. That was how my career started.

I remember decades ago when a hunting article I wrote came out, the publisher included a bio that incorrectly said that I was a warehouse supervisor instead of the lead. One petty co-worker, Tim, highlighted it, laughing loud while telling everyone, "Cam thinks he's a supervisor. He's only a lead." In the end, the same day I officially got promoted to supervisor, I accepted a job on the construction crew at the place I work now. Except now I'm the superintendent. Still laughing, Tim?

When I got a job offer to work for the Springfield Utility Board (SUB) on the construction crew in 1996, it was for less money than I was making at the Coast-to-Coast distribution center as a supervisor, but I took it anyway. Everybody knows that working for the city, the state, or a municipality is a good and stable job, so even though it was a bit of a sacrifice, my younger self actually made a good decision. It was a great decision, actually. I've been working for Springfield Utility Board ever since.

At the time, I thought that if I got a good job like this, I would have everything I ever wanted. A good job with good benefits working for a great company. After I started working, I felt like the luckiest guy in the world. I was now going to take care of my family. We'd bought our first house for $64,000 and I fixed it up and sold it for $91,000. We then used that equity to move into a slightly larger house in a modest neighborhood. Things were headed in the right direction.

However, the new job meant I had no vacation time built up yet, so I could no longer hunt in the wilderness for ten days like I'd been doing for the prior few seasons. I needed to be a "weekend warrior" instead. It was just one more sacrifice I was willing to make.

This poem was written by the late Jimmie Osburn, a friend who grew up with me and my brother Pete. The three of us, along with Jeff Peck and Donnie Mannila, all grew up on Wendling Road in Marcola, Oregon, and were the best of friends and fiercely competitive. Life in our high school days revolved around sports, with a big emphasis on football. Playing football, Donnie and I were "The Connection" because he was the quarterback and I was a wide receiver. We hooked up for a lot of touchdowns. Pete and Jimmie were a couple years younger and dubbed themselves "The Connection II," believing they were better than the original. Maybe they were? The point is we pretty much saw each other every single day for years and were very close.

After high school, hunting took precedence over most everything. In the off-season, Jimmie and I went through a period when every weekend we'd ride horses into the country where we deer hunted. We would load up our saddle bags and spend the entire day in the mountains, trying to be like the Man from Snowy River. I have a lot of great memories from those days.

When Jim was killed in a freak accident on his horse at the age of twenty-eight, many were devastated. Especially his wife, Wendy, and his three young kids, who he'd be very proud of if he could see them today. Jim has been gone for over twenty years now but his memory lives on. A man taken in the prime of his life like Jim has always been hard for me to make sense of. I just know we need more guys like Jim Osburn—tough, hardworking, loyal and smart.

Jim's poem here comes from his experiences at "Elk Camp." I've always liked this poem as it allows me to envision the camaraderie and tradition of an annual Elk Camp. My only elk hunting experiences have come by way of bow and arrow, where solo hunting is the name of the game, or at least it has been for me. So I never got to spend a week at a big Elk Camp, where hard mountain hunting ruled the day and canvas tents, a wood stove, big meals, poker, and cold beer made the nights fun and memorable. I wanted to share Jim's poem and the photo of him from his funeral program.

If you have a friend like Jimmie Osburn, consider yourself lucky.

ELK HUNTERS SPECIAL

Look forward all summer
To this time of year
Loaded the truck
And bought a little beer.

Pull into camp
Under beautiful skies
Set up the tent
And start tellin' lies.

Cut and stack the wood
And everything's a go
Scout a few elk
And it's lookin' like snow.

Well the fun's all over
And the work starts here
Gotta get out your knife
And put down your beer.

Didn't fire a round
But packed meat all day
All I got's stories
Of the one that got away.

Whether it's the time you got the rack
Or the year of the big snow
You got some good memories
And a few pictures to show.

Well when it's all over
You got an elk or not
You start plannin' next year
To give it another shot.

Jim Osburn

I still remember some of those weekends. I would mountain-bike into the logging country I grew up hunting in, parking at the gate on the mainline and riding for hours before daylight so I could be miles in as the sun came up. I wanted to be farther in than anyone else so I could hunt undisturbed animals.

I didn't need to be somewhere like Eagle Cap to want to get as far away from other hunters as possible.

One fateful morning, as a late summer rain fell gently, I glassed up a herd of elk miles away from my high vantage point. I was on the 9,000 line and the elk were back off the 5,000 which meant I'd ridden past them. It also meant that other hunters who didn't go as far in as me could be closer to them. I hopped on my bike, bombed down, hit the mainline and made like a bowhunting Lance Armstrong hammering my pedals, eating up the miles. When I got to the 5,000 line it was all uphill to the road that would take me closest to the herd I'd spotted. My quads were on fire as I kept my ass in the seat, pushing hard on those pedals. If you stand up and pedal, the back tire will dig up the rocks, as there's not enough weight on it. So you sit and grind. I'd been scouting up there all summer, so my legs were strong, meaning I got to the elk quickly.

I had cheap optics, so I couldn't really tell how big the bull was from a distance, but I knew he was bedded at the top end of the herd. I eased close to where I'd last seen them, with an arrow nocked. My plan worked perfectly. As

Long range practice has become one of my bowhunting preparation staples. Here I'm shooting at 140-yards, over the trucks, to the furthest target. My goal is to become proficient shooting at a distance twice that I'd ever shoot an animal at. For instance if I can be accurate at 140-yards while practicing then I'd feel comfortable shooting an arrow at an animal at 70-yards while hunting.

the bull was still bedded, I slowly stalked closer. The bull was facing toward me as I came to full draw. I expected him to stand, as he looked in my direction the moment I settled in for the shot. Instead, he stayed bedded. At forty-three yards I had a lot of confidence in my shot, built over time and repetition, so I locked my forty-yard pin high, just above the gap where his shoulder and sternum meet, and released. The arrow drove home perfectly to the nock. The big-bodied bull stood as blood fell from the hole in his chest. It was a heart shot, so he didn't go far before piling up in the thick reprod.

A great shot for a weekend warrior.

I still was called to the wilderness so I'd bomb to the other side of the state, when I could. Some weekend scouting or hunting trips looked like this: On Friday afternoon, I left work around 4:00 p.m., driving north through Portland and arriving at 1:00 a.m. at my Eagle Cap trailhead. I'd load up my pack and start walking, trying to get back twelve miles or so by first light. I wouldn't sleep. I'd get back to the backcountry by first light on Saturday morning and be able to hunt or scout until Sunday. Then I would hike out and drive home on Sunday night, being back at work on Monday morning.

Two nights of no sleep for two days of scouting, or hunting if it was season, was worth it. These trips gave me the confidence to do my long solo hunts. I was testing myself, and passing each test.

As time went on, and as elk hunting became such a passion—an obsession—that I eventually used all my vacation time, my boss at the time said I couldn't miss another day of work. I wasn't on the crew anymore; I was now the buyer, so I had more flexibility as other crew members weren't relying on me. As a buyer, if I was gone, the work would just stack up until I got back. But even so, I was out of vacation time. I told them it looked like we had a decision to make. If I hadn't earned their trust and confidence and proved my worth, they'd likely have thought I wasn't worth the ultimatum. Instead, they let me go hunting and I made up the time when I got back.

Would most people risk their jobs—their steady, good jobs—just to pursue a passion? Probably not. Most people are smarter and more realistic than me.

I'm glad I did.

Don't make excuses.
Give it your all.
Show up when you're supposed to show up.
Speak your mind.
Own up to your mistakes.
Think with perspective.
This is how you live a life worth remembering. That's what I was starting to do.

The world will never forget August 31, 1997, and neither will I. Of course, I'm not like the rest of the world.

This was my eighth season as a bowhunter, and on that fateful day my world revolved around survival, eating, drinking, shelter, and of course, killing a bull.

That was it.

Nothing else mattered.

I was coming back from a hunt with news I couldn't wait to tell my wife. When I got in my Toyota and finally got cell service on the highway, I called her.

"Hey, Trace. I killed a six-by-six bull."

It was the best bull I'd ever killed. Her response wasn't what I expected.

"Princess Diana died."

"What?"

"Princess Di died. She was in a car crash in Paris."

"Who cares?" I said.

I know that might sound heartless, but look . . . when you're back in the wilderness and kill a six-by-six bull, nothing else matters. Princess Diana was beautiful and had a big heart. She was an icon to the highest degree, and it was a tragedy that she died. Approximately 2.5 billion people watched her funeral. I understand.

But to twenty-nine-year-old me, in late August of '97, my only focus was arrowing a good wilderness bull. And at that time, this six-by-six was my best.

Forgive me for being selfish, Princess Di.

With Roy and his family living in Alaska, we stayed in touch by calling each other on the phone and giving updates on our hunting adventures. I would tell him about my kills and share a few stories, and Roy would tell me about his hunting and guiding adventures. Sometimes we'd call each other just to BS. We tried to get together at least once a year to make something epic happen. My first two expeditions to Alaska were hunting Sitka blacktail deer on Kodiak Island in 1997 and black bear on Prince of Wales Island in 1999. All together I probably hunted in Alaska thirty times over the years. We had epic adventures together.

I still recall driving for fifteen hours on the Dalton Highway up toward the Prudhoe Bay Oil Field in northern Alaska. That's basically where the highway ends up reaching the top of the earth. It's way up there. If you got to a certain vantage point, you imagined you could see the curvature of the earth. There was nothing up there but great, wild hunting, which was enough for us. We did a big forty-mile float trip on our own and we each killed caribou with our bows, I got chased by a grizzly, and we lived on the edge for a week.

From day one, our journey was fueled by big dreams. When we were younger, Roy and I were very competitive, even with each other. I remember bumping each other out of the way as we fought to get a shot at a big bull elk when I was twenty and Roy was twenty-two. Just as brothers might, we argued about tactics, gear, everything. As hunters, we were successful on the small scale that matched the small town and world we called home. We also know that oftentimes success breeds jealousy, so some people tried to tear down our bow-hunting accomplishments in the early years. All this did was inspire us to push harder and made us not only stronger as individuals, but as bowhunting brothers, our bond became unbreakable.

I believe this unwavering union was forged because, for many years early on, our mindset was, "It's us against everyone else," in regard to bowhunting. Truth is, it wasn't. While people may have talked smack, talking only gets a smack-talker so far. We knew there wasn't really any head-to-head

The shirt aptly captures the key to any success I've experienced. The only talent I've ever had is to put in my time and more effort than the competition. Because skill-wise, I don't measure up.

competition in bowhunting when we were in big, remote country. It's just man versus animal, the country, and himself. Either way, the us-versus-them mind games kept us focused and always wanting to outwork the fictional bowhunting beasts we competed with in our minds.

Roy was the only other person I've ever hunted with who truly had no limits. If I wanted to go farther, so did he. If he wanted push harder, past where most would quit, so did I. The pain we had to endure meant nothing. We dealt with a lot of both physical and mental pain while surviving hard hunts in those early years.

This was probably why I never found someone else to go hunting with.

Roy and I both had our families, and we both had jobs to support them. But everyday life was pretty mundane for us, something we regularly joked about every time we were together. We knew everyone was good at something. Some men were good insurance salesmen, builders, teachers, and doctors; we were good at getting it done on difficult bowhunts.

"Cam, it's what we do."

Roy often said this when we bucked insane odds and tested ourselves. This was what we lived for. Our regular lives couldn't have been any more the polar opposite from what stirred our souls.

Bowhunting was a challenge that defined Roy and me and gave us an identity for many years. Sometimes, early on, I know we probably both were too consumed with hunting. Over the years, while the love of the mountains still called to him passionately, Roy did a better job prioritizing than I did. Like all things in my life, I have grown to be better at it over time.

I've been working at the same company for twenty-five years.

I've never called in sick.

I've never missed a day that I wasn't scheduled to be gone.

Knowing that I make more money from my side hustle of bowhunting, people always ask why I don't just quit my day job. Since my work ethic is the only reason I excel, and my job at the utility company has been a huge part of developing that work ethic, I feel called to stay and continue working there. I really like the guys who work for me. I believe in them and want them to succeed. Maybe I'm just loyal?

Also, I don't quit things. And I'm not going to start now.

Getting that job meant the world to me, so I would have a hard time saying, "Hey, I'm putting in my two weeks' notice so I can be a full-time bow-hunter." I don't know if I can ever do that. I still use my vacation time to go on hunts and make appearances. Balancing it all just means I have to grind harder every day. I love working where I work, so it doesn't feel like there is really a choice to make. This is what I do.

I'm a worker.

The truth is that I've always worked really hard because I've never really felt like I had a ton of natural skills or talent. It would feel unnatural to me not to have a regular job. I feel like such a life is reserved for someone who's a star, and I don't think I've got that, so I grind it out. I grind it out at training and I grind it out at work.

Not taking a day off is my only edge. I can't just say, "You know, today, I'm not gonna run. I've sacrificed enough."

No.

That's what everybody does. Everybody has an excuse. Everybody has a reason. You can always come up with a reason to not go after a challenge. So I've learned to never care what the excuse is. It's never valid. That's my attitude, and that's my edge. It's how I've built endurance and fostered resiliency. There are no rest days in my schedule. And that is the reason I excel.

"I don't have talent. I have tenacity."

—Henry Rollins

It's not talent. Not luck. Not know-how.

It's discipline. Endurance. Work ethic.

I've heard the same sort of excuses the last thirty-plus years.

"Yeah, I would do badass bowhunts, too. But I have kids."

So do I.

"I wish I could train like you and shoot my bow all the time, but I have a full-time job."

Yeah, me too.

I've always been a hard worker, but that's just the start. You can't just have a work ethic; you have to earn it. Discipline and excellence aren't something you can just think about and achieve. Decide to do something every day for a year. Whether it's running a mile, reading a chapter, writing a paragraph, eating breakfast, or drinking a gallon of water: find something that will help you improve yourself and do it every day for a year.

That's how you build a work ethic.

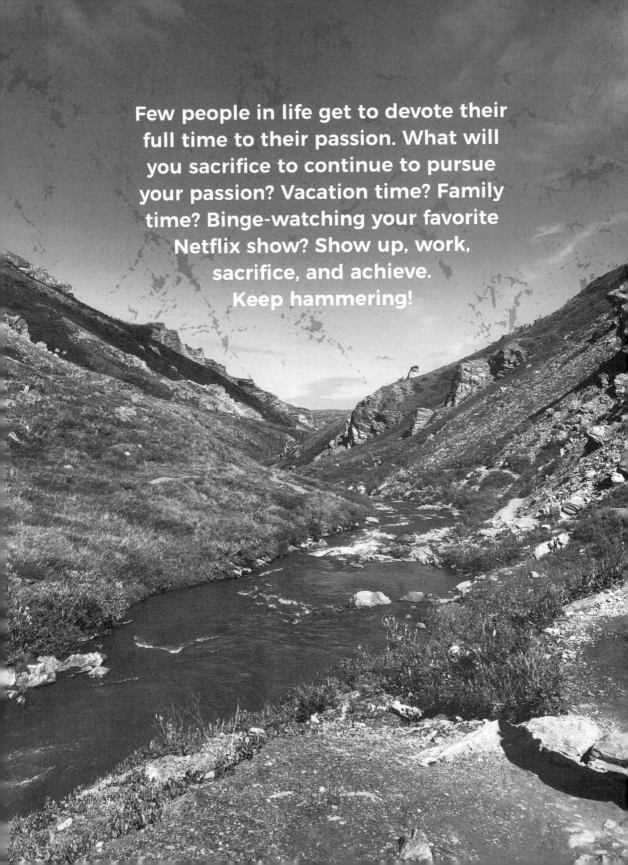

Few people in life get to devote their full time to their passion. What will you sacrifice to continue to pursue your passion? Vacation time? Family time? Binge-watching your favorite Netflix show? Show up, work, sacrifice, and achieve.
Keep hammering!

If you set high goals, make sure they are fueled by a passion for the journey. No great achievement ever comes easily, so you have to love the hard work you're going to have to put in along the way. If not, the pursuit will be a futile one.

There are lots of people out there who see the images of the beautiful and picturesque country and the pictures of the trophy animals, who watch videos chronicling these hunts and who read articles about these life-changing adventures. They tell themselves and others, "This is what I've always wanted to do."

But a ten-minute video of a hunt or a 2,000-word article cannot do justice to a ten-day hunt. All you're seeing are the highlights. And in the highlights, chances are you're missing the blood, sweat, and tears.

Doing a hunt by yourself means the hunt starts and ends with you. You have to do the research, pore over the details of the maps, test the gear, scout the country, and find the animals, all before finally tasting success if, and only if, that arrow strikes home.

Before making that kill, the time in the country is full of silence, bouts of homesickness, and likely second-guessing the decision to take in such a monumental challenge. Endless hiking in rugged and unforgiving country with the sun beating down on you or the wind drying your face, cracking your lips, or maybe your fire for the hunt being literally and figuratively doused by rain, while looking for an animal, can end up producing doubts and fears inside of you. And that's just during the day. The nights are obviously darker but can be an even greater test to the wandering mind and loneliness.

The question ultimately becomes . . . do you love hunting enough to endure?

The backcountry can defeat guys who aren't more than physically fit because mentally, after a couple of days on their own, without any distractions of normal life, they become wrecks.

What is your lifelong ambition? What is your long-term goal?

Whatever it might be, whether it's becoming a solo backcountry hunter or a doctor or a musician, just know that all rewards have to be earned the hard way.

There are no shortcuts to success in the mountains, and in life.

Those who work the hardest are successful, period.

Get to work.

EASY SUCKS

Since my early, clueless days, I've enjoyed some elk-hunting success, and along the way I've learned that achievement often involves some blood.

My own.

Bowhunting is not easy, which is perfect. I despise easy.

Easy does nothing for my spirit.

Easy can't change my life.

No one tells an epic story about an easy path they've traveled.

That's why I love backcountry bowhunting. It is not easy. It is a powerful mental, physical, and spiritual journey. It is life-changing. Arrowing a big six-by-six bull in the mountains brings extraordinary satisfaction, but it's never going to be easy. You can get lucky once, but if you expect every-year success like I do, you're going to have to work.

"Train hard, hunt easy" means I want my training to be so hard that even the most difficult of hunts are easy by comparison. Long mountain runs make me dig deep in training and give me mental strength and physical endurance.

Training hard is not easy.

It'd be really easy not to run every day.

It'd be really easy not to lift every day.

It'd be really easy not to shoot my bow every day.

Only problem: Easy sucks!

You don't wake up and see a new person in the mirror. There are no overnight transformations or dramatic improvements. Just little tweaks along the way.

Nothing makes it easy, though. Everything I do is very hard. Bowhunting. Running. Lifting. No shortcuts in any of it.

It just takes time and effort.

Try to make training as hard as possible and you will go a long way toward succeeding on those ball-busting hunts. I shoot my bow every day of the year anyway, but I believe the reps that really count are when I shoot after running an ultra or after a tough lifting session, when I am beat down, tired, weak, and mentally exhausted, much like I get on those long mountain hunts. I know if I practice putting the arrow on its mark when feeling like this, I'll be that much more proficient come crunch time.

People typically look for the easy way out, me included at times. The human body is capable of amazing things if we get out of our own way mentally. For those who say it's "too much" to hammer every day with all you have, I can't relate to that mindset. And I don't want to.

Life ain't easy. Just gotta keep grinding.

CHAPTER 6

OBSESSED OR AVERAGE

Most people won't give up all. I will.

Get better and grow, or throw in the towel. These are two choices we're faced with on a daily basis. Sometimes growth might be something as simple as spontaneously deciding to go run outside in the rain, or it might be some deep-rooted desire you've carried from your childhood.

Hunting isn't the only thing I have been passionate about since I was a kid. A good elk steak is enough to inspire anyone, but the written word has always been a big inspiration to me as well. I grew up enamored with good writing, mostly as it pertained to hunting, but the subject really didn't matter. Words that could paint a picture fascinated me. I was never that good at writing, but I wanted to be and tried really hard. As I mentioned earlier, one of my favorite books is *Hunting with the Bow and Arrow* by Saxton Pope, with a special introduction by Fred Bear. My dad bought me the title on one of his many Salvation Army bargain searches. I buried myself in that book, and its images are burned deep in my mind.

As a teenager, I bought and read every hunting magazine on the rack. I've always loved the feel, smell, photos, and, of course, the words that fill good hunting magazines. I have framed magazine articles and filled albums with cutout magazine articles. I have full collections of hunting magazines—stacks that drive my wife crazy—that I could never dream of getting rid of. To me, they are an indelible part of history—my bowhunting heritage, if you will. As a kid, I would ease through the timber of western Oregon and recall anecdotes my favorite hunting writers shared. This was a special time for me. All the magazines had great writers; I seemed to connect best with the articles in *Bowhunter* magazine. I was young, but to me it was the biggest, best, and most legit magazine out there.

In the same way kids today are enamored with professional athletes, I looked up to my "hunting idols." They were larger than life to me. In my dark living room back in the late 1980s, the TV flickered and emitted sounds of screaming bull elk as I watched my grainy *Elk Fever* VHS tape so many times that I could recite virtually every line Dwight Schuh and Larry D. Jones spoke.

Me and my younger brother, Pete. Our grandpa Bob trained, raced, and bred quarter horses in eastern Oregon. I worked there when I got older and will admit he was tough, even by cowboy standards. Maybe this was why, when Pete was in high school, he had a bumper sticker on his truck that said, "If you ain't cowboy, you ain't shit."

I recall vividly the "pinecones-in-the-boot" prank, as well as all the incredible bowhunting action. I bought green wool gloves like Dwight's and fletched my arrows with red and white vanes just as he did. I wore camo face paint with white and gray colors mixed in like Larry, and I have always submitted my hunting articles with my middle initial in the byline, just as Larry D. Jones did.

Back then M. R. James, the editor, ran the magazine I loved so much, and to a kid who bled bowhunting, he too was an influencing figure. I even wore a bandana around my neck when bowhunting during those early years, just as I'd seen M. R. do in many magazine articles.

My infatuation wasn't limited to just my *Bowhunter* magazine idols. With my first few kills, I didn't smile at all, trying to emulate a big name in bowhunting at the time, Myles Keller. Of course, Chuck Adams was the bowhunting king, and I took great pride in the fact that he grew up hunting blacktails, just as I did.

For hometown heroes, the late Billy Cruise, founder of Oregon Bow and an elk-hunting legend in Oregon's Eagle Cap Wilderness, was godlike to me. In my early years, Billy's amazing stories of his backcountry success in the same wilderness and exact same drainages I bowhunted for big bulls inspired me to be tougher and to endure more than I ever would have otherwise. I started shooting an Oregon Bow because of him, and I will never forget being featured in my first magazine advertisement for Oregon Bow. The passion I had for bowhunting governed my life in those days. Little has changed.

I wrote my first hunting article back in 1990, published not long after my first bow season in 1989. I wrote a story called "Bulls, Bugles and Botches" about the spike bull I killed my first season as a bowhunter, after blowing my chance at a monster.

I had everything in my own little world all figured out. Or so I thought.

Everybody needs feedback. But it's not always easy getting honest critiquing. Most people would read my stuff and say, "Yeah, I think it sounds really good. Nice work." That drove me crazy because I knew it wasn't that great but couldn't put a finger on why.

Carl Allen didn't mind giving it to me straight. I worked with him at the same warehouse where I met Trace. Carl was an interesting character in a workplace full of them. He and his wife would yell at each other over the warehouse intercom and they threw trash cans at each other while working and squabbling. He was a hippie, and a bit of a lunatic. He wasn't a hunter, but he was well read and smart. I decided one day to have him read an article I wrote for *Western Bowhunter*. I knew writers wanted and needed feedback. You put your heart out there, so you eventually have to ask the question to somebody:

What do you think about my heart?

So I asked Carl if he would read my article. Even though he couldn't relate to going into the wilderness to hunt for elk, he understood good writing.

He read it and didn't offer up the cursory "Good job." Instead he asked, "When you are stalking the animal, what is it like? What noises do you hear? When you make steps, what do they sound like? Can you put me there? Can you let me know what it was like to be you in the moment, how you felt?"

Carl's input was incredibly helpful.

"I want to be there with you on the hunt," he said. "I want you to paint that picture with your words and put me there."

I simply said, "Okay." Then I realized, *Oh my God, he's right. I've gotta put people right there with me on these hunts. I need to let them know how it feels to stalk a buck with an arrow nocked, wind blowing gently on my face, assuring me my scent won't make it to the deer before my arrow does.*

Carl's input gave me the insight and encouragement to dive deeper into my prose. I was so used to venturing farther into the wilderness when I was hunting, so I felt at home pushing deeper into my writing. Trying to do a better job on the details. Trying to paint a better picture through the words on the page.

After finally receiving constructive criticism, the first step to improvement is acting on it.

I was committed.

I earned my stripes as a writer penning many how-to articles along with editing a hunting magazine, *Eastmans' Bowhunting Journal*, but all I really wanted to do was write hunting adventure pieces because, as a reader, that's what I loved. The magazine business required technical writings and how-tos but honestly, I was fully vested only when I was writing of grand undertakings, so before I worked for *Eastmans'* I tried to go big.

To aptly write of grand adventure, one must be a talented writer. And,

March 4, 1996

Cameron Hanes
3241 Montebello Ave.
Springfield, OR 97477

Dear Cameron:

We appreciate your loyalty to Easton over the years. We're proud of the quality and integrity we build in to our entire line of arrow shafts and accessories. And it says a great deal about a product when the consumer is the one shouting its praise.

Enclosed is a new Team Easton camo cap and one of our new window stickers. We hope you will continue to support the bowhunting publications with your hunting stories, and that you will continue to use Easton arrows in all your bowhunting adventures.

Good hunting!

Sincerely,

Randy A. Schoeck
Director of Marketing

Hunting had never been about making money for me. This is good because, as this letter indicates, most begin earning a way in the industry by getting paid with stickers and hats.

I killed this buck in 1994 in a logging unit not far from my home. It was one of my best blacktail at the time and was featured on the cover of my first book, Bowhunting Trophy Blacktail.

as I'd done most of my life, I had put the cart before the horse.

To me, the best first step to launching my writing career was to get an article published in the very best bowhunting magazine in the world, *Bowhunter*. So, after having a good season back in 1994, which included arrowing two Pope & Young blacktail bucks, I put a manuscript package together and sent it off to M. R. James. I was excited about my first potential *Bowhunter* feature.

A few weeks after sending my article to M. R., I started calling home every day from work, asking Tracey if anything came in the mail from the magazine. Day after day I got the same response from my wife: "Nope, Cam, nothing today."

Then, one day a couple months later, it finally happened. I remember it as if it were yesterday. After heading upstairs to the lunchroom of the warehouse for my afternoon break, I dialed home. Tracey answered the phone and said, "You got something from *Bowhunter*."

With butterflies in my stomach, I told her to open it. I heard ripping and tearing, the phone banging around, and then Tracey saying I got a letter and some other stuff from somebody named M. R. James. She started reading the note.

"Dear Cameron, Thanks for sending me your 'Bonus Bucks' manuscript. Congratulations on taking a couple of fine bowhunting trophies. I'm returning your article and photos along with an invitation to rewrite and resubmit it."

A full page of great advice followed this, and the letter ultimately concluded with these sentences:

"Rewrite your article and try us again. You do have the makings of a good deer article, but it is going to take some effort to get this ready for publication in *Bowhunter*. Good luck and give a shout if you need some specific editorial advice. Sincerely, M. R. James."

Well, after Tracey read me the second sentence, I knew where the letter was headed. I was crushed. Since killing my first deer at age fifteen and writing a story about it in English class, I had held the dream of being an outdoors writer. Now my dreams were shattered.

Rewrite and resubmit?

I didn't want to rewrite anything. I had worked very hard on that article, poured my heart and soul into it, and knew every single word was just right.

With an "I'll show you" attitude, I bitterly sent the article, unchanged, to a local hunting magazine, which published it and sent me a big fat check for twenty-five dollars.

Truth is, that was about twenty-five dollars more than the article was worth. My article was nothing more than a hunting story about a guy who got lucky and killed two good bucks. It didn't teach the reader anything, and it didn't offer any powerful insights or share any poignant lessons. While at the time I was angry and frustrated, M. R. was right. My article wasn't up to *Bowhunter* standards. However, this sour disappointment was necessary to my development as a writer. I took a chance and was faced with either getting better and growing, or throwing in the towel.

I chose to keep hammering.

What are you willing to sacrifice?

In order to achieve anything in this life, you have to make sacrifices. Not just the typical ones we think about, such as money and time. Sometimes you sacrifice your emotional energy, or others' trust and belief in you. All for the sake of a dream.

The dreams of one individual are never identical to another. The British scholar, writer, and soldier T. E. Lawrence, also known as Lawrence of Arabia, once said this about dreams: "All men dream: but not equally. Those who dream by night in the dusty recesses of their minds wake in the day to find that it was vanity: but the dreamers of the day are dangerous men, for they may act their dreams with open eyes, to make it possible."

The only way to make dreams possible is to sacrifice.

Back in the mid-1990s, when nobody knew me, I was writing for a magazine called *Western Bowhunter* for free. Being a writer was all I wanted to be, but I wasn't really one. When Doug Walker, the editor of *Western Bowhunter*, asked if I wanted to go on a writer's hunt he was setting up, I decided to participate even though it would cost me about $3,000. At the time, I had no business traveling to bowhunt, but I didn't care. My dreams were bigger than my abilities, and definitely my finances.

At the time, we were poor. We had just welcomed our first child (Tanner) into our family, so Trace was off for six weeks on maternity leave while I was earning around twelve dollars an hour. We were on a nutritional food program known as WIC during those six weeks until Trace went back to work. Spending $300 would have been a stretch, but $3,000? That would have been, and was, ludicrous.

One part of me knew this was an opportunity, but another part told me I would never be getting that money back. Even if I got paid twenty-five dollars per article, which I did when I wrote for *Oregon Hunter*, how many articles would I need to write to earn back $3,000? How many articles is that per year? I was hunting only in Oregon at the time, so how many articles would I really be writing? I didn't have to be a genius to know the math on this looked bad.

After my in-laws gave me $200 toward the hunt, I decided

Newly married, my wife Tracey and I had to adjust quickly with the birth of Tanner. She's always been the stabilizing force of our family and without her, I couldn't have achieved what I have.

to put the rest of the cost on my credit card and consider it a business investment. I could use this hunt as an opportunity to earn a name and start selling hunting articles to pay the monthly credit card payment. It would take only about ten years to get the hunt paid off.

Ah, to be young and full of unrealistic dreams.

Yeah, for the short term, I realize it was a pretty terrible decision. In the end, I worked as many hours as I could at the warehouse I was employed at, sometimes up to sixteen hours a day, just to pay off that hunt. I spent probably a hundred times more money than I ever made being a hunting writer, until I wrote my books.

I remember the hunt in great detail. It was on a great piece of land in Texas—the YO Ranch, which was so big that kills qualified as free range, which isn't always typical in Texas. For what I paid I could kill two whitetail deer. One was just a small eight-point; the other was a management seven-point buck. But I went on the trip and never regretted it.

This is the sort of mentality you have to have.

Are you willing to take a chance on yourself?

Are you willing and able to be stupid like that?

I knew it wasn't a smart thing to do, but I did stuff like this often and would justify to myself that someday it would pay off. I didn't obsess about whether I would be getting my money back and how quickly I would get it? I didn't question where this was going to put me.

My mentality was to go. To believe. To take a chance. To be foolhardy and try over and over again.

Obsession is lonely. For thirty-three Septembers now, bowhunting has been my obsession.

Some people will look at me and talk shit. They have no clue about the sacrifices and struggles I've made for decades. I've learned that the people who talk the most won't sacrifice what I have, and those who will don't talk shit. Because they get it.

All I know is you don't need anyone to believe in your dream. With tunnel-visioned focus, you can be whatever you want to be.

I'm a writer, and when I document something it becomes part of my personal archives. I like writing when the feelings of success, failure, pain, or victory are fresh so that my words are the most accurate and poignant. I don't want time to water down whatever experience I'm trying to capture. I'm also somebody that can only give 100 percent at anything I do. Either I'm going to give 100 percent or I'm going to give zero. I'm never going to do anything halfway.

These two traits came together when I decided to write my first book, *Bowhunting Trophy Blacktail*.

nd we were down at halftime thirteen to z

half we came out and scored fourteen point

y caught one pass, but it was for a two-po

ked up our fifth straight victory from the

ked Oakridge. Donnie had an excellent gam

two-hundred yards, he also threw for three

I caught two touchdowns and a two-point

All together I caught five passes for on

d thirteen yards.

we beat Oakridge, we thought nobody could

ve and one and on a five game win streak.

ng Crow, who were four and three. We were

em twenty-eight to six. When we got there

wn rain and the field was in about six inch

id'nt play that ~~good~~ well and they got some luck

s eighteen to twelve in overtime. The offic

p either. Donnie really could'nt throw tha

, but when he could it worked well. I caug

ninety-six yards and one touchdown.

ur last victory of the season we played Low

an excellent game and killed them nineteen

Donnie did ~~good~~ well passing and I caught four p

seven yards and one touchdown.

year was Mr. Kaster's most successful year o

e has had and he got coach of the year for

I've always loved to write. Not saying I was ever great at it, but I have always enjoyed sharing my experiences through the written word.

There was never any grand plan. One day I decided I wanted to write a book and I wanted it to be badass. Hardback and full color. Nobody had ever done a book about bowhunting blacktail, so that's what I set out to do. That was as far as it went. How much would it cost? I figured it out, then priced up how much it would cost to print them and what I should charge for each copy.

It turned out to cost $50,000 to print 5,000 copies. That was about $50,000 more than I had. I decided to go ahead and publish the book anyway. I had to borrow money from my whole family. My grandma Ruby, as the biggest investor, ended up giving me around $15,000.

Was this a stupid decision to go ahead with a full-color hardcover book? Yeah. But I paid everybody back, including my grandma. When I did, she was so shocked that I gave her the money. She never had anybody in her family pay her back because, unfortunately, that's usually how family works. It's always like, "Yeah, I'll pay you back," but then things come up. But paying off my debt is exactly what I did. I've always been someone who is going to do what I say. The only thing I ask is that others live up to their end of the bargain, no matter what it might be.

It took me a long time, but I sold all 5,000 copies of *Bowhunting Trophy Blacktail*. For a long time we had lots of cases of books in the house, and I even had to move them once to a new house. I didn't really think things through before publishing it, and that's why it wasn't that profitable. I didn't sit down with a business plan or anything like that. I just had a belief and a determination that I needed to write and self-publish that book.

By the time I wrote my second book, *Backcountry Bowhunting*, in 2005, I had a bigger name and a publisher, and that particular title blew up. It is now in its ninth printing and has sold 90,000 copies. Those two books represented two more big chances I took on myself, and not just in the field of bowhunting but in my other passion of writing.

It took me twenty years to finally earn a few pages in *Bowhunter*. After twenty long, hard years I finally had a featured column titled "Bleed" in the September 2009 issue, complete with the byline "Cameron R. Hanes" listed in the table of contents. During those two decades, I wrote hundreds of magazine articles, authored two books, served as editor of a bowhunting magazine for ten years, honed my bowhunting and writing skills, and worked my hardest to raise three kids as best I can—all with the unwavering support of my wife, Tracey. And now, coming full circle on this odyssey, I was finally blessed with the chance to write a regular column for my favorite bowhunting magazine.

Bowhunting has made me who I am today. When I think of bowhunting, I think of hiking up faint pack trails in the wilderness that lead me to lonely, rugged mountains. Nothing about the backcountry hunts I love is easy. In my world, bowhunting will make you want to cry at times, have you dripping with sweat more often than not, and will probably require you to bleed a little for success.

Not long ago I was going through some things in my office at work and happened upon a flyer Eastmans' made to promote my book, *Backcountry Bowhunting*. I looked it over it and a couple thoughts came to mind as I read the personal endorsements my book garnered from icons.

First, I bet there are some on social media these days who might not know Chuck Adams, Mike Eastman, Randy Ulmer, or Dwight Schuh. They are all hunting legends and were my heroes growing up, learning the ropes as a bowhunter and writer. They paved the way for many in the hunting industry and made a huge impact on me personally. In the mountains, stalking, arrow at the ready, eyes scanning, I would think of Chuck Adams and those Sitka blacktails he'd hunt in the late summer on Kodiak Island, or that famous photo of him with his giant bow-killed brown bear. I'd think of his beanie, his smile, and by today's standards, those seemingly gigantic aluminum arrows. I wanted to be Chuck Adams. His tunnel-vision focus was something I tried to emulate. I didn't have deep pockets, and I was very green to bowhunting, but I made up for it with effort. I learned more than thirty years ago that, with extraordinary effort, I could experience above-average results when hunting.

Hunters like Chuck Adams and Randy Ulmer simply set the bar for exceptional bowhunting. I read their articles and studied their photos for years, longing for the experiences they'd lived. I still do. Mike Eastman believed in me when few others did and gave me a career-altering opportunity when he offered me a job at Eastmans'. The late Dwight Schuh showed me what the "power of the pen" meant. His writing inspired me for decades. And, as great a writer as he was, he was an even better man. I was honored to have known him.

The second thought I had was how the kind and complimentary words they wrote about me and my book seemed surreal when this flyer came out. They still do even today. One thing I've noticed that sometimes jealousy and envy permeate and taints the outdoor industry. Instead of building each other up and becoming a stronger group of unified, passionate, and focused hunters with a common interest, our egos have us tearing one another down. With our low numbers, we can't really afford to segment ourselves. We need one another. What these four pioneers said about me as I fought to earn my way says a lot. They built me up and didn't have to. To me this says so much about the men they are, and in my opinion, it goes a long way in explaining why they've cemented themselves as hunting, writing, and outdoors icons.

I am still humbled, honored, and appreciative that those legends helped lead the way for me.

On December 10, 1962, John Steinbeck took the podium to receive the Nobel Prize in Literature "for his realistic and imaginative writings, combining as they do sympathetic humor and keen social perception." His opening remarks made it clear that he felt a bit like an impostor by earning this prize.

"In my heart there may be doubt that I deserve the Nobel award over other men of letters whom I hold in respect and reverence—but there is no question of my pleasure and pride in having it for myself,"

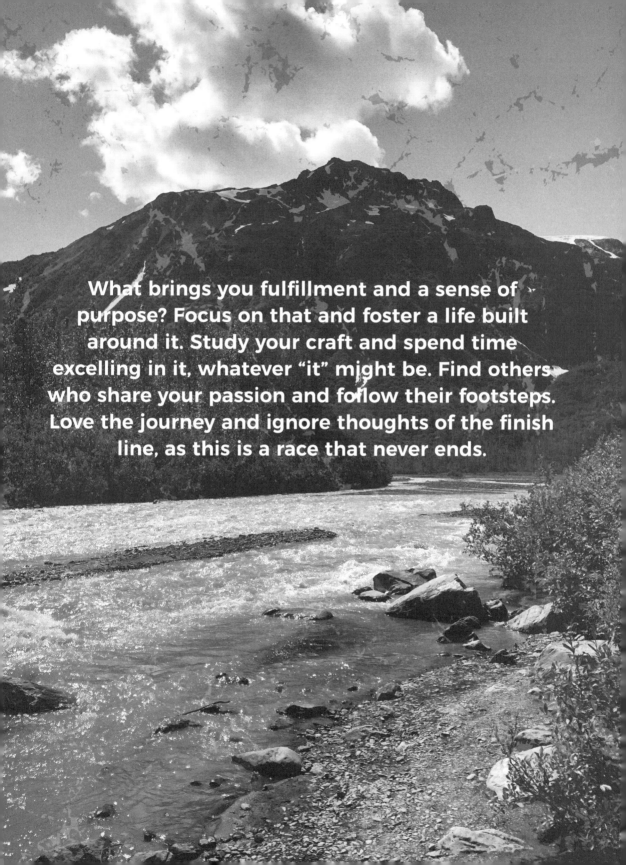

What brings you fulfillment and a sense of purpose? Focus on that and foster a life built around it. Study your craft and spend time excelling in it, whatever "it" might be. Find others who share your passion and follow their footsteps. Love the journey and ignore thoughts of the finish line, as this is a race that never ends.

I have felt like an impostor myself, and that has forced me to work even harder at what I do. Running, training, hunting, even writing.

I love another quote from Steinbeck: "The writer is delegated to declare and to celebrate man's proven capacity for greatness of heart and spirit—for gallantry in defeat, for courage, compassion, and love. In the endless war against weakness and despair, these are the bright rally flags of hope and of emulation. I hold that a writer who does not believe in the perfectibility of man has no dedication nor any membership in literature."

Steinbeck isn't referring to being "perfect" but rather the journey and dedication to the pursuit of perfection. This reminds me of my own journey.

My desire for perfection in bowhunting.

My dreams for publishing stories about those adventures.

This perfectibility of man reminds me of the first 100-mile endurance race I ran in 2009. I think of the passion I see in others, and in watching the success others have.

What is your dream? Mine is to be the "perfect" bowhunter. I want to be successful on every hunt and release a perfect arrow on every hunt that results in a quick and merciful death of the animals I pursue. I realize bowhunting probably isn't something one can master, but that's my goal.

That was how my journey in running and training began to ramp up. Greatness only comes with grinding it out. Striving for perfection means you have to put everything you have into your dreams.

It was time to truly become obsessed.

NOBODY CARES

You make a good shot this season?
Nobody cares. Work harder!
You miss this season?
Nobody cares. Work harder!
You got a promotion at work?
Nobody cares. Work harder!
Your dog died?
Nobody cares. Work harder!
You won the Super Bowl?
Nobody cares. Work harder!
Your battery died?
Nobody cares. Work harder!
You couldn't finish the marathon?
Nobody cares. Work harder!
You won the marathon?
Nobody cares. Work harder!
Run to the monument at the
top of Mount Pisgah?
Nobody cares. Work harder!
Nobody really cares about your goals.
Nobody cares about your excuses for not achieving
what you said you would or what you thought you deserved.
You want people to care? Then do something special. Do something
that people can't ignore, easily dismiss, or one-up.
Recent success? Yesterday means nothing.
Recent failure? Yesterday means nothing.
Yesterday means NOTHING.
Give all you have to today.
Worry about tomorrow, tomorrow.
What you've accomplished in the past means nothing. We don't rest
on laurels here. Time to work!!!!
You killed your first bull? Okay, now that I care about! Now work
harder and build on that success.

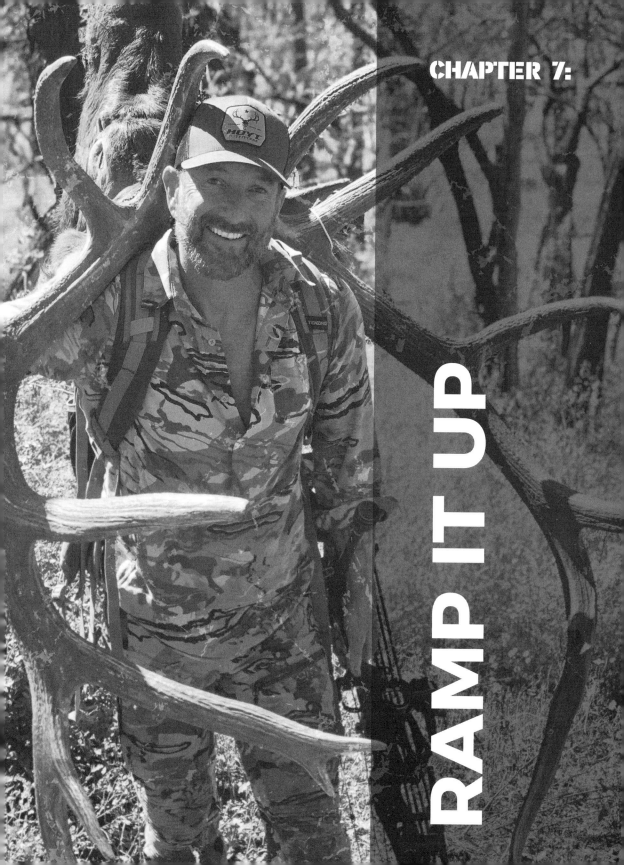

CHAPTER 7

RAMP IT UP

Long endurance races can strip one down to their core, physically and mentally. But on the other side of the challenge is increased strength and confidence to overcome typical daily challenges, which after conquering an ultramarathon, don't seem all that daunting. This photo was taken during the Antelope Island 100 in Utah. I finished the 100-mile foot race in 22 hours and 41 minutes.

Yㅗou have to walk before you run.

Years ago, hunting and running went together like oil and water. I ran to get in shape and knew it helped my hunting, but no one ever talked about exercise for the hunter. There surely was no huge athletic performance apparel outfit like Under Armour making the highest-quality gear for the active hunter and projecting to all who will listen, "Athletes hunt."

I started running just for the test, just to push myself.

Up to the year 2000, the most I had ever run was a 10K. Then one time I entered a 7.3-mile race in Salem, Oregon, and guys thought I was crazy for running that far just to get in shape to hunt the blacktail woods around home. Then I ran a half-marathon, and then in 2003, I ran my first marathon and finished third overall.

This was about the time I really began to notice that my physical condition could play a huge impact in the hunting woods. This was where I could improve my game. I might hike twenty miles or more in a single day during a hunt, so building endurance is crucial. Generally speaking, the better shape I was in, the easier success came. And I've really found no ceiling to this approach. I'm trying though.

Since that first marathon, I have competed in ultramarathons and when in peak shape just prior to bow season, I run at least twenty miles a day. I've ramped it up in an effort to gain not only physical but mental strength and it's paid off with many years of consistent success. I love endurance running for many of the same reasons I love bowhunting. At times, both disciplines will push even the toughest of human beings to the brink. And over the long haul in both endeavors, justice is always served as the people who work the hardest and sacrifice the most reap the rewards.

Trust me, however, when I say this wasn't easy. And believe me when I also state that if I did this, so can you.

No matter where you start, you have to put in consistent work.

I wasn't born a naturally good runner. Once upon a time I struggled to run three miles. I know what it feels like.

Before you can grind up to the top of a mountain, you have to first get up off the couch and start moving.

So where do you start?

As I'll say time and time again, I don't give advice, I just share what I do. And I know what I do is not for everybody. Maybe it's not for *anybody* else. That said, to see where your journey can take you, first you must start. My whole thing is I don't care what you do—if you run or hike—so long as you're simply walking and moving, it's all good.

If you've never run, that's okay. Get outside and take a walk around your neighborhood. Go somewhere and do something simply to burn some calories and get your metabolism jacked up. Walk when you can, even if it's for a half hour; you'll feel good doing that. In just a couple of weeks of regularly going out to walk, you will be pleasantly surprised to see how far you've come. Then start to incorporate some running. Walk for five minutes, run for five, walk for another five and then run for five. Slowly you'll start running more. Walk for five minutes and run for ten, then walk five and run ten.

Soon you'll find yourself running for the entire time. Then you can throw some hills in there but take things slow. Not many people can run a hill. It's awesome if you can, but you don't start off heading uphill.

I love nothing more than running the mountains, but I've built up to this. I see a lot of guys who begin running, and they start up out of the gate too hard and then oftentimes get shin splints. Then they can't do anything. You're working muscles that you're normally not using in everyday life, and you have to develop them before going crazy. With running, you have to ease into it, and you've got to put in the time and effort.

My running was an evolution. When I began to put in fifty miles a week,

This photo was captured on Mount Pisgah outside of Eugene, Oregon. I run here nearly every day as I haven't found anything that prepares my body for the challenges of the hunt like running a mountain will.

soon I could run a half-marathon under 1:20. After finishing third in my first marathon, I still didn't believe that I was talented or naturally gifted as a runner. I just knew that I worked really hard, and I could work even harder.

There was no limit if I ramped it up.

I am not blessed with insane talent. My secret is time. And I've been grinding for years to get where I am at.

During my first year in the woods with bow in hand, I figured it out real quickly. I remember thinking it was going to be completely impossible to get within bow range of a bull elk and get him on the ground with one of my arrows. No one told me I would feel utterly harmless in the elk-inhabited woods with my stick and string. I kept plugging away, though, and each day I learned.

"You have to wonder at times what you're doing out there. Over the years, I've given myself a thousand reasons to keep running, but it always comes back to where it started. It comes down to self-satisfaction and a sense of achievement."

—Steve Prefontaine

Day, after day, after day, after day.

Finally, with each passing day, I was starting to get it, and the effort paid off when I arrowed a spike bull elk after eighteen straight days of bowhunting. The key to that success? Time. It took me nearly three weeks straight of elk hunting, every day a supreme effort, to take that young bull. But with something as difficult as bowhunting, nothing happens overnight.

In terms of my ability, I am probably ten times the bowhunter now compared to then. The biggest reason for this is I'm never satisfied. I am always trying to get better. Get in better shape, become a better shot and a smarter hunter.

This takes time.

You can't expect results overnight like everyone does in this day and age of instant gratification.

Of course, at the start, I expected those immediate results right away, like most do. That was just part of being young and dumb.

I had a lot to learn. And as the famous Michelangelo quote goes, "I am still learning."

I always challenge myself and look for a bigger and tougher test. After realizing I could run in marathons, I began to look into ultramarathons. In 2005 I ran in the McDonald Forest 50K, which is 32 miles. Once again, people in my little circle thought I was crazy, and while I was running, I had a few thoughts that they were right. It was the hardest thing I had ever done up to that moment, and I vowed to never do it again. Of course, I regularly ran in the event in the years that followed.

In 2007, I decided to run in the Bighorn Trail Run. In the three weeks before the race, I shared a daily "Day in the Life" on my blog where I showed how I prepared for the big race. Here's an excerpt from ten days before the race:

4:00 a.m.: I'm up, couldn't sleep. Shower, emails, eat cereal soaked in water, read the paper, check a couple forums, coffee on the way to work. On the way out the door my wife had to remind me today is our 15th anniversary. Man, talk about having a pit in my stomach. Not saying I forgot, but it has been a very busy time.

Supplements: Multivitamin, calcium, magnesium, vitamin D, Vitamineral Green drink mix, and fish oil capsule.

6:00 a.m.: Work, fire off 30 pull-ups right out of the gate. Feeling not-so-fresh yet this morning. It was a short night of sleep.

10:00 a.m.: Coffee and a whole wheat roll.

12:00 p.m.: Eat two chicken and black bean burritos, watermelon, two pieces of wheat bread with no butter that Tracey delivered, like every day. She is the best. Drink water.

4:00 p.m.: Get home and chill out with the kids. Eat a little steak and whole wheat noodles. Light meal. Take off on a run with a Spott Hogg SDP sight with wrap that I will drop off at the Bow Rack during my run.

Wayne set up my Vectrix and Vectrix XL with the red, white, and blue custom string. I did shoot a couple times before heading home. MONEY through paper in two shots with the Vectrix. God, that is a sweet feeling. Run home (this is an easy six-mile run all together), shoot the Vulcan 24 times before running out the door, taking a hand-off from Trace of a bowlful of noodles and steak as I go. I shovel it down on the way to the first of Tanner's two summer league basketball games.

6:30 to 9:30 p.m.: Watch B-ball (Tanner played well) and work on the computer. Emails. Lots of emails to get back to. This daily blog has really stirred interest. I love it. I can talk about bowhunting and conditioning as it relates to bowhunting all day and night. It sure seems like more guys are wanting to do all they can to prepare themselves for the rigors of the backcountry these days. This will result in bowhunting effectiveness, and more success means the tradition of bowhunting grows. That is my number one objective.

One thing I'd like to share in this space: Do not think you need to go on 10-, 20-, or 80-mile runs to be a successful bowhunter. I do think the more you can do, the better off you'll be. Especially in the mountains. That being said, many many guys kill animals with their bows and don't run a step before season. For that matter, there are guys who arrow animals every year who dusted off their bows a week before the opener. The problem in keeping up that routine is that those guys might not kill anything for five or ten more years. For the average guy, if you don't prepare your body and you don't practice, if you kill anything with a bow, it will be in large part because of LUCK.

Bowhunting is all about preparation, and my goal is to hopefully inspire guys to ramp up what they are currently doing to prepare. If you run three miles once a week, maybe this blog will motivate you to run three times a week? If you shoot your bow twice a week, maybe after reading this you will shoot four times a week? Look, I am not saying what I do, you should too. I am saying whatever we have called the "norm," we can do more. That is me, you, everyone. Do this and bowhunting wins. Again, success and sharing positive experiences grows bowhunting. Pump the passion for the sport. Are you doing all you can?

As always, I shared what I was doing instead of telling others what they should do. The number one thing anybody could see was that if I set a goal, I was committed 100 percent, physically and mentally, to be the very best I can be. My goal was gearing up to run the crazy-tough, 32.4-mile Bighorn Trail Run in the Bighorn Mountains of Wyoming and complete the run with my best-ever ultramarathon finish. (By the way, an ultramarathon is a race longer than 26 miles.) My best before this race had been a sixth-place finish at the 2006 Siskiyou Out & Back Trail Run (aka the SOB) in Ashland, Oregon. The by-product of this goal for running the Bighorn (where I got second, if memory serves) was to hopefully show those who might have the wrong impression of hunters that we are a passionate group of people. All the effort I expended in regard to conditioning was for bowhunting, period.

If we are all heroes and heroines on quests and journeys like Joseph Campbell wrote about in *The Hero with a Thousand Faces*, we experience and accept that call to adventure. I had accepted mine when I decided to pursue bowhunting as a passion and to become the best hunter I could be. Eventually we reach a point of no return where we must overcome any obstacles in our way that prevent us from moving forward. These can be deep-rooted fears or discouraging excuses that hold us back. Campbell calls this "crossing the first threshold."

> **"The adventure is always and everywhere a passage beyond the veil of the known into the unknown; the powers that watch at the boundary are dangerous; to deal with them is risky; yet for anyone with competence and courage the danger fades."**
>
> **—Joseph Campbell,** *The Hero with a Thousand Faces*

When you're getting off that proverbial couch and out the proverbial door, it's easy not to want to venture further into the unknown, knowing that whatever comes is going to be more difficult. I had done this when I began to bowhunt, and I continued to do this when I began backcountry bowhunting on my own after Roy moved. Now I was pushing myself further with running longer distances.

Ultramarathons? What was I thinking?

I stood at the gateway where, just beyond it, as Campbell wrote, exists "darkness, the unknown, and danger." Of course, something like that excited me. Nobody else might understand this except Roy Roth.

No mountain is too high and no challenge is too great and danger is a non-factor.

Roy, while not a runner like me, clearly understood the spirit residing in my soul that spurred me on to compete in the Bighorn Trail Run.

I was ready.

I began the race with a plan. My goal was to go out hard and try to "break" all the other runners by hammering out the first fourteen miles, which included some tough ascents (up to 9,000 feet) and brutal descents on game trails. Jumping over logs, slipping through the mud, sloshing through snow—this section had it all. I went down hard twice. Tripping on the steep downhill and flying like Superman, except not really flying. I was skidding down the hill over rocks, sticks, and mud with my arms out. That last part was like Superman.

It ended up being very wet up there, so my shoes were soaking and muddy and remained like that for the entire 32-mile run. This was hard on my feet as the wet conditions softened the skin; I had lots of painful blisters for most of the run. This ultra had me hurting and more banged up than I had ever been on a run. I moved into first place at about mile 7, as we were running on an elk trail and must have spooked a herd. There were fresh tracks running down the trail; this gave me a shot of motivation. I was in my element.

This part of the race took me back to times when I had to hustle to head off a herd of elk while in the wilderness. I envisioned myself running with my bow down the trail casting glances through the dark timber for any sign of elk. It was awesome and I knew that after passing the guy who had been leading, he was going to be non-factor—a bowhunter running in some of Wyoming's best elk country was a tough guy to beat. This section included a long five-mile uphill section where the runners behind me would be able to see me from a great distance. I made it a point to hammer out this section as hard as I could, hoping their spirits would say that I was unbeatable.

Damn, that Under Armour guy from Oregon is a machine. The race is for second.

I arrived at the top of the hill after completing the 14-mile section with at least a four- or five-minute lead. Perfect. I grabbed a few goodies, shed my shirt since it was warming up fast, and was off. The bad part about hammering out that portion was that my quads and calves were on fire. I had to be onstage though—there were still eighteen miles left. I needed to pretend that it was all good to squash the hopes of the guys behind me, who were no doubt looking for a sign I was spent. Any sign, like hands on the head, bent over, hands on knees, whatever. My plan worked . . . almost.

I led the race until mile 24 or 25. The problem was the race didn't end at mile 24 or 25. I stopped at an aid station to refuel, feeling like crap. I had stomach issues and wondered if it could have been the altitude. Living at sea level, I wasn't accustomed to running at 9,000 feet. I even ended up hurling a couple of times postrace. Two runners zipped in, grabbed some stuff, and were gone before I was.

There were spirits already broken in this ultra, but it wasn't theirs.

Two things I enjoy, mountain adventures and running. To combine the two makes for a great day. This photo was captured during a 28-mile mountain run with my brother Taylor Spike and Ashley Nordell.

I kept hammering away, catching the guy for second, but never reaching the winner. It was no wonder; he was an endurance machine. Matt Hart out of Seattle, Washington. He was slated to run a 100-mile race but decided to run my race instead. I wish he would have run the 100.

My good friend and bowhunting mentor Dwight Schuh ran the same Bighorn race in his first-ever ultra. And he picked a tough one. At sixty-two years old, he was no doubt in his prime. When the gun went off, we all started together, and Dwight was on his way. Six hours and 51 minutes and 37 seconds later, he broke the finish line after a great and noteworthy run. He looked like a stud out there—a real mountain ultra runner. Guy Eastman, who came over the hill to film, and I were very impressed with how strong Dwight looked. He inspired and motivated many to believe they can achieve more as he placed third in his age group.

I finished second overall with a time of 4 hours, 53 seconds. It was a great day to be alive. Despite the misery on the run, I felt so grateful to have the ability to run in the mountains. It gave me so much confidence for my true passion of bowhunting. Both disciplines are so similar. They are very difficult, and there are many mini-mental battles that go on over the course of a race or a hunt. In both, success finds those that prepare the most, work the hardest, and are the strongest mentally.

On almost all the races I run, at some time or another, I want to stop and throw in the towel. Similarly, on many tough hunts, I want to quit and go home to the good life. To my family. Mountain hunting had made me tough, and that helped me on the runs. The runs made me tough in another way, and that helped me in the mountains.

So why don't I quit? What resides in me to keep going?

Maybe it's because I don't want to let people down. Because I'm a regular guy coming from a regular small town who dared to dream about being special and finding some success in life.

Maybe I've always felt like proving people wrong. As I started running marathons, I realized the connection between endurance racing and hunting, because in both disciplines, you're facing huge barriers that make you want to quit. Nobody's going to judge you if you quit a hunt; most people fail on a hunt. The same goes for an ultramarathon. Not many could call you a failure if you didn't last to the finish of a long ultra, because most people you know likely wouldn't even toe the starting line. But to me, failure feels like all those people who've doubted me over the years were right. I can't have that.

All I thought about was success. All I trained for was to do whatever it took to succeed against all odds and circumstances.

"It's all mental."
I say this all the time, and it's true.
If you believe you can do it, you can.
We all have virtually limitless potential.
Our bodies are capable of so much more than what we ask of them.
Take off the mental handcuffs, get out there, and start on your way today.
What is your passion? You can become better at it.
Committing yourself to fitness only fuels your beliefs.
You gotta believe to achieve.

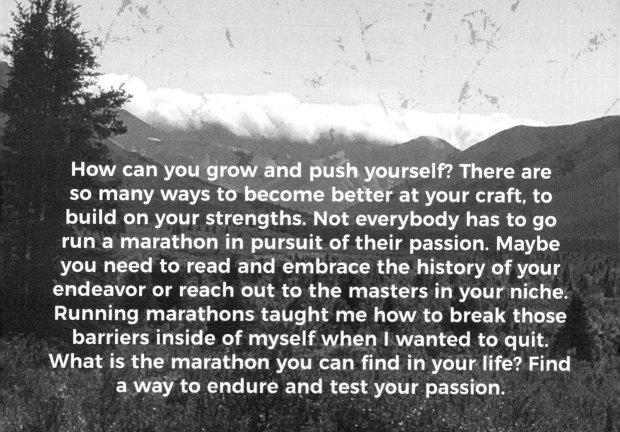

How can you grow and push yourself? There are so many ways to become better at your craft, to build on your strengths. Not everybody has to go run a marathon in pursuit of their passion. Maybe you need to read and embrace the history of your endeavor or reach out to the masters in your niche. Running marathons taught me how to break those barriers inside of myself when I wanted to quit. What is the marathon you can find in your life? Find a way to endure and test your passion.

PREPARING FOR THE PACK OUT

I haven't been good at much throughout life, but getting animals on the ground by arrow is one area I've been able to experience long-term success. The hunt doesn't end there, however. Packing the meat from your kill out of the mountains comes next.

Killing bulls with a bow is a ridiculously hard challenge on its own, but right behind that is breaking down the bull. This is the hard work I love and live for. Regardless of how it may appear to those who don't hunt—or don't hunt the backcountry anyway—there is an art to butchering a bull in the field.

But, art or not, it's a process I'm addicted to.

You start by getting the hide off, then the quarters. Continue with the neck meat, backstraps, rib meat, and tenderloins. Finally, the cape and head are pulled off. Your best bet is to hang the meat in the dark timber (thicker, bigger, enclosed canopy of trees) on the north side of a draw to keep the meat cool as you pack it out quarter by quarter, which is work that takes time.

You want to hang the quarters so the air can flow around them, helping to "glaze" the meat. Also, you want to make it at least halfway hard for bears to get the meat, but with any luck you won't be away for long between pack trips or to fetch the pack animals. If you are, because the pack out and turnaround can take hours, leave a shirt or coat with your scent on it as a deterrent. This will cause most predators to shy away until you've returned for another heavy pack or to load up the panniers.

If you have animals or friends or family members to help you, then you have the ability to potentially pack out the meat and antlers in one trip, but otherwise you have to quarter it and make several trips yourself.

I train daily for these exact moments: packing out heavy loads of wild game meat for miles from the big game animals I kill with one perfectly placed arrow. That is, if the plan works . . .

This is why I don't get the head shakers—the guys who are overly critical of training for hunting by saying physical conditioning has little or nothing to do with killing big game. Our bodies and minds are tools to use in the woods, and training hones those tools—simple as that. The better the tools you pack into the mountains—pack, sleeping bag, stove, bow, binoculars, body, mind—the more success you'll have. So I prepare . . .

Running thousands of miles a year in the mountains to build endurance.

Lifting thousands of pounds of weight in the offseason to build strength.

Shooting at minimum 15,000 arrows total in advance of bow season to build confidence in my craft.

This process gives my life purpose and direction. I put in the work because that's what I'm good at. This work results in success for me and puts a smile on my face, even when there's a heavy load on my shoulders.

I am thankful bowhunting allows me to be the provider I was born to be.

CHAPTER 8

BELIEVE TO ACHIEVE

"I dreamt this so clearly, so precisely, and so frequently that it has manifested itself into reality."

—Conor McGregor

My performance described below predates this quote by Mystic Mac, but his mindset is exactly what I tried to emulate in 2008.

"Believe it, then achieve it."

I think of this as I spot him around mile 7 of the Boston Marathon. He's in the middle of a big group of runners, wearing a gold jersey.

There he is. That's him.

In 2008 I ran my first Boston Marathon, a dream I'd held for a while. What marathoner doesn't dream of the Boston Marathon? Shortly before the race, I learned that famed American cyclist Lance Armstrong would be competing in the marathon as well, so I was excited and told my kids about it.

"I'm going find Lance in Boston and run with him for a while," I said to my boys, Tanner and Truett. "Maybe someone will take a photo of us. I just want one. And then if I have anything left at the end, I'll push as hard as I can and sneak over the finish line just ahead of him."

My kids smiled and laughed when I said this.

"You actually think you can beat Lance Armstrong?" Tanner asked.

We'd watched him for years dominate the Tour de France on TV, so the boys knew of his superhero status.

"You're just a dad," Truett added. "He's Lance."

I understood their disbelief.

Lance Armstrong was an icon and an endurance-racing legend. While he was fairly new to marathons at the time, he was an Olympic medal winner, seven-time Tour de France champion, and the greatest endurance athlete of all time.

Back then he was not only my hero but almost everyone else's too. Performing on the bike was one thing, but his greatest claim to fame may have been beating an advanced form of testicular cancer that had also spread to his lungs and brain, which was potentially fatal.

A couple years earlier in 2006, I ran another race with Lance, this time in the New York City Marathon. I finished in 2 hours, 50 minutes, and 21 seconds, averaging about 6 minutes and 30 seconds per mile for 26.2 miles. That time I passed Lance at the one-mile mark and never saw him again. As someone who looked up to Lance and loved watching him race in the Tour de France every year, I was thrilled to beat the greatest ever in an endurance

I ran alongside endurance legend Lance Armstrong for about half of the 2008 Boston Marathon, which pushed me to my second-best marathon finish: 2 hours and 50 minutes.

event. Of course, it wasn't really a race between us, but everyone knew Lance and wanted to feign a race, one way as it might be.

By 2008 Lance was training hard and really coming into his own as a marathoner. At a marathon leading up to Boston, he ran faster (2 hours and 46 minutes) than I ever have for 26.2 miles. His goal for Boston was getting in the 2:40s. Race day in Boston is Patriot's Day, the third Monday in April,

> **"Anything is possible. You can be told that you have a 90 percent chance or a 50 percent chance or a 1 percent chance, whatever it is you have to believe, and you have to fight."**
>
> **—Lance Armstrong**

which in my estimation made the 2:40s too lofty for me at that stage of my training for the year. I was coming off show season, and lots of travel makes it difficult to get in the miles. Plus, I'm just a backcountry bowhunter from Oregon, four years Lance's senior. The numbers don't really add up for my dream to come true, but that wouldn't stop me from visualizing what would actually come to pass.

At the start of the Boston Marathon, I saw Lance way up ahead on the line with the elite runners. There were thousands of people between us, so I had some work to do to catch up to him. But I was feeling good, more confident than normal, and sure enough, seven miles into the race I had Armstrong in my sights. I couldn't believe it.

I caught up to his group and settled in at their pace. I was running a little slower than I normally start, but then again, I always start too fast, blow up, and find myself scratching, clawing, and hurting like hell just to finish. I am not a smart marathoner. Lance's pacers were dialing him right in on a steady pace. I figured, unlike me, they likely had a solid strategy.

At about mile 14, we started to get into some hills. From what I could tell, Lance's pacers were gone, but he was still hammering away. He was a monster going up the hills. There was no way I could keep up his pace. I was hurting bad and started to beat myself up.

I can't believe I have the chance to run with Lance and now I'm letting him pull away.

Leaving me back with the masses of runners. Faceless, nameless strangers to me.

I have nothing left. Nothing.

Hopefully somebody got a picture of me with him somewhere along the way.

This was one of those moments in life, those defining moments we look back to, when we had a choice to make. When we have to decide to either give up or keep on going.

Lance knew all too well about those sorts of moments, as he wrote about them in his 2000 book, *It's Not about the Bike: My Journey Back to Life*.

"Pain is temporary. It may last a minute, or an hour, or a day, or a year, but eventually it will subside and something else will take its place. If I quit, however, it lasts forever."

I was just about ready to throw in the towel, thinking I had given it all I had. Self-doubt started to seep in.

I fixate on his calves hammering away in front of me.

God, why couldn't I have been an Olympic athlete? Why couldn't I have had that kind of talent?

I'm no different from anyone else. Some days it's hard. My body hurts, my spirit wavers, and my mind is weak. During those times, it would be a lot easier to go home and chill out, but I never do.

I always show up and grind it out. So that's what I decided to do.

Armstrong once said in an interview on CNN, "I believe that the mind powers the body, and once the mind says we want to do it, then the body will follow."

I want this. I'm going to give it all I've got. I'm going to catch up with Lance. If I puke or pass out or whatever, at least I'll be going down in flames.

Running as hard as I could, I picked up my pace to try to close the gap. My legs didn't have much snap and they felt heavy, but by God I was slowly catching up. Sure as anything, I started feeling a little better. I couldn't believe it.

I was back on Lance's heels just in time for the toughest hills on the course. He powered up them, leaving me a little, then we topped out and I caught back up, as it seemed as if I could run the downhills easier than he could. At about mile 19 we climbed a fairly substantial grade, and Lance asked me a question.

Theodore Roosevelt said, "We admire the man who embodies victorious effort; the man who never wrongs his neighbor, who is prompt to help a friend, but who has those virile qualities necessary to win in the stern strife of actual life." Where are the places in your life where you can achieve a victory? It doesn't have to be the Boston Marathon; it can be building a bridge to a relationship or beginning a journey to recovery. Addicts and alcoholics record their sobriety not for sound bites but rather as triumphs. What can you do with your passion to achieve important benchmarks of success?

"Was that Heartbreak Hill?"

"No," I tell him. "Heartbreak is still a couple miles out. Mile 21."

"Then what the hell was that?"

I didn't know, but it hurt.

"How are you feeling?" I asked as we steadily moved together.

"I'm fucking dying!" Lance said.

Thank God, I thought, *because I'm dying too, but this gives me hope. Misery loves company.*

We stayed together, or close, exchanging a few short comments back and forth along the way as we clicked off the miles. Running got easier then. I definitely had my second wind.

"Hey, I lost my pacers," he said. "How fast are you going to run today?"

"Probably 2:50," I say.

"I'll just stay with you if you don't care."

"Yeah, that's cool."

Understatement of my life.

The fans were loud. Amazingly loud and almost deafening. They saw Lance coming and went crazy. He had been one of the most recognizable faces in the world at the time, which had people in a frenzy. At the water stations, each volunteer excitedly tried to be the one to hand Lance a cup of water. I heard fans, lining the course, yelling, "Lance!" 10,000 times as we ran through the city. It was surreal.

I ran beside a legend, beside someone who'd inspired millions all over the world. That man overcame so much. He stared death in the face and battled back to be the very best.

It was a beautiful day in Boston. For the last few miles there was a motorcycle with a cameraman on the back, filming every one of Lance's steps. Fans were reaching out, and I wondered if it reminded him of the Tour?

As we came around the corner nearing the finish line, I told myself, *Well, here we go*. Lance had his own finish line and tape to break for the cameras, so we drifted apart.

Then I dug deep and immersed myself in the pain.

Amazingly, I ended up coming in twelve seconds ahead of Lance. My time, 2:50:46.

After the race, there was a moment when Lance pointed to me. As crazy as it sounds, it felt like we sort of formed a pseudo bond while running the marathon. I pointed back, then headed over and shook his hand, telling him it was an honor to run with him. Not sure he'd even remember me, but I'll never forget that day and that special marathon.

After the race, I hustled off to the airport to get back to work the next day. I was excited to talk with those at home about the race. After checking in at the airport, I dug my phone out, listened to voicemails and checked emails. I was overwhelmed. I couldn't believe how many people had seen the footage of me and Lance running together. After the elite men and women were done with the race, the main story was Lance, so the camera was locked on him—and me—by default.

The most welcome of all the voicemails came from Tracey. My wife's voice was thick with emotion as she spoke.

"Cam, I am watching you on TV right now and I can't believe it. You are running stride for stride with Lance, and I just want to tell you how good you look, how strong you are running, and how proud I am of you. I have tears welling up in my eyes watching you, because I know how hard you have worked to do what you are doing right now. Call me."

It's still the sweetest, most heartfelt message I've ever received. I stood there in the bustle of the airport, absorbing every single word she said, shaking my head thinking what a lucky man I am. Later on, Tracey told me that Truett, our youngest son, just sat on the couch and watched me on television with a big smile on his beaming face, not saying a word. I learned later that Tanner and Truett's school gave an announcement over the intercom saying their dad ran with Lance Armstrong in the Boston Marathon, and beat him.

Truly an incredible day.

That happened in 2008, back when Lance was a sports god, back when the world revered him, including me. Before the doping scandal and the public outrage and everything that followed. Did any of that diminish my thoughts on running the marathon with him?

Absolutely not.

Here's the deal. It's over. Lance paid the price for his misdeeds. He was stripped of his wins, forfeited millions of dollars, and lost more in respect.

Running with him for the entire second half of that race was surreal. It was also an honor. All the stuff that has come out about him since then doesn't tarnish my memory of running with Lance.

That was also around the same time I started getting hated on for putting too much emphasis on training with regard to mountain hunting. That criticism lives on but just like back then, it doesn't have any impact on the amount of drive I have to best prepare my body and mind for the test that is bowhunting.

Not long ago I watched the ESPN documentary *Lance* and loved it. I know everyone probably has a different take on Lance, but for me he was a legend and is still a transcendent icon despite his rocky past. It probably has a lot to do with my age and where the "Legend of Lance," who at one time was considered the "greatest endurance athlete of all time," fit in my life. I saw in that documentary that Lance still has the same fire burning inside of him.

I remain a fan.

Visualize success.

Over the years, I've talked about that with respect to bowhunting. Expecting success, working tirelessly to perform in crunch time, giving nothing less than your very best—these are the ways bowhunters achieve their dreams. Anything is possible. Dreams can become reality to the goal-orientated hunter. This fact is proven time and time again in the rugged mountains of the West each and every fall.

In the Boston Marathon, I put the visualization theory to the test. Runners and hunters share common threads. To be successful in each discipline requires many of the same attributes: commitment, dedication, and above all, damn hard work. Endurance events like marathons or ultramarathons ratchet this commitment up another level. Much like backcountry bowhunting.

To run a 10K, you can prepare by running a few miles a day, three days a week. It is really not that tough. To run a marathon, you should be running five or six days a week, seven to ten miles a day on average, with long runs occasionally over twenty miles. There is nothing easy about that, and that's the draw. Easy seldom makes memories. Similarly, backcountry bowhunting is not something you do successfully on a whim. Many have tried and many have failed. But, to those who have ramped up what they expect of themselves in the mountains, geared their training to maximize every ounce of their ability, and ultimately find success, well, it is a powerful experience to say the least. To some, life-changing. All I have to do is look in the mirror to see an example of what I am referring to.

For many years a 10K was the farthest I'd ever run. Then I consciously made my off-season training match my hunting in terms of intensity. I

I was exhausted here but only halfway through the Bigfoot 200 endurance race in Washington. I finished the 205-mile mountain race in 78 hours and in eighth place overall. This was my first 200+-mile footrace.

expect a lot of myself in the backcountry and I figured the best way to prepare for the difficult challenge of mountain bowhunting would be to put myself through hell training during the spring and summer.

"Cry in training, laugh in battle." That pretty much summed up my newly defined approach to excel in bowhunting back in those days.

One reason I respect Lance Armstrong is that if anybody gets the above statement, it's him. I love some of the things he has said about training and determination.

"I'm not happy if I'm not doing some physical suffering, like going out on a bike ride or running," Lance told *Time* magazine. "First, it's good for you. Number two, it sort of clears my mind on a daily basis. And it's a job. My job is to suffer. I make the suffering in training hard so that the races are not full of suffering."

Not only did Lance train hard but he also was one of the fiercest competitors ever. After winning his fifth Tour de France in 2003, he defiantly said, "No one trains like me. No one rides like me. This jersey's mine. I live for this jersey. It's my life. No one's taking it away from me. This fucking jersey's mine."

Lance didn't just visualize success. He also visualized crushing his competitors.

I respect that mindset.

There was someone else who celebrated my run in Boston that day: my dad. Since I had always felt like we had a connection that came through track and running, racing in the Boston Marathon next to Lance Armstrong was a thrill for him. My dad knew what it took to sacrifice and try to be the best. He loved seeing me on TV running with the legend.

Up till then, he had never really given me credit for my hunting. As I mentioned earlier, he liked to tell me that every time I killed an animal, I lost brain cells. Instead of getting credit, I usually got dismissed for my outdoor adventures. Running was different. Now he finally had something about me that he could brag about with others.

"You know . . . my son beat Lance Armstrong."

To my dad, this was a lot more exciting than talking about the biggest buck I ever killed. Everybody knew Lance. Just to be in an endurance event with him was kind of cool.

As I've said, the only hero I had growing up was my dad. Now that I had officially beaten America's hero, mine was beyond proud.

When *The Oregonian* newspaper ran an article about me and Lance in the marathon, I loved where it acknowledged me simply as "Bowhunter."

BOWHUNTER BEATS ARMSTRONG the headline read. That is exactly how I like it . . . I'm simply a bowhunter, nothing more, nothing less, and I'll be a bowhunter until the day I die.

What does running the Boston Marathon have to do with bowhunting? Everything.

Oh, I can hear the chorus of guys who offer up the same old tired statement time and time again.

"You don't need to be able to run a marathon to kill with a bow."

I agree. You don't need to do a lot of things to kill animals with a bow, but one thing I do know: The better shape you are in, the better your chances are for staying 100 percent committed, mentally and physically, to your bowhunting goals.

I've obsessed about mountain bowhunting so much, for so long, I feel like the comparisons and similarities I've concocted are valid and worth sharing. In my opinion, mountain bowhunting is not that much different from other performance sports like basketball, football, and running in regard to evolution. I think the ultimate performance endeavor, bareknuckle bowhunting, is evolving and progressing in much the same way as those other sports.

A few decades back, professional football players wore leather helmets, and I remember seeing an old NFL locker-room photo in which the players looked like they could have been talking politics or, at six feet, 175 pounds, they could have been insurance salesmen talking about the benefits of higher deductibles. Compare that with images of NFL players today. They're beasts. Solid muscle and track-star fast, they rewrite the record books with ever-increasing skills—and definitely no leather helmets.

Basketball, same deal. Have you ever seen old footage of Bob Cousy dribbling a basketball and shooting? I have, and I don't remember ever seeing him touch the ball with his left hand. No disrespect intended, because during his day he was The Man, but his shot reminded me of my wife's

when she is out shooting hoops with our boys. Yes, the game has evolved big time.

Running, same deal. Pretty much every single running record is broken every few years. And in my favored sport, ultramarathon running, men and women are running faster and farther every year. Similarly in bowhunting, yesterday's legends might struggle to keep up with today's hunter athletes. And shooting, there's some archery snipers out there these days.

Let me clarify one thing: Backcountry bow-

Mount Pisgah, Eugene, Oregon

hunters are athletes, but they will face challenges other athletes will not. For most sports the training and goals are pretty straightforward. Sprinters train to increase speed. Weight lifters train to get stronger. The goals are easily defined, the results easily measured and tracked. And cheering crowds justify the effort.

At some point in every long run, I want to quit, and the same holds true on tough bowhunts. Many times I've wanted to cry, *"No más!"* By no means am I a great hunter or a world-class archer. What sets me apart is my ability to suffer. I love every minute of bowhunting, but I have yet to be on an easy backcountry bowhunt. So I train like a professional athlete. I train to bleed.

Some people like to take what I say and turn it into "Cam says everybody needs to be able to run a marathon or they won't kill an elk." I've never said anything close to that.

Listen . . . I don't care what you do.

For me, this is how I feel and what works for me. Does that mean everybody should do what I do? No way.

Do whatever you want to do. Whatever gives you confidence, whatever makes you feel good, whatever makes you feel empowered—do that. If that's shooting your bow, do that. If that's playing chess, go for it. Do something that inspires you and makes you work hard. I'm inspired by people who give their best every day.

Those people believe what I believe:

Anything, and I mean *anything*, is possible.

THANK YOUR CRITICS

From the bottom of my heart, thank you.
Thank you for your unsolicited advice on how I train.
I appreciate your comments on my rest and recovery.
It's nice to know your suggestions about how much I should sleep.
I love learning about how I should lift.
It's nice to know where you stand on politics and where I shouldn't stand.
Remind me a few more times why I shouldn't be running.
And yes, my deepest and most sincere gratitude for your critique of my music.

May I respectfully just add one little thought . . .
Unless you can help me put a broadhead-led arrow through the vitals of a big bull, bear, buck, or buffalo, your opinion doesn't mean much to me. And by "much" I mean absolutely nothing. Bowhunting is my purpose and the only thing I've ever been good at. I'm not a runner, so criticize my running all you want. I'm not a weight lifter, so critique my lifting and my strength as it means nothing to me. Hell, you don't hunt? Go ahead and judge me for hunting and killing animals to feed myself. If you're a fellow hunter, bash me to make yourself look better. I'm good with it. Because in the mountains come September, if my arrow lands true, I'll be bent over a fallen bull elk putting my knife to work and all your opinions of me won't make you any happier or make me feel any less fulfilled in my journey as a bowhunter and provider.

If you're a fellow honorable diehard and live to roam bow in hand, you have my respect. Or, if you're a new-to-the-fray archer, welcome to the brotherhood. Bowhunting can change your trajectory and give you a new perspective on life.

If you're a critic and a couch life coach, please keep your comments and criticism coming. I love being entertained and appreciate the fuel. See ya at the top!

CHAPTER 9

TRAIN HARD, HUNT EASY

"The gods of the valley are not the gods of the hills, and you shall understand it."
—Ethan Allen

"**C**am, can't you just do the 50-miler?"

I was on the cusp of my first-ever 100-mile mountain run in 2009 when Tracey said this. I still couldn't believe I was only days away from the Bighorn 100, taking place in the rugged Bighorn Mountains of Wyoming. With over 17,000 feet of elevation gain, the Bighorn 100 was one of the toughest 100-mile footraces in the United States. It would be my first ultra over 50 miles; the previous year at the Bighorn 50, I finished third overall. It would also be the first race where I would be required to run through the night. A full day of running followed by a full night of mountain running sounded intimidating among other things.

My wife was having second thoughts and tried to persuade me to reconsider.

"You could do really well in a 50-miler," she said. "You won't have to run at night, but that race will still drive your message home. And I've read people have kidney failure sometimes on those crazy long runs."

She made some good points and she almost had me a couple of times, but I remained determined.

"I've already done a 50-miler," I said. "My goal is to find out exactly what I can do, to find where's my breaking point."

Not long after this conversation, my dad called me at night with the same sort of concern.

"Cam, you don't have anything left to prove. No one cares if you do a 100-miler."

"Ah, but Dad, you're wrong. I know full well not many will ever do a 100-miler or even have it as a goal, but many guys could be influenced by the standard it sets. Guys who on their regular run are feeling fatigued might think about my race and the challenges associated and find themselves pushing just that much more to finish their workout."

I know this type of influence goes both ways. The stories I hear from those who follow me online inspire me to be the very best I can be every day. I appreciate each and every one of them for their support and sharing with me their journey of bowhunting success and personal growth.

Of course, there are the usual guys that offer other thoughts.

"Cam is a crazy idiot. Why in the hell would anyone have to run 100 miles in order to bowhunt?"

Great question. As I've already said, my answer has always been: You don't. I don't have to do this and nobody else needs to, either. I just knew that if I didn't push myself, I wouldn't be where I am today. Conventional wisdom in regard to hunt preparation suggested the typical twenty minutes of exercise a day, three times a week and shooting at forty yards a couple months before season would suffice. Such a regimen doesn't ruffle feathers, doesn't challenge the norm, doesn't make other men uncomfortable by introducing the concept that maybe they could do more to prepare?

At this stage of my life the "norm" wasn't enough for me or for a lot of other guys who hunt the rugged West.

Getting out of your comfort zone and finding out what you are really capable of is almost an awakening of sorts. I know I am an entirely different guy from who I was twenty-five years ago and I owe it all to pushing my limits, expecting more of myself, and increasing my pain threshold all in the name of hunting. Now I would rather quit hunting than go halfway in preparation. It is all I got or nothing.

I was ready for the Bighorn 100.

This is for one day. Just one day of my life. I can get through anything for a day.

My last big preparation weekend (three days, as I had Friday off work) couldn't have gone better. In trying to prepare my body for the Bighorn 100, I told myself, *The more misery I withstand this weekend, the bigger payoff I will have during the race*. I wanted to break myself down all the way mentally and physically, knowing I had twelve days to recover, which to

Bighorn 100 finish line. My first 100-mile mountain race: 29 hours of pain and growth.

me was a lifetime. I knew my body had a short recovery period. My "pile on the miles" plan originally was going to cover two full days. I figured if I did a tough 20 miles one day, followed up by a 30-miler the next, I would be good to go for the Bighorn, given the previous races I'd run this season. This included back-to-back marathons in the last month.

My problem is accepting when enough is enough.

After that 24-mile Friday, I logged on to Map My Run and outlined a sweet 33-mile course with some great hill work thrown in. I figured if I just cruised and made the run last, it would take me about six hours. Perfect, I needed a six-hour run after the four-hour, 24-mile first leg the day before. The only problem was that left Sunday. What the heck was I supposed to do all day Sunday? Yard work, grocery shopping? No.

I understood the obsessive/compulsive tendencies I had been known to exhibit when working in endeavors I am passionate about. I got obsessive about shooting my bow, to the point where I wouldn't quit until I felt infallible. Maybe I was overly confident, but mentally, this was where I had been before and a place I loved to be.

With running, especially extreme endurance running, I had never been in this place. Not until this Sunday evening.

I had the bright idea of getting some night running in, so I set my alarm for 2:30 a.m. The satanic alarm snapped me out of a deep, deep sleep. After throwing on some clothes and lacing up my UA runners, I was out the door doing a nice one-hour loop on the dead-quiet, ghost town–like streets. Seven more miles added on to my total. I felt okay afterward.

If I can break myself down even further, now's the time to do it.

I went back to bed for a few hours, then got up with Trace to have some breakfast and read the paper. Finally I was able to head out the door. My plan was to head to the Prefontaine Classic over at Hayward Field where some of the world's most elite athletes were running and my dad was officiating the jumps. I made it over there, nine miles into my run, just as the meet was concluding.

Watching those world-class guys always inspired me. I had been going to the Pre since I was a grade schooler, sometimes just peeking through the fence since I didn't have any money for a ticket. The electricity of the meet made its way to me even way back when, and it did just the same on this Sunday. Running by Hayward, I thought of Pre's quote, "To give anything less than your best is to sacrifice the gift." Hammering away up the sidewalk from Hayward, I was energized.

I passed my grandma's house and was reminded how much I missed her since she had passed. This was where I'd spent a lot of time listening to the roar of Hayward just a couple blocks away. I powered up the steep grade of a street just beyond where Grandma Heloise lived. Making short work of the hill, I pounced down the back side, through Amazon Park, by South Eugene High, to Skinner Butte Park, where Tanner then met me on his Trek to ride home with me as I ran. The boys wanted me to take them to Will Ferrell's *Land of the Lost*, so Tanner wanted to help get me home quicker. It actually helped. With more spring in my step, I finished off the last five miles of my 20-mile run with increased effort.

"Dad, you seem like you are in a pretty good mood," Tanner told me.

I was. I had done everything I set out to do on this last prep weekend before the Bighorn. But this was when my psycho-ness started to creep in. I have a hard time feeling satisfied. Ever. I was sure there was an official diagnosis for this.

There was every reason for me to feel content. After logging eighty-five miles in the last three days, which was equivalent to running more than a 26.2-mile marathon three days in a row, I expected I would be spent. Not able to walk another step. Stiff and blistered. Granted, I was tired, but not exhausted.

I didn't hurt.

I expected to hurt and wanted to hurt. To me this would signify that there was no question my considerable effort did its job. But I felt no pain, so I was disappointed. Naturally this made me want to run even more.

After a nice carb-loaded dinner with the family, the boys and I headed to the movies. I bought their tickets, their goodies, got them set up in the theater and leaned down telling them, "I'll be right back. I am going to go do that five-mile loop along the river real fast, then come back in, get a Slurpee, and watch the rest of the movie with you. I will be back in forty minutes, tops." They were fine with it and weren't surprised in the least. They knew me.

Outside once again, I took off on a perfect running night, and I ran. It was crazy, because I felt great. My legs definitely felt like I'd done something, but I could still stride out and run strong. Not super fast, but fluid.

I was so pumped.

A smile crossed my face, the same sort I had on hunts when I was in a zone. This was the feeling I chased every day.

I want to keep going. Get in another 20-miler.

Then I thought of the boys waiting for me. Looking into the dark of the theater for my silhouette to appear.

As I made my way back to them, I reflected on my weekend. As it was, I pushed my three-day total to right at ninety miles. Everything was going so

My daily run takes me here, to the monument that sits atop Mount Pisgah. Photo by Travis Thompson.

well that I became a little afraid that something would go haywire. A blown Achilles tendon or something like that. I kept my fingers crossed.

I knew I had to fight the urge over the next twelve days not to overtrain heading into the Bighorn. When I felt this good, I wanted to push it. Hard.

Bighorn, however, would push back. Even harder.

One hundred brutal miles.
Over 17,000 feet of total elevation gain.
Twenty-nine straight hours spent.
Twenty thousand calories burned.
All in the name of better bowhunting.
Man, did I have so much to learn.

As I lined up for the Bighorn Mountain Trail 100-mile endurance run, I was pumped. But honestly, I was also really nervous.

This had been called the fourth-toughest ultramarathon in the world. The Bighorn 100 was an out-and-back run consisting of 76 miles of single-track trail, 16 miles of rugged double-track jeep trail, and 8 miles of gravel road with approximately 17,500 feet of climb and 18,000 feet of descent. What that meant was basically you were either running up or running down. Only a fraction of the course was level.

I couldn't help thinking about how far 100 miles was. This was my third year in a row competing in a Bighorn race, but my first for this distance. It was a long way to run in any conditions, let alone the high-elevation Bighorn Mountains of Wyoming.

One hundred miles . . . That's the distance from Eugene to Portland, OR.

I hated driving to Portland. Now I was going to run that far? Not on a drive I detested but on a nasty-tough course? At least I knew I'd be running in some beautiful country.

The race began at 11:00 a.m. under sunny skies and amid perfect running conditions. For the first hour or so I thought I was running smart, but I was not. Too fast. Also, I was wearing a borrowed CamelBak, which I had never run with. Dumb. It started rubbing immediately and didn't stop for 29 hours. Yup, that rubbed some hide off my lower back and became bleeding silver-dollar-size hot spots.

After only twenty miles into the race, I began to wonder if I would be able to finish. It was 1:30 p.m. and I had just topped out after a big 4,000-foot climb; now we were headed down the big drainage on the other side. I hurt already and had eighty miles to go.

I decided that I wasn't nearly as tough as I thought I was.

In the race packet, the organizers mentioned to be prepared for about anything weather-wise and they were spot on. We ran in the baking sun, mid-80s, through knee-deep mud as well as at least a couple miles of postholing through wet, shoe-soaking snow as the course climbed up and over 9,000 feet. By mile 30 around 5:00 that afternoon, things weren't too bad. Despite lots of pounding on my body coming down, and in places where it was too steep to even run, I actually started to feel better. I took in some calories in the form of about a half of a peanut butter and bacon sandwich Trace packed for me at home. I was back on pace.

Truthfully, I shouldn't have been thinking about time at all. A 100-mile run is not one against the clock for most; it is a race against your body and mind.

At 7:00 p.m., I began feeling like crap again. I started the big 18-mile climb to the turnaround at Porcupine, mile 48. As night fell, I realized I had screwed up thinking I would get to the 9,000-foot-plus aid station sooner, since I didn't have any of my cold-weather UA and no headlamp. I was good until about 10:00 p.m., then it was too dark to see. I stumbled around in the dark timber, in the snow, falling about every third step. This was not helping my declining attitude. Also, I was freezing as the wind up top was whipping over the ridge. Finally I got behind someone with a headlamp and rode them into the aid station.

The best part of the race came at 11:00 p.m. at mile 48. I ate some soup, slipped my cold-weather stuff on, got my feet bandaged up, and headed back out. The aid station looked like an infirmary. There were some hurting runners in there, but the staff was awesome. I had a nurse put some second-skin type stuff on a couple of blisters I developed from running for miles and miles in wet, muddy shoes. That made a big difference. I weighed in (they check your body weight to see if you're dehydrated) and checked out okay, so I was back on course. I lost some weight but not too much. I bombed out of there, intent on making up some time.

It was biting cold up at the race's 48-mile turnaround, in the 30s for certain. The howling wind, approaching midnight and daunting beyond, combined to make the Porcupine Aid Station a real convenient spot for DNFers. That was the official notation on the race results for runners who quit. DNF, Did Not Finish.

Me and my oldest son, Tanner. I took him with me to Wyoming for my first 100-mile ultra. I knew if my son was there, I couldn't quit or fail. I needed to be The Example of endurance, to show him how one overcomes challenge.

I saw guys at Porcupine, tough guys obviously (I mean, hell—to get there they just ran 48 miles, the last 18 all uphill to the tune of a 4,500-foot gain) looking like they were on their deathbeds. Wrapped in blankets, being attended to by medics. It was at Porcupine that many called it a race. But that wasn't the only place guys quit. At almost every aid station, even the most remote, there were runners sitting there having turned in their race bib. To get hauled out from the remote stations, it was going to have to be on horseback, but it didn't matter. They simply weren't going to or couldn't run another step.

Before this race, I could never see myself quitting. Now I had a new appreciation for just how far down you could go. Not only physically, but most importantly, mentally. I believe most of the guys quit because mentally it was too much. Granted, there were some who battled hypothermia and straight-up exhaustion, but more than anything they lost the battle between their ears. On this note, I ran for a time with one old boy who was doing his thirty-fifth 100-mile ultra. I thought to myself as we ran through the mountains, someone that tough, there is no way he's ever quit a race. So, I asked him and yup, he'd had to bail out of three 100s over the years.

This had to be one of the most intense events ever.

By 2:00 a.m., fifteen hours of running was a new experience for me, and so far, not real enjoyable. It was at this time I became envious of those who had a pacer or a crew there supporting them. Some runners had a friend or a family member run critical segments of the race with them. I was crewless and right about now it sucked. I had a nice Eminem mix that Tanner had put together for me on my iPod, and while his "me against the world" shtick motivates me most of the time, right now I was just feeling sorry for myself. There were times when I had a hard time even walking. Everything hurt. I had no energy. I planned on knocking out this eighteen miles back to the bottom quickly, but now it seemed like I was losing time. Yes, I was losing the battle, but the war was not yet over.

"Cam, why do you have to go overboard on everything? Can't you just do a regular marathon or something not so extreme? Stuff like that is too hard on your body. I don't think it is a good idea."

I could hear Trace's words, and now I was asking myself those same questions. It reminded me of one of my early wilderness trips I took by myself. Before leaving, a doctor had found a blood infection in my leg and told me I couldn't go, but I still went. On that hunt, I found myself alone in the cold and the snow, sitting in the wilderness and questioning why I was there. I felt pretty selfish for being away from my family.

Is this necessary?

It was one thing to read some stranger on social media asking me this, but now it was my own voice I heard.

Yeah, it's necessary, I answered back silently.

I need to be out of my comfort zone. You never forget experiences like this. They help you to grow.

The Bighorn race packet contained a warning, one I ignored.

"To ensure a sufficiently experienced and trained field of participants, each runner should be aware of the extremely rugged terrain and difficulty this course presents. This will increase the likelihood that the participants will be prepared to deal with a rugged course and unpredictable mountain weather to safely participate in the event. It is important for the participant to recognize the potential physical and mental stresses which may evolve from participation in this race. The runners may be subject to extreme temperatures of heat and cold, hypothermia, heat stroke, kidney failure, seizures, low blood sugar, disorientation, injury, falling rock or trees, wild animal or reptile attack, or even death from their participation in this event."

I thought this was a little good old-fashioned hyperbole before I ran. It is not.

This race would teach me something. I could fake my way through 50Ks and even 50-milers, but I could not fake it through a 100.

Hundred-mile runs are tough, much tougher than I gave them credit for. Not only did this test my physical abilities, but it also pushed my mental capabilities. I could run and did fairly well, if I didn't have to use any intelligence. I could run a regular 26.2-mile marathon like Boston, New York, or Eugene, never thinking, barely drinking, just hammering it out. If I had to be smart, game over.

A 100 required being smart. But I wasn't finished with the game. Not yet.

I had entered the race thinking that I should be able to get in around 24 hours given this and that . . . referring to my baseless logic.

Well, last year my third-place overall finish in the Bighorn 50-mile brought me in just under 9 hours. Cool, double 9, add a little for fatigue, and bingo: 24.

You failed the class, Cam.

I ran the SOB 31-mile 50K with 7,000 feet of gain in right at 4 hours. I can bust 100 miles out in 24 hours just by staying steady.

Nope.

Mine was a flawed math.

There was a huge difference between running for 4 hours or even 9 hours and 24 or more. Besides, 9 hours was the longest I had ever run in my life, and I did it only one time.

Even after I had told myself a million times that there was one mistake I desperately needed to avoid, I took off way too fast. I also didn't eat or drink the way I should have, and after about forty miles, I blew up. I recovered a bit at the turnaround, then told myself I was going to go make up some time heading back down the hill to Footbridge at mile 66.

Not so fast.

For a couple hours I had a hard time even walking. I was sick, I was dehydrated, or maybe overhydrated after drinking a ton at the turnaround. My hands were all swollen, I was by myself, and the lowest of lows was at about 3:00 a.m., when I was trying to make it down to the bottom of the canyon. I was hurting as bad as I had ever hurt, up to that time in my life. After that, I hurt worse.

At 6:00 a.m., I finally made it to mile 66. I weighed in, was still down but still okay. I ate a pancake and sausage, knowing there were 34 more miles to go and another brutal 17-mile climb up Dry Fork. There were parts of this that were nasty steep, but I never stopped. There was no way you could run it—power hiking was the only option. I hammered away and actually caught and passed some runners near the Dry Fork aid station.

I can safely say, that six-hour climb was one of the longest of my life. It was unrelenting.

At 12:00 p.m., I topped out at mile 82. I felt pretty pumped. Every ounce of me hurt, but I tried to keep a smile on my face. Sean M. from Sisters, Oregon gave me this tip: No matter how bad things are going, smiling always helps. I thought I'd try it on my next tough hunt.

I was at 25 hours now. My 24-hour goal was long gone, but I didn't care in the least. I had readjusted and now, I was going to finish in the 20s. Even if it was 29 hours, 59 minutes, and 59 seconds, I would get it done. I had 5 hours to get the last 18 miles. Seemed doable enough, so long as my body

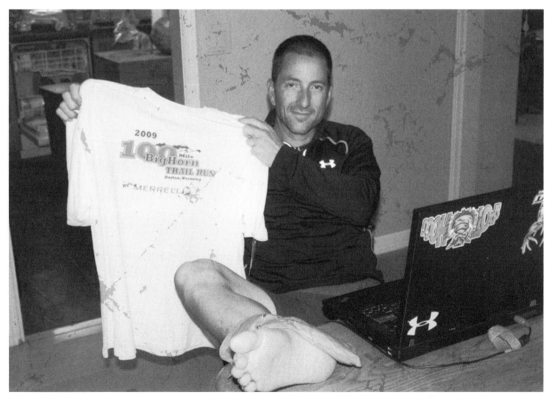

Rest and recovery the day after my first 100-mile endurance run, the Bighorn 100 in Dayton, Wyoming.

When I first started down the road as an ultramarathon runner all I did was run, 20 miles a day. I soon realized that being lean (skinny), while making me an efficient runner, hindered my mountain hunting ability in terms of packing heavy loads of meat if successful or survival gear when hunting deep in the backcountry. I needed muscle AND endurance. I needed to be a hybrid athlete so I married the two; endurance running and strength training. With this shift I achieved the bowhunting success I'd been dreaming of.

held up. That was a problem. Now I was really dried out. I weighed in at 153, ten pounds down from my official weigh-in of 163 the day before. I needed to take in some fluids, which was a common theme for me during this race. I ate some watermelon, a PB&J, chatted with a few bowhunters, said hi to Dennis from Oregon who had been progressing right along with me for the past twelve hours or so, then hit the road.

Here was what I learned: eighteen miles, while compared to 82, was not much, but it was still a LONG way. Thankfully I proved something else to myself . . .

I am tougher than I thought I was.

The New York Times wrote this about the race:
"And a few humbling realizations: That the Bighorn Mountains could not be conquered by a mere human being on foot. That shoe-sucking mud and thigh-deep snow banks, and steep climbs that sometimes felt as if they would never end, were things that at best could be fought only to a draw,

and even then only with luck. And that as tough as you think you are, there is always somebody tougher and faster, and that the course itself, in the end, would always be tougher still."

No matter how tough I might think I am, I know the mountains will always be tougher.

The mountain will always have the upper hand.

By 3:10 p.m., I reached the last aid station at mile 95. I came bombing off the hill and down 4,000 feet as best I could, but that thirteen miles hurt. My right Achilles was really acting up. After the race, I realized something was seriously wrong with it after that ankle swelled to twice the size as my left and I couldn't walk. Speaking of my left ankle, it felt like it had a bone sticking out the top of my foot, which I just ignored, pushed on, and it felt "better." Perhaps I could be a doctor? My right knee had a catch, so if I stopped running, I could hardly get started again.

I kept thinking of a favorite quote from Mexican revolutionary Emiliano Zapata: "It is better to die on your feet than to live on your knees." I knew I had to push through the pain.

When I got to mile 95, Tanner was there waiting for me and ran the last five with his old man. That-a-boy. I told him I couldn't stop because of my knee and said we had 1 hour and 50 minutes to run five miles. That just sounded weird. Normally at home, I could click off five miles in less than thirty minutes. Different time, different place. Off we went, running slowly, walking fast, just moving forward. Always. That was one thing I did the entire race, and I have to thank Under Armour's Anne Bonney. In an email before the race, she advised RFP—Relentless Forward Progress. I never stopped one time on the course, only to change shoes at the aid stations. Tanner and I joked around. After about two miles of our run together, he said he was tired. He also said he was surprised how good a mood I was in.

Looks can be deceiving.

At 4:20 p.m., 100 miles were in the books. Official time: 29 hours, 20 minutes. I was a 100-mile ultramarathoner! I earned my first 100-miler belt buckle.

It wasn't long ago that the thought of me running 100 miles in the mountains wasn't possible. I was pumped for the future. For new challenges, new tests, new dreams.

No matter what happened in my life, the highs and lows, no one could ever take this from me. I felt like I did when I arrowed my first six-by-six bull.

Of course, my inner demon attempted to steal a bit of my thunder. Twenty-seventh place wasn't where I dreamt to finish. But I knew all too well that adversity and shattered dreams were great teachers.

You can either get to work and get better, or wallow.

A good testament to just how difficult this race could be, even to seasoned ultramarathoners, was that only about 60 percent of the confirmed entrants finished the race, and just 34 runners came in under 30 hours.

I remembered finishing twenty-ninth in my first ever ultra (50K) back in 2005. From there I slowly chipped away and got better at the shorter ultras. Reaching new heights, achieving more, and gaining confidence allowed me to get to this point here, which again, years from now I would look back and say, "I remember my first 100. I learned a lot from that race."

Bowhunting was the same way. Years ago, I wanted to kill big bulls and bucks, and travel to Alaska and other exotic places and countries. The problem was, I couldn't go from a rookie bowhunter to the success I longed for in one giant leap.

Earn your breaks.

Hone your skills.

Develop a talent.

Eventually your dreams will become a reality.

The lessons I learned in the mountains of Wyoming that weekend were fresh and painful. They were also necessary.

I am thankful for every second I have spent in the Bighorn Mountains.

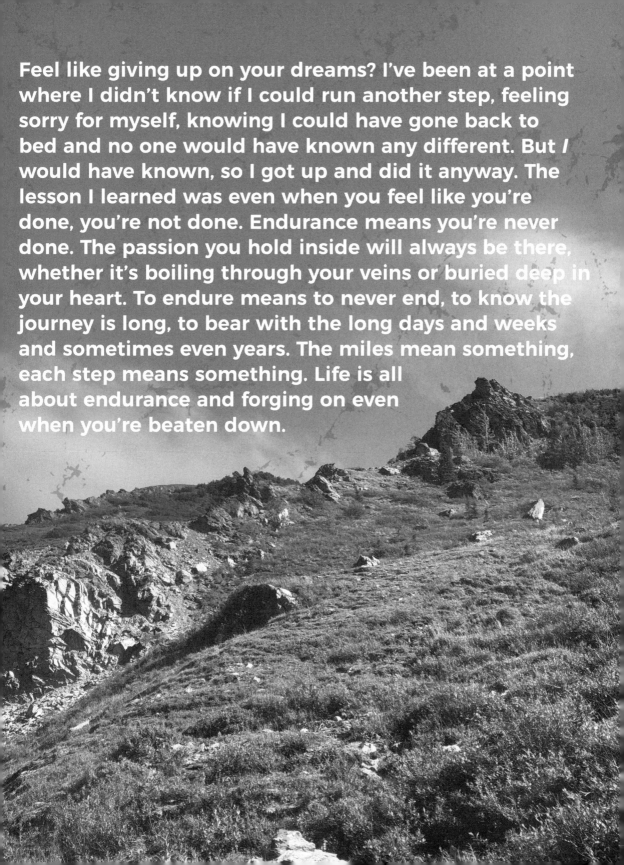

Feel like giving up on your dreams? I've been at a point where I didn't know if I could run another step, feeling sorry for myself, knowing I could have gone back to bed and no one would have known any different. But *I* would have known, so I got up and did it anyway. The lesson I learned was even when you feel like you're done, you're not done. Endurance means you're never done. The passion you hold inside will always be there, whether it's boiling through your veins or buried deep in your heart. To endure means to never end, to know the journey is long, to bear with the long days and weeks and sometimes even years. The miles mean something, each step means something. Life is all about endurance and forging on even when you're beaten down.

FIND COMFORT IN BEING UNCOMFORTABLE

"It is better to die on your feet than to live on your knees."

—Emiliano Zapata

Words can be fuel, and phrases can become fire. Some inspire me to go out on my feet fighting, working, digging deep for all I am worth, not on my knees bowing down to physical weakness, life's setbacks, discomfort, or fear.

Sometimes I need to repeat quotes like that as if they're mantras.

"It's better to die—" I tell myself as I hammer away, stride after stride.

Sometimes before the crack of dawn.

Sometimes on tough, steep, and muddy trails.

Sometimes when I want to quit in the worst way.

Excuses are easy to come by. Pushing through is not.

With ultramarathons, I know I will be miserable. No doubt. But I've found that I can handle misery. My good friend Misery and I have become real close over the years.

I've also found that your body will respond and adapt to almost any challenge you put before it. I have learned this in the mountains on long hunts, on the race course, and in training in the blistering heat or in the driving rain.

Our bodies are capable of amazing things if we take off the shackles of doubt, toughen up, sacrifice, and dig deep. Our spirits are capable of the same.

Dare to be defiant.

Dare others to doubt your abilities.

Damn the conventional wisdom from skeptics and experts and morons.

It is better to die on your feet . . .

People might think ultramarathons are too psycho, unrealistic, self-serving, or unnecessary, and that is cool. I've heard it all. What works for some does not work for others. My only suggestion is to find something that helps you to be the very best you can be.

Find inspiration somewhere.

Find what works for you.

Then give it all you have.

"I'd rather be dead than average."

I saw this quote on Mark Bell's Instagram page and agree: "I simply can't give a half-ass, average effort to anything I'm passionate about. I gotta go hard and give all I got."

I'm not talented.

I'm just a bowhunter like many others.

The only thing that sets me apart is my drive to do more and expect more from myself all while ignoring the doubters and naysayers that are always there trying to sabotage us dream chasers. My average, God-given talent, coupled with an average effort, would yield average results and, therefore, unfulfilled dreams . . .

With that I'd rather be dead. Because what's worse than unfulfilled potential?

The good news is I believe each one of us is capable of greatness in something. Have you found that something? The only reason people know my name is because I found bowhunting many years ago and was consumed with being the best I could be. It's changed my life for the better and helped me provide a better life for my family. Bowhunting led me to writing, magazine editing, TV hosting, sponsorships, endurance racing, and having a connection with all of you through social media, of which I am so grateful because your passion has, in turn, pushed me to greater heights.

Your "bowhunting" is out there. I promise. It will open doors for you as well. But be warned: when you become obsessed, it takes over your life. This obsessive approach works for me. It has changed my life, impacted others positively, and most importantly has taught my kids that anything is possible.

Dreams come true every single day. Yours can come true, too, but it is going to take some damn hard work.

If you're like me, that is fine. Just keep telling yourself the mantra: It is better to die on your feet than to live on your knees.

Go out fighting!

CHAPTER 10

LAST LOAD

In 2009, my dad was the first inductee into South Eugene High School's athletic Hall of Fame.

South Eugene High School

SE

ATHLETIC
HALL of FAME
Inaugural Inductee

Robert Hanes
Student Athlete - Coach

2009

Have you ever just stopped and asked yourself in what ways the world is better because you are in it?

How are you impacting the people and places around you?

What is your influence?

What will they say at your funeral?

How will you be remembered?

Strength and courage. They inspire people. Physical strength and bravery in the heat of battle. But even the physically weakest individuals can exhibit these traits.

In the final year of my dad's life, he reminded me once again how much I respected and admired him. From the moment doctors discovered a lump on his liver, Bob Hanes began his fight with cancer. It was an aggressive form of cancer, but he never gave up. For eighteen months, he waged a war against it.

"I'm going to beat it," he told me.

Everybody who gets cancer says this, and sometimes they do. Other times it seems like they will beat it because doctors begin pumping them with chemo and it hammers the cancer down. It seems like they're winning, but they're not, because they can't take that chemo forever. It's poison. Oftentimes, after the chemo stops, cancer comes back; and when it does, it's even worse than before.

After being diagnosed at the start of 2009, my dad had been saying he was going to beat liver cancer, and in the spring of 2010, doctors couldn't believe how good he was doing. Throughout this time, he still tried to coach and do everything he always did. The chemo temporarily worked, but the side effects were rough. He was so exhausted, yet he could never rest. There was a constant ringing in his ears. He clung on, but with something like liver cancer, this was an impossible battle to win.

Dad never beat it. But he continued to inspire me and others who knew him, even in those last months and weeks and days of his life.

While I look up to many, my dad was the only true hero I've ever had. He showed me why during those last tough months.

We love to see when people persevere. My dad continued to hang on to hope during his battle.

One of the hardest things I've experienced in my life was seeing my dad slowly die. Cancer is a devastating disease; and while there is nothing positive about losing your dad to cancer, the one thing I was thankful for was the chance to have many quality, loving, heartfelt, and sometimes emotional talks with my dad. While he battled, we bonded. Those talks with him are moments in my life I will always hold dear.

My dad, clowning with my boys. Truett gave my dad the medal he was awarded for running the Eugene Marathon as a 13-year-old, in 3 hours, 30 minutes. Tanner, in the background, ran a few miles with Truett during the race as a pacer.

Another thing that stood out to me was the way my dad fought. There were times when he was scared and depressed that he was going to be leaving us, because truthfully he didn't want to. Regardless of his fears, he never quit. He kept fighting.

Why do you do what you do? Why do you run or compete?

For Truett, my youngest son, he ran his first marathon for Grandpa Bob and he crushed it. Even though Truett was only thirteen, instead of the marathon minimum age of sixteen (which meant I had to lie just to get him in) he ran the 26.2-mile Eugene Marathon in 3 hours, 30 minutes, and 41 seconds. I was really proud of him. I finished in 3 hours and 1 minute, and Trace did the half in 1 hour and 49 minutes. Tanner also got in on the action, pacing his little brother for about 8 miles of the race.

An even prouder parenting moment came when Truett gave his marathon finishers' medal to my dad. He was very pleased with Truett for getting that marathon done.

I've come to love the struggle. And every struggle—physical, emotional, spiritual—pushes us past our breaking points.

The most coveted award in the ultramarathoning world is the silver buckle awarded at the Western States Endurance Run. It's the most famous 100-mile race in the world because of its history and competitiveness. I earned my buckle in my second 100-miler by finishing in under 24 hours, at 22 hours and 41 minutes. In my world, if there was ever a comparison to an Olympic gold medal, it would be this silver buckle. I felt like it was my greatest personal athletic achievement, but it came at this bittersweet time of my life.

All through the race, I thought of my dad, who was fighting hard for each extra day he could on this earth.

His obituary would read:

Robert "Bob" Hanes, born on January 2nd, 1948 in Seattle to Lester and Heloise Wilmsen Hanes. After graduating from South Eugene High School, he attended the University of Oregon. At one time he worked as a baker, then had a job in sporting goods sales. He owned and operated a record store in Portland. His true passion, however, was coaching track and field pole vaulters and jumpers.

I remember as a little boy looking through his athletic scrapbook hundreds of times. The newspaper clippings, medals, plaques . . . He was my hero. Unlike me, he had awesome athletic ability. Coming out of South Eugene High, he was a D-1 athlete (meaning a collegiate athlete at the highest level) in both track and field and gymnastics. My dad seemed to have it all. He was smart, talented, and everyone in Eugene knew him. To me, his oldest son, Bob Hanes was larger than life.

While putting in miles training for the Western States race, I would think of how my dad refused to give up battling inoperable liver cancer. I admired his strength and courage. Whenever I didn't want to run, lift, or shoot my bow, I pictured his frail and failing body and thought, *Who am I to be lazy?*

On the drive down to where the race started in Olympic Valley, California, I talked to my dad on the phone, and he didn't sound good. He'd been battling cancer for a year and a half, so I knew in my heart he was nearing the end of his fight. As I ran, I took some solace in knowing he was following my progress live on the ws100.com website.

Earning my coveted silver Western States 100 buckle just days before my dad's passing.

What running Western States proved to me was that I could achieve all my mountain bowhunting dreams. I convinced myself that if I could run 100 miles through the Sierra Nevada Mountains with 41,000 feet of total elevation change, in over 90-degree heat, while battling mental and physical fatigue and despair, in less than one day, I could do just about anything. I'd put in the work, now it was time to reap the rewards.

At 3:41 a.m., I crossed the finish line in Auburn, California, and in doing so, earned my silver Western States buckle. I just logged a nearly seven-hour improvement over my first 100-mile race. I started out the race supremely confident, but during those 22 hours and 41 minutes of reflection while running, doubt crept in more than once. Through those struggles I kept telling myself that my pain was temporary. In a few days' time I would be healed up and richer from the experience. For my dad, there would be no healing. There would only be deeper and more debilitating pain and sickness, then death.

I finished the race Sunday morning and we drove home that day, getting home very late. I went to work the next day, then headed over to my dad's house, eager to tell him in person that I loved him and give him a hug on the heels of my successful race. As a lifelong track guy, he appreciated a solid athletic performance as much as anyone. Dad and I had started out my life's journey together, then through circumstances and challenge, had drifted apart, but things were back in order. My brother, Pete, spent a lot of time with Dad during the past few months, which warmed my heart. From back when I was five years old, when my mom and dad divorced, I'd always just wanted us all back together.

I will never forget looking into Dad's eyes upon my return from the race and saying, "Dad, I wish I could give you some of my strength."

"Don't give up on me," he told me. "Not yet."

He still thought he was going to beat it.

I will never forget his will to live.

A handful of days after I had earned my silver buckle in the Western States race, my dad passed on early in the day on July 5. The pain of losing him was much worse than any I'd felt before from races, life, or anything.

My dad's greatest reward came in helping others achieve their full potential. He also loved sharing a beautiful, masterful piece of music with them. He believed it could enrich their lives. Music was as much, or more, a part of his life than anything. He had a passion and love for track and field, but music for my dad was a spiritual journey at times.

Music spoke to my dad, especially the work of Brian Wilson, creator, songwriter, and producer of his favorite group, the Beach Boys. As a young man, he started listening to the Beach Boys like just about everyone else did for the fun, summer-themed tracks they put out. Then he really began to appreciate the other side of Brian Wilson's spectrum of music. He became an unofficial Beach Boys historian and was friends with Brian Wilson. My dad most enjoyed the songs with deeper meanings, like "In My Room," "God Only Knows," and many of the tracks off *Smile*, which Dad himself helped compile. My dad, along with many others in the music industry, saw Brian Wilson as a genius. Maybe a touch eccentric. Most geniuses are, they say. But still an amazingly gifted man. Brian's music was powerful medicine to my dad.

I will never forget seeing Dad standing there at his reel-to-reel deck, the Beach Boys rolling, cranked to deafening levels. He would sing with all his heart, eyes closed, head back, more a part of the music than one could ever be. Then he would turn to whomever was there with him, with a look that said, "Are you getting this too? Are you feeling this?"

That was my dad as much as anything else.

A couple of nights before my dad's funeral, I bought a new Beach Boys greatest hits CD. I had listened to the Beach Boys songs hundreds and thousands of times over the years, but listening to those familiar songs in my truck brought my dad back to me in some little way. There is nothing quite like music in that regard.

At my dad's funeral, I spoke to the crowd gathered in the South Eugene High School gymnasium to celebrate Bob Hanes's life.

"I know for certain my dad, Bob Hanes, would be overjoyed with this get-together today," I said. "Friends, family, music, and memories. I hope he is looking down on us now smiling, feeling the love that fills this gym."

The people I spoke to were all giving up a part of their day to honor my dad. Their presence meant so much to me and the rest of my family.

"To me it means my dad has either impacted you, or maybe just someone close to you. For instance, I know for a fact there are some here who only met my dad once in his life, but because they care for me and my family and know what my dad meant to us, they are here showing their love and support. My dad is gone, but he is bringing people together. He is still making an impact."

I shared several memories and reflections of my dad that I would never forget. Especially the memories of the small, impressionable boy I once was.

"I vividly remember my mom telling me that my dad's legs were so strong and muscular they were as hard as tree trunks. Then I would poke at them and of course, she was right. I also remember late one night when he got home from a softball game, just he and I were up. We were eating cereal, me in a little wood rocking chair and him leaning over his bowl, seated on the edge of the couch. He watched TV; I watched him. His knee was bleeding pretty good from sliding into a base. I remember sitting there staring at the bloody wound, mesmerized by his seeming invincibility."

I reminded everybody sitting in the gym that, just like them, my dad wasn't perfect.

"I will never forget how he would take his experiences and use them to help others. He had been there and done that, so to speak. He competed on the

Speaking at my dad's funeral wasn't easy, but I felt it necessary to honor him and celebrate what he meant to so many.

field and in life, won some battles and lost others. He wasn't afraid to own up to the mistakes he made when I was growing up. He was up front and honest with everyone, which is an approach that helped build trust in many of the young adults he mentored. He talked and shared; they listened and learned. I would guess many times they walked away thinking of what he'd told them. I know I did. Maybe they still think of the advice he'd given. As a rule, kids like to blow adults off. The key is to get them to listen, and he could, because he spoke from the heart and had no agenda other than to simply help them navigate successfully through life. Plus, the way he spoke, with unwavering confidence, looking you in the eye, you'd believe anything he told you."

As I shared my dad's passion for music and the Beach Boys, we had a special surprise for everybody. I had received a special musical tribute from Brian Wilson of the Beach Boys, which I played at the service. He sang "God Only Knows" acoustic and ended it with, "We love you, Bob." My dad would have been so happy to hear that personal tribute to him from the iconic Brian Wilson. We were so thankful he took to the time to acknowledge Bob Hanes.

I shared a story with the crowd about a guy I had worked for a couple years prior who treated people like crap and he knew it. In fact, one night over a few beers he wondered if anyone would come to his funeral. He asked me, "Will you come?" Of course, I answered that yes, I'd be there. What was I supposed to say? I was an employee. He still had doubts. I would never forget him writing a contract on a napkin saying that I agreed to come to his funeral. Partly it was in jest, but there was some truth to it. He was genuinely concerned and rightfully so.

My dad didn't need to be concerned about attendance at his funeral. Here were hundreds of people gathered together for no other reason than the love we felt for Bob Hanes. Whether they knew him as Dad—as Pete, Justin, and I did—or as a husband, as my stepmon Kandy did. Or as a coach like all his athletes did, or as "Beach Boy Bob," or just as a friend, everyone there would acknowledge that my dad, if given a chance, could enrich their lives.

"If helping others realizing their dreams and enriching lives isn't the true definition of success, I don't know what is. My dad's life proves to me that strength of character is a lot more important than worldly riches."

A week after the memorial service, I hunted the Nevada wilderness for eight brutally tough days. It was one of the least productive hunts I had ever been on; I saw twenty deer total. Luckily, I had a good partner and cameraman, Jody Cyr, who was tough as nails.

Leaving for the hunt was not easy for me so soon after losing my dad. Ideally, when leaving for a tough hunt, a guy wants everything in order, to be focused on the challenging task at hand, having a heightened sense of things. Such was not the case. But regardless, bowhunting is what I do. It's who I am, so I loaded up my pack and gave it everything I had.

Two months later, I found myself flying home from British Columbia on my birthday, October 2. I had a few voicemails and texts wishing me a good b-day, but all I could think about was that, for the first time ever in my life, my dad wouldn't be calling or giving me a hug, telling me he loved me and to have a happy birthday.

I knew that people lose loved ones, and that at some point, everyone is going to lose their dad. I was not unique in that regard. But my dad dying was the worst heartache I had ever felt. Honoring him was what gave me strength when I was at my weakest. And I needed that strength throughout the 2010 hunting season . . . no elk in Wyoming, no breaks for a while in Colorado, through the pouring rain and tough hunting in Oregon and finally, BC. Week after week on the road, grinding away in the unrelenting mountains.

All throughout these weeks, my dad's courage to fight as long as he could inspired me every day.

As a kid, I missed having a dad to share things with growing up and it hurt, but I was able to use the pain for motivation. Now that he was gone forever, I vowed to succeed, whether it be in bowhunting or ultra running, in his honor.

The Beach Boys played in my ear buds as I ran.

"If you should ever leave me / Though life would still go on, believe me."

Ever since my Dad died in 2010, every time I run a race in Eugene, I spend most of the time thinking about him. There are so many things that remind me of him.

Hayward Field, of course, where he competed as an athlete and officiated for years.

Amazon Parkway, a major street in Eugene, which is close to where he last lived.

The house he lived in before that on Ferry Street.

South Eugene High School, where he graduated and coached for decades, my grandma's old house, where he grew up, on 24th and Emerald, where I spent many days growing up myself.

I will never forget my dad's eagerness for life, his thirst for knowledge as reflected in his extensive and widely varied library. He was easily the smartest, most well-read person I've ever met. We had many interesting conversations—me being a bowhunting redneck, him being a South Eugene liberal. I loved the bantering. He thought the NBA playoffs were fixed, every year. I always just laughed saying, "Come on, Dad," but secretly gave some credence to his theory.

There are so many memories of those I love and miss every day, but those same memories helped push me yesterday, power me through today, and will be there for me tomorrow.

I miss and love you, Dad.

God only knows what I'd be without you.

Do you have a passion that's neglected or unfulfilled? Have you given up on the dreams you once held when you were younger? My dad never competed in the Olympics, yet he took his passion and gifts to the world of track and field and he helped others achieve their full potential. Unachieved goals don't have to result in unused gifts.

PART 3

ALL MY DREAMS AND
GOALS HAVE ALWAYS
CENTERED AROUND
SUCCESS IN THE
WOODS, BEING
ABLE TO TELL
A STORY AND
SHARING A
JOURNEY.

THE ULTIMATE
PREDATOR

CHAPTER 11

THE BEST NEVER REST

Courtney Dauwalter,
endurance legend
and one of my
inspirations

"Outliers are those who have been given opportunities—
and who have had the strength and presence of mind
to seize them."

—Malcolm Gladwell

What is possible if we take off the shackles of comfort? There are a few select individuals out there who know what's possible when they move beyond their discomfort, when they master their pain, and when they sacrifice their lives to be the best at their craft.

They are runners. Like ultramarathoner Courtney Dauwalter.

"I refuse to give my physical pain any value," Courtney told Zach Davis of TheTrek.com . "I shove the pain aside, focus on something different, and force myself to keep moving . . . I keep repeating over in my head, 'Keep moving. Keep moving. Keep moving.' Or sometimes it's, 'You're fine. You're fine. You're fine.' If I'm being nice to myself, sometimes I will cheer myself on and repeat, 'You're doing a good job. You're doing a good job. You're doing a good job.'"

They are fighters. Like martial arts athlete Michael Chandler.

"Life is about saying yes," Michael was quoted in an article at MMAfighting.com. "Life is about performance, especially in this industry. I've said yes to every opportunity. I've said yes at the drop of a hat with the UFC (Ultimate Fighting Championship) thinking, 'Holy cow, this guy's a little bit nuts for saying yes to this, but I love it.'"

They are Olympians. Like Emma Coburn.

"I don't take a day off; I probably run nine times a week," Emma told ESPN. "I find that the best way to connect with people is to run with them. I have someone that I'm running with at least eight of those nine runs a week, if not nine of nine, so it's a great time to catch up with friends. My training partners are my friends."

They are winners. Like Conor McGregor.

""I don't give a shit what people say. I never did. I never do. I told you before the fight I was the shit and I'm telling you right now, I'm the shit."

They are warriors. Like ultramarathoner David Goggins.

"Be more than motivated, be more than driven, become literally obsessed to the point where people think you're fucking nuts," he wrote in his book *Can't Hurt Me*.

They are outliers. Legends. Freaks. People who push the bounds of what is humanly possible. And they are who I follow, not just on social media but in real life, into the soaring mountains and the scorching deserts.

Each and every day, I am motivated to improve myself in some way. Usually that amounts to just putting in work on my own. In general, I am obsessed with learning from elites in their field, or as you might say simply, the "winners." Over the years, there have been times when I've been lucky enough to spend time with true legends. In those instances, I've wanted to know what makes them legendary.

Why are they different from everybody else?

What pushes them to the heights—and depths—they reach?

What makes them true icons?

I've wanted to unlock the code and see why they are beasts, then apply their mindset to my own journey. If I can learn one thing that will translate over into my craft that ultimately makes me a better, more successful, consistent, insightful, or merciful bowhunter, I feel like my journey will have been worthwhile. To me that's the point of life—learn, experience, share, value, teach, and build.

I could fill an entire book full of the outliers I've met and what I've learned from them. I'll share a few of my favorites.

It's not often that we meet someone who challenges the norms of society. A person who pulls back the curtain and exposes the masses to a new realm of what's possible with physical and mental discipline. David Goggins is as I've described, and it's an honor to call him a friend. In my eyes, he's making

David Goggins, whose goal has been to be "one of the baddest m*therf*ckers to ever walk the earth" (that's his quote), has become a friend who gets how my brain works and loves to push himself. He has impacted me greatly. Here I'm introducing him to the world of archery.

a huge impact on people who grew up with the odds stacked against them, just like he grew up.

In Goggins's words, "You can be born in a fucking sewer and still be the baddest motherfucker on earth." He knows because he just so happens to be that. A rough childhood turned him into a depressed and overweight young man, but he was the only member of the US Armed Forces to complete SEAL training as well as the Army Ranger School and Air Force Tactical Air Controller training. He is also known for competing in ultramarathons and triathlons.

Being around someone like Goggins makes me realize that I have so much more to give, that I haven't sacrificed enough. As he often says, most of us only tap into 40 percent of our ability. We all have so much more to give than we know. I understood this once, when I ran 240 miles. Upon finishing, I realized that I actually felt fine. During the race I felt terrible, but at the end I was smiling and saying it was great. So I wasn't even close to being done. That wasn't the limit.

Goggins pushes his limits as far as they can go.

In his savage book *Can't Hurt Me*, Goggins shares his story and offers insight into how anyone can reach their full potential. "A lot of us surround ourselves with people who speak to our desire for comfort," Goggins writes. "Who would rather treat the pain of our wounds and prevent further injury than help us callous over them and try again. We need to surround ourselves with people who will tell us what we need to hear, not what we want to hear, but at the same time not make us feel we're up against the impossible."

> **"Sometimes your motivation needs to be because no one else wants to fucking do it. We need doctors, we need lawyers, we need dentists, we need teachers. We also need fucking savages."**
> **—David Goggins on Instagram**

Goggins is someone who pushes me simply by what he stands for and his unfiltered, unapologetic way he attacks life. His mindset might make some uneasy. I've noticed that true outliers sometimes make those that embrace mediocrity uncomfortable. But Goggins has neither time nor patience for mediocrity.

"Mediocrity feels so fucking good!" Goggins posted. "If you wake up and don't want to work out, all you have to say is 'Fuck it, I don't give a shit!' And if you're mediocre, you are probably hanging around other mediocre people, so they are happy that you don't add pressure to their life! One big happy soft-ass family!!! People don't like hanging around that motherfucker who makes them feel uncomfortable or like an underachiever on a regular basis! We stay away from the fucking savage who wakes up at 0330 regardless the weather, if they got a good night's sleep, if their life sucks and times are hard. People stay clear of that cat! Those kind of people make you question yourself. They also let you know where your life ends and their life begins!"

Some people love to criticize him, but he is *doing* it, making a real impact on society, and they are making excuses or simply trying to dull his shine. I'm inspired by people like David Goggins who are fighting, bleeding, and sacrificing comfort every day as they scratch and claw toward their full potential.

If I see someone who's been ultra successful, I'll never complain, "It must be nice." Rather I study, ask questions, learn, and see if I can use their approach to help me get to the next level. When I meet people who are more successful than me, I get excited. I'm fired up to find out what makes them tick. Why are they the best at their craft, and how can I harness that to be *my* best? I don't waste time being jealous or petty or trying to discredit their spot on the top of the mountain and the effort expended to get there. There's room for others too.

I know I'm not some amazing athlete. I'm not the best shot in the world—I guarantee that there are better hunters than me. But I won't stop, that's the difference. What I'm good at is not a talent. I'll just do more and work harder than most others are willing to.

I know what it's like to be average and to define myself by my limitations, but over the course of my life, I've pulled the curtain back on the people who push boundaries. They are freaks, but they're human too. We're the same species. And now I'm running and training and learning from those freaks.

When you surround yourself with people who are pushing the limits, you will be motivated either by inspiration or competition to push yourself beyond what you thought possible. When people around you have the same goal of self-improvement and the same dedication to that goal, it is easier to challenge yourself.

I love celebrating greatness. I crave being around people who have excelled in their field and who have characteristics that I'm obsessed with emulating. I'm always looking for ways to rub elbows with winners, hoping some of their greatness rubs off on me. Courtney Dauwalter is one such person. She's the number-one women's ultra runner in the world. The only things that rival her running talent are her positive attitude and her smile.

The truth is, I train hard all year to hopefully get in good enough shape so she doesn't have to wait on me too long when we run together.

I first heard Courtney's name when we both ran the Moab 240, which she won. I didn't know I was competing against someone who *The New York Times* would call "The woman who outruns the men, 200 miles at a time." I mean . . . damn. The newspaper reported that in the Moab 240, "Dauwalter obliterated the competition."

I can vouch for that.

In the race, when I took off, I told myself, *You gotta be smart*. As I've said, I'm not the smartest runner out there. I usually take off in these races way too fast. For the first 200-mile race I did, the Bigfoot 200, I was leading by hours the first day, but I went too fast. Then I dried out (got dehydrated) and blew up (faded fast). So I decided to be conservative with Moab, and to keep track of the leaders knowing it's a long race taking place over several days. I knew I had time. I remember getting to an aid station and asking someone who was in the lead.

"Courtney Dauwalter."

"Who?" I asked. "Where's she at?"

When they told me she was ten miles ahead of everybody, I assumed she must have gone the wrong way.

There's no way she's that far ahead of us. She had to miss a turn or gone off course.

But no . . . Courtney just *crushed* the 238.3 miles of Moab and won the race and beat every man and woman out there.

Joe Rogan was following along to see how I was progressing during that race, as there was live tracking available to keep tabs on the racers. In doing so, he saw her incredible performance and was like, "Holy shit, I need to talk to this Courtney." He had her on his podcast, and that's when I began to get to know her story. That's when a lot of people finally figured out who she was and came to realize she's one of the best ultra runners ever. She's won the Western States, the most famous 100-miler, the Ultra-Trail du Mont-Blanc ultramarathon in Europe, and the Tarawera Ultra in New Zealand.

> **"The human body and our brains are such an amazing combination. I am always intrigued by our ability to complete these big mileages and that keeps me coming back for more. What else can we do? How fast can we go? How much physical pain can we push past by being strong in our minds?"**
>
> **—Courtney Dauwalter**

Without question, Courtney's a legend. We've had some really great trips. One of the best days I've ever had was when Courtney and I went rim-to-rim-to-rim in the Grand Canyon.

Courtney understands how huge the mental aspect is on her sport. "For me, this is the most interesting part of ultrarunning," she said in a 2020 interview. "During my first 100-mile attempt, I ended up dropping out of the race around mile 60 because my legs hurt really bad and I didn't know how to shift gears to the mental game. Now, when it becomes physically painful, which is inevitable, I try to remind myself that by staying tough in my head, by not giving up on myself and by continuing to push forward, I can mentally overpower the physical pain."

See why I love running with her?

In 2020, Courtney attempted to break the record for running the 490-mile Colorado Trail. During her attempt, I ran with her for twenty-six hours. At one point, she looked at me and asked if I was feeling okay. She had been running for four days, yet she asked me if I was doing okay? I couldn't help laughing.

"I'm not falling for this shit," I said, smiling. "You're not asking me how I'm doing when you've been running for four days! You don't worry about me."

Taking in the dry mountain air for days on end, nonstop, at over 10,000 feet elevation ended up drying out her lungs. Her nose was also bleeding constantly but it was the deep, raspy cough that was causing concern. She's incredibly tough though, and while her legs were still strong after 309 miles, she went to the ER where they said her oxygen level was very low and they told her she was suffering from acute bronchitis. They stressed that she couldn't go back out, and when asked what would happen if she did, the doctor stated, "Well, she could die on the trail."

I've said I want to find my limits, to find out what happens when I push myself too far. Courtney has found hers. She has been there at least one time. But that was her limit given those circumstances; she's not done yet. I'll bet money 309 miles is not her breaking point. The promised land of her potential is far beyond that.

I've learned from her that we can all push it so far past what we thought was possible. She's simply amazing.

The outliers know that sometimes your body says, "Not this time."

To get it done takes your mind, body, and spirit all to be in synch, which is why when it goes well, it's so special. It's powerful.

This life-altering endeavor—despite the pain that comes from laying it all on the line and the possible heartache knowing there is a real risk of crashing and coming up short—is so amazing, you can't help but want to come back for more.

A select few keep coming back.

Those are the few I want to keep finding and following.

We are all inspired by the best athletes: Jordan. Kobe. Brady. Tiger. LeBron. Gretzky. Pelé. If you're known by only one name, that means you outworked everybody around you. You became a legend by being fanatical. I love the great examples of that. That's what I love more than anything. I think of Olympians like Usain Bolt. I think of stars like Serena Williams. People who push the limits far beyond anyone who came before them. Seemingly superhuman. Outliers. Freaks.

Many have talent, but few are obsessed.

> **"No man has the right to be an amateur in the matter of physical training. It is a shame for a man to grow old without seeing the beauty and strength of which his body is capable."**
> **—Socrates**

One thing I can relate to with Michael Jordan is his competitive nature. I remember back when I was fighting my way up in the hunting industry, some of my friends would say I was "too competitive." They were probably right, and I haven't changed a bit. Only thing is now, instead of competing against everyone else, I battle only myself. No one else is even on my radar other than for inspiration. Unless they talk smack of course. And, while I don't really put much stock into what the haters say, I *never* forget, which is also MJ-esque.

One group that inspires me the most is the elite athletes of the UFC. Now I know . . . what do UFC fighters have to do with world class ultramarathoners and mountain bowhunters. Seems like an odd combination, right? Maybe so, but the common thread is that each discipline is incredibly difficult to master, and success only comes to those who put in blood, sweat, and tears. There are no shortcuts and no substitutes for hard work!

Why, when I listen to those insanely dedicated to a craft or art, do I link their thought process to my chosen passion, bowhunting? Conor McGregor is a great example of that.

Every time Conor talks, he is sharing the mindset of a fighter, a warrior. I hear lessons that an open-minded bowhunter could, or actually should, embrace.

Conor knows you can't talk your way to the top.

Conor realizes hard work rises.

When Conor asks, "who is going out there, time and time again, back-to-back-to-back-to-back, putting it all on the line and continuing to show up?" he might as well be reading the audiobook to my life's story.

"I had to work my fucking bollocks off to get it, and here I am still working," Conor said in a 2016 interview. "While they're talking . . . I'm talking, but I'm fucking walking a hell of a lot more than I'm talking."

Conor McGregor embodies the winning mindset—and a champion's mindset that can apply to any worthwhile endeavor. I always say that I don't have a blueprint for success, but Conor's story unveils a time-honored blueprint for one.

First, you have to work, sweat, and bleed with unbridled passion. And you have to exhibit tunnel-visioned focus on your craft.

Second, you have to change the way you think and believe that with every single breath you take that you are the best you can be.

Last, like Conor had, it helps to have someone in your life who believes in you with all their heart and will never doubt you.

With that formula in place, the sky's the limit.

Speaking of the UFC and the sky being the limit, let me brag about Michael Chandler and Colby Covington. I've trained with both of them, and those have been some of the most memorable workout sessions I've ever experienced.

Michael Chandler quite literally burst on the scene when he knocked out Dan Hooker in the UFC 257 (in 2021) inside of three minutes. How far he had come, however, was a miracle.

"I've earned my way in this sport over the last 12 years, over the last 27 fights. A lot of dominant victories, tons of first-round finishes, tons of exciting fights," he said in an interview.

Chandler didn't mince words after his first big victory: "Conor McGregor. Surprise, surprise. There's a new king in the lightweight division. Dustin Poirier, your time is coming. And Khabib, if you ever do see fit to grace us with your presence back here in the UFC Octagon, in your quest for 30–0 you've got to beat somebody, so beat me if you can."

> "I just saw this Rumi quote that I love: 'Set your life on fire. Seek those who fan your flames.' The Philly translation of that is don't be hanging with no jankass jokers that don't help you shine. The prerequisite for spending time with any person is that they nourish and inspire you. They feed your flame. Look at your last five text messages. Are those people feeding your flames or dousing your fire? Put your phone down for just a second and look around. Look to the people around you. Are those people throwing logs on your fire or are they pissing on it? The people that you spend time with are going to make or break your dreams. Everybody don't deserve to be around you. You got to defend your life with your life. So who are the people in your life that are fanning the flames? Shout them out."
>
> —Will Smith on Instagram

I went to San Diego and trained with him. We trained hard, and this is an athlete who's in his prime as a fighter. Chandler still says it was one of his hardest workouts. It was great. It hurt. Here was the menu:

Medicine ball slam x 12
Lateral band walk x 12
Band upright row x 12
Band face pull x 12
Band core rotation x 12 each side
Goliath Shoelaces circuit
Medicine ball bucket toss X 10
Medicine ball power punch X 10
Bench press + chain x 5–10
Sprinting sled pushes in the parking lot 2 up and backs

Colby "Chaos" Covington believes that if someone has a passion for something, they'll find a way. He's worked out with me and run the mountain with me. He knows the secret: It requires hard work and dedication.

Colby has ascended to the top of the UFC and is currently, as I'm writing, number one in the UFC welterweight ranking. So it's amazing to be able to do reps in the gym with this beast or to ascend Mount Pisgah with him. It's even more amazing to hear him say comments like the following:

"I'm inspired by people like you. You know—you're the people that give me hope and drive. You came from this small town and you're a larger-than-life figure now. That's what inspires me to keep pushing and keep chasing dreams and leaving a legacy just like you."

What can I say to that? I feel the same way about him. Colby and Michael inspire me. They give me hope and drive. THEY are the ones that are larger-than-life figures, and they inspire me to keep pushing and keep chasing dreams and keep hammering.

Working out with freaks like them are my favorite workouts. They're not exercises. It's not about the reps or the weights. It's about the company I'm with.

Surround yourself with those who push you to be a better human.

Strive to find people you can model yourself after and you can see qualities and characteristics that you want to possess yourself.

They show me firsthand that good is the enemy of great.

I know personally, and have been lucky enough now, to have spent time with people who are truly *great* at their craft, be it hunting, running, endurance racing, lifting, training, writing, or motivation, and I've been fascinated. I can't get enough of true greatness.

I am not great at anything. On my best day I'm good at one or two endeavors. I can't be satisfied with "good" because I've learned the greats are never satisfied. They are always working, learning, growing, and giving more. They are disciplined in their drive to keep pushing, getting to the next level. So in following their lead I find myself doing the one thing that in my mind means discipline . . . I run. When I run, I feel like I've put in work, and working in one aspect makes me want to work in all aspects.

In all likelihood, if I'm being honest, I know I'll never reach the level I dream of in anything, as many people don't. That said, I'll never stop trying.

"How you do anything is how you do everything."

Sure, it's a pretty simple statement. But doesn't it seem odd that "winners" seem to find a way to win at everything they do? They win at life. I think it's because they put the same amazing energy, effort, and focus into everything they touch . . . work, training, their craft, mental strength/growth, diet, etc. They never make excuses. Instead, they will push themselves to excel and win.

I love following people like this.

Most people don't want to compare themselves to greatness; instead, they will compare themselves to average and think they're great.

They are wrong.

I'm the opposite. I want to see greatness, to train, run, and experience greatness firsthand. I want to see if I can steal bits of the formula here and there. But even so, without my own hard work and obsession, nothing will be gained.

There is a dangerous tipping point regarding potential . . .

Putting in half-assed effort that you tell yourself is hard work is the wrong side of the pivot. Here, you'll never change.

If you grind hard on the right side of that pivot, consistently over time, then the sky's the limit.

It's a mindset.

There's a mindset and a mentality that all of the greats have. Courtney carries it. So do Goggins and Michael Chandler and Colby.

I need to know what drives them. What makes them tick. This is what drives me. They are what make me tick.

I want to see if I can reach another level. I want to know what that looks like.

These outliers and many others have shown me this. So has Emma Coburn. The challenge has been keeping up with them, especially when Emma is the most dominant steeplechase runner in US history.

Nothing quite compares to hammering out miles on the trails above Crested Butte with Emma. For the most part, I found it hard just to keep up on our mountain runs. After seeing her work firsthand, I believe that not only her training at elevation but also running trails for years has really translated into useful strength for her specialty. Navigating uneven trails, rocks, tree roots, etc. while running a quick pace has seemingly enhanced her natural athletic power, which allows her to not only get over, but come off those barriers better than her competition.

I've trained with three-time Olympian Emma Coburn in Crested Butte, Colorado, and she's run my mountain with me here in Oregon. I am a long way from Olympic-level athleticism, but I've tried to learn what I can from Emma's winning mindset and apply it to my craft.

Emma won the bronze at the 2016 Olympics and ran well at the 2020 US Olympic Trials, winning the steeplechase and setting a new trials record in the process. Unfortunately she fell during the steeplechase Olympic final and was disqualified, but one race won't define her. All I can say is that she's perfected her craft. She's a freaking beast.

I remember watching her running an outdoor mile in Colorado Springs, which is 7,000 feet in elevation. That makes running fast for distance harder than normal as there's less oxygen to use. Emma was somewhat in the back after three laps as they approached the final turn. Shortly before that final

turn, she started to close the gap and began to reel people in. It was amazing to watch. I asked her about that race.

I wanted to know what made her click, what motivated her to crush it.

I knew in the race, Emma could have easily thought, *Well, it's 7,000 feet. I just don't have it today. I'm running against milers and I'm not a miler. I'm a 3,000-meter runner. This isn't my day*. She could have just settled in and come in with the pack and still had a good time. Still had a 4:30 mile, which is fast. Or she could have told herself, *It's gonna hurt, but I don't care.*

There was some moment, some decision she made where she decided to give it all she had, knowing it was going to hurt very bad.

Nobody would know.

Nobody would question whether she was giving 85 percent or 90 percent or 99 percent.

Emma turned it up, passed every other woman down the stretch, and won the race. I asked her about that decision she made.

Emma Coburn during one of our training runs in Crested Butte, Colorado. She ran the trails outside of Crested Butte as a young girl and as a 3-time Olympian she still runs them in preparation to compete against the best in the world on the biggest stage.

What was it like? She simply shook her head and told me there was no decision. This was what she was trained to do.

She's not trained to make decisions, as in deciding she's not going to give it her all. She's trained to win.

This is where my mentality to run comes from. I'm going to go running, and I don't care if I'm tired or if the weather is bad . . . I will run.

I love Emma's mindset.

"Why?"

It's a question I get often. In fact, while back at an event at Under Armour one day, I was asked this question by one of the best athletes ever in the history of her sport.

Why do I like to run so much and so far?

"I know you like pain, right?" she asked.

I do, but that's not why I like running. In regard to pain, I like to hurt because it's only then that I know I am sacrificing and pushing past where most would quit. I've convinced myself that's the only advantage I have. The ability to deal with pain. And I'll lobby that almost all who run 100-mile ultras like I have also have a very high pain threshold. Pain is part of the deal in extreme endurance racing.

I told the superstar athlete that I like running because being able to run hard for hours through the mountains makes me feel invincible. I get the same feeling when holding my bow while facing a grizzly bear, a Cape buffalo, a lion, and so on. In reality, am I invincible? Obviously not, but in my mind I am, and that's all that matters.

I feel lucky. Really lucky.

I get that it's weird. This guy who made a name for himself as a bowhunter suddenly running with these legends.

I don't really deserve to hang out with Olympians, icons, performance freaks, but for some reason I get to. And I train with them. They're the best in the world at what they do, but as a runner, I am definitely not. There are many other people who deserve to be running and training with them.

But shouldn't the best be training with the best?

Here's the thing. I don't feel like I'm the best bowhunter in the world. I feel like I'm on the verge of not succeeding every year. If I kill an animal, I don't pat myself on the back and nod and shout "GOAT!" Instead, I acknowledge the facts.

You just did what you're supposed to do, Cam. You didn't do anything great. You're supposed to be good and train, hunt, kill, and eat elk.

But I'm always like, until I get that first kill, I'm second-guessing and hearing the demons of doubt.

This might be the year when the rug's pulled out and the truth is exposed.

That's why I work so hard. That's why I run with the outliers. I don't feel like I have talent. I feel I've been lucky. Sometimes I feel like I've been lucky for thirty years.

Who are the people in your life that have inspired you? That have poured into you and others? What lessons can you learn from them? Every day I am inspired by people I hear from, and I am blessed to be able to inspire others. It means a lot to me when I get messages that include words like "inspiration" and "motivation." What can you take from those who motivate you, and in turn, how can you motivate others?

Pretty soon the luck's going to run out and the truth is going to be exposed and everybody's going to know you're a fake.

All I have . . .

All I can bring to the table . . .

All I can do is to outwork everybody. Otherwise, everybody will know the truth and I'll be back where I'm supposed to be, doing some mediocre thing that I deserve and dreaming mediocre dreams.

Every day I gotta put the work in. And I'm never going to be satisfied.

I can't rely on my natural ability or accept that I've done enough.

I can't allow myself to feel like I deserve to take a day off.

No way.

I need to keep figuring out ways to get better, to push harder, to train with people, to take something from them, to increase what I do.

If I don't, this shit's going to end.

I don't feel special, but there are people out there who look to me for motivation. So I don't want to let them down.

We all have to make a positive impact, because if you're not striving to make one, what's the point in life?

The best of the best and the toughest of the toughest.

It's a rough world full of rugged and ragged people vying to be at the top of the mountain.

So why do I run with the best and hang with the outliers and train with the freaks? Maybe it's because I got spoiled early on doing exactly that all the time with Roy Roth.

People would see Roy as this big guy, but if anybody thought he was an "average" man, they'd be dead wrong. Anyone who hunted with Roy quickly realized he'd outwalk, outwork, outhunt, outproblem-solve and out-tough even the most elite mountain athlete, let alone your typical hunter.

Whenever people minimized his talents by telling me something like, "Roy could get it done with a bow and he wasn't a gym rat," I'd would always say, "Yeah, maybe so, but *you're* not Roy."

Nobody was Roy. He was a different breed. I knew this firsthand and I wanted others to know it, which is why I loved writing articles that celebrated his accomplishments.

Roy made me get used to being around different breeds. Maybe that's why I continue to seek them out . . .

Because Roy is no longer here.

If you can talk with crowds and keep your virtue,
 Or walk with kings—nor lose the common touch;
If neither foes nor loving friends can hurt you;
 If all men count with you, but none too much;
If you can fill the unforgiving minute
With sixty seconds' worth of distance run—
 Yours is the Earth and everything that's in it,
And—which is more—you'll be a Man, my son!

—Excerpt from "If" by Rudyard Kipling

MUST BE NICE

Winning comes with a price.

The accomplished and the focused and the best all know this truth about the battle. Victory only comes through weathering the unpleasant and the distressing and the dismal. Yet all along the way, a group of spectators spout out the same three words.

"Must be nice."

They don't get it.

Their eight-to-five schedules don't work for me.

Their asses parked on the couch don't get it.

The only marathon they know is binge-watching Netflix.

The only focus they have is on their newly downloaded app.

Sleeping in and sick days and satisfaction with life don't equal success in my eyes.

"Must be nice."

Nice has nothing to do with this. Not one damned thing.

Time and time and time again, I state my case, but daily I hear the derision.

"You don't need to run a marathon to kill an elk or lift weights or be that obsessed."

Even after decades of proven results and success, I still hear the same broken record of questions and statements that give people an out, thinking I don't see the game they're playing.

"Don't you spend time with your family?"

"I'd bowhunt too if I was sponsored."

"How much sleep are you getting?"

"You're going to ruin your knees and body."

"Must be nice to get free bows and your hunts paid for."

"Do you do your own lawn work?"

Here's a fact: I can pay others to do my lawn, but I can't pay others to run miles for me, lift weights for me, or shoot my bow every day.

There is nothing *nice* about fifteen-to-twenty-hour days.

There is nothing *nice* about waking up before the rest of the world opens it eyes.

There is nothing *nice* about working on the weekends, or missing family time, or sacrificing life for a singular passion. But that's the choice I made.

The must-be-nicers never want to think about any of that. A lot of those guys who utter, "Oh, I'd love to be able to do that" really and truly wouldn't love it. If you put them under that pressure, I guarantee you, they wouldn't love it at all. They wouldn't even remotely like it.

It's too much.

It's too hard.

For me, success has come at a high, sometimes not-so-nice price.

For me, "Must be nice" is the swan song of incompetence.

"Must be nice" is the white flag of defeat.

There is nothing nice and light and sweet about success.

Heavy lies the crown, and it comes with a not-so-nice price.

CHAPTER 12

BEAST MODE

"All you need for a workout is a mountain and a rock."

I like to say this when I get asked specific questions about working out and running. But the statement is true.

Once I was doing a seminar at Cabela's, and I told everybody about how I run up Mount Pisgah every day. There was a good-size rock on the side of the trail about halfway up the hill that I passed every day, so I asked the crowd, after the seminar, who wanted to come with me to the mountain and watch me carry this rock up the hill. I figured it probably weighed around seventy pounds. *That would be a good test*, I thought.

After the seminar, a bunch of guys and I headed to Pisgah and started making our way up the mountain. After hiking and running for about fifteen minutes, we arrived at the rock, sitting stoically in the grass off the right side of the trail. I went over to the rock and picked it up. The moment I lifted it, I knew immediately I'd underestimated its weight.

Oh my God—this isn't 70 pounds. It's way more than that.

I had a small crowd of men watching me, so I couldn't let them down. I ended up carrying the rock up the mountain, and it was terrible. Excruciating. It wasn't a nice and smooth rock, either; it had sharp, jagged edges. My shoulders ached as it sat first on one until it hurt too bad, then on the other, then back. I'd hold that damn rock in front of my body against my stomach until my forearms locked up and hands quit working from gripping too long. Each slow, hard-earned step sucked my strength.

Eric McCormack has been helping me train for many years. There was a time when I would just run to get in shape for mountain bowhunting but I have learned that I also need muscle to be at my best, so I lift weights as well. Photo by Travis Thompson.

It is a mile and a half from the bottom to the top of the mountain. Hauling my rock took two hours, whereas I can run the same trail in fifteen minutes.

Carrying the rock was so simple and so painful, it was perfect.

I set it at the top of Mount Pisgah, and thus a tradition began. The next week when I was running Mount Pisgah, I carried it back down the mountain.

I decided I would haul the rock back and forth once a week.

Sometimes people glanced at me with furrowed brows and asked what I was doing as they passed me and my rock on the trail.

"Trying to get tough," I told them.

Some laughed to themselves or simply shook their heads as they strode off, leaving me to continue to struggle with my rock. I began to hear the voices of question and doubt from others.

"Why would you do that?"

"You're going to get hurt."

"You're going to feel stupid when you drop it on your foot."

And the best . . .

"What a waste of time."

Exactly.

I want to do what no one else wants to do, what no one else finds the value in doing. That's the only edge I have.

I didn't find out until after a few trips up and down over the subsequent weeks how much the rock actually weighed. After hauling it down one time, I took the rock to the gym and carefully placed it on the scale.

It weighed 130 pounds.

Some might view me and my rock-carrying exploits as silly or just plain stupid, but doing it and enduring the pain and fatigue were things I enjoyed. Sure, my seventy-pound estimation was a little bit off. But when I came up there and carried the rock, I told myself that if I could do that about ten times, I would feel like I'd done something.

Fun fact: a video of this jocularity was one of the videos Joe Rogan saw of me years ago on my YouTube channel. *What's this guy carrying this rock for?* he thought. Rogan was intrigued and tweeted out an invite to join him on the podcast. We've been great buddies ever since.

There's the familiar phrase to leave no stone unturned, to try every way and action to achieve the thing you want. That's the way I am now. And in some cases, I *literally* leave no stone unturned. Uncarried, too.

From the moment I decided to start getting into shape in order to be the best bowhunter I could be, my fitness regimen began to change, and it's evolved over time. I've referred to it as Beast Mode; Lift, Run, Shoot; and Train Hard, Hunt Easy. I remember when I first began to imagine what it might look like if, for eleven months a year, I was running, lifting, and shooting with one goal in mind: to arrow a big bull in September, the month of mountain elk hunting.

Did I need to do this?

I asked myself the same thing about the greatest athletes of the day.

Did Kobe Bryant really need to shoot 1,000 jumpers a day?

Did boxer Manny Pacquiao really need to run ten miles every morning, do 2,000 sit-ups a day, and train like a man possessed for eight weeks straight?

Did UFC fighter Georges St-Pierre really need to do pull-ups with a 120-pound dumbbell attached to his waist and carry only 5 percent body fat?

Does anyone *really* need to run, lift, and shoot every single day getting ready for bowhunting in the mountains?

"No" was the answer to all these questions, but I began to wonder what it would look like if someone did do all that stuff. So that's what I began doing. I would start off the day running and getting reps in before work. At lunch I would take another run, then in the evening I would shoot my bow and work out in the gym.

Over time, I ramped up my fitness. Today, if you told thirty-year-old me my current workout routine, he would say, "No, that's impossible." But I've just pushed my body more and more and more to try to find the limit of what I can do to give me the ultimate edge over everyone.

That's why I try to go to muscle failure eight or nine times a day. That's why on the days I don't run a full marathon and maybe only do twenty miles, I make up for it with an hour of lifting weights in the gym. That's why I set aside time every day for target practice with my compound bow. That's why I try to fit in as many miles as I can . . . to find that ultimate threshold of where I'm at my best.

> **"I found a world where I belonged. But every once in a while I think, 'What am I doing out here running, busting myself up? Life could be so much easier. The other guys are out having fun, doing other things, why not me?'"**
>
> **—Steve Prefontaine**

There are no rest days. As irrational as it may seem, in my mind, I'm not good enough to take a day off. And I never will be.

Running, training, and bow shooting have always been a therapy of sorts for me. It's my release. Over the years, I have run the mountains with people who love the challenge or I've run by myself. I've shot bows by myself or with others who share a true love of archery. I have lifted weights with my sons or with friends who push me to be better and stronger and more grateful. For us, the harder the workout, the happier we are.

What I call my Lift, Run, Shoot lifestyle is a means to an end, and that end is hunting. Preparation is key to achieving any goal. You cannot fall back on luck or talent; those will leave you empty-handed every time. When you push your body and find your limit, or think you have, have you really though? Goggins said most people quit at 40 percent of their true ability, and I believe him. But let's pretend you're one of the few who push as hard as Courtney does. Even pushing too far sometimes helps you become the best you can be. It helps you find your "limit," real or perceived, so that you can slowly train to push past it and find a new one.

There's no substitute for daily dedication to your craft, whatever it may be. My definition of that is punching the time clock every day, giving everything I have seven days a week, and refusing to ever be satisfied.

I love being exhausted.

I love being depleted.

I love knowing I have nothing else to give.

That is dedication.

I never get bored running all those miles or lifting all those reps or shooting all those arrows.

I'm on the path I've always envisioned.

In *Atomic Habits*, James Clear sums up the difference between amateurs and professionals:

"Professionals stick to the schedule; amateurs let life get in the way. Professionals know what is important to them and work toward it with purpose; amateurs get pulled off course by the urgencies of life . . . When a habit is truly important to you, you have to be willing to stick to it in any mood. Professionals take action even when the mood isn't right. They might not enjoy it, but they find a way to put the reps in."

Dedication creates atomic habits like this. Being a professional means you'll do the necessary work, time and time again.

Do you want the instructions for being a beast? Want me to write down my daily routine? Are you curious to see how long I run and how many reps I take? Do you want my secret?

I've already shared it 10,000 times.

What I'll tell you is this. If you're not the hardest-working person you know, you're not working hard enough. An outlier will never allow someone to outwork them.

That said, here are some beliefs of mine that fit into my Beast Mode mentality, that race alongside my Lift, Run, Shoot days. This is what I know and understand. This is why I keep hammering.

Running and pounding out miles by myself is therapeutic and keeps me focused.

Smiling is a good thing, and you can't help doing it when you see the sun rising on those morning runs. I love starting the day working up a sweat, getting mentally right before heading to work. Releasing a few arrows might actually be better than coffee for clearing the head. However, a nice cup of both is probably best.

Reaching the summit is always a win, right? Even on my worst days, I always end up grateful to see the monument at the summit of the mountain.

Sharing quality time with my family is mandatory.

Training for misery is the only way to train, the only way to find my limits.

Pushing through pain allows you to run when your ankles or knees or hips or feet don't want you to.

Lifting weights is something I love. I love the pump, the veins, the burn. I love being sore, feeling strong and undeniable in the backcountry; and to be honest, I enjoy looking fit. I love it when people see me and ask what I do.

"What do you mean?" I ask.

"I mean what are you in such good shape for? Training for something?"

"Yes. Bowhunting."

I love when all the hard work starts paying off.

Focusing on the reps is the important thing in lifting. Weight doesn't matter. It's all about reps and endurance.

Shooting a bow looks cool and feels empowering.

Shooting bows with friends is something special.

Shooting every day is a must.

Sensing pain means you're sacrificing, and sacrificing sets you up for a big reward. I've found that your body will respond to whatever you ask of it. Humans are amazingly capable of so much. Push your limits.

Hunting is the pinnacle for me. Preparing for that first hunt of the season is the goal. Pushing myself harder each and every year helps me get more and more prepared.

Being in Beast Mode is when it feels like you're in a superhuman state of being, when in your mind you're playing at a level above everybody else. Is this reality? Doesn't matter. If you believe you are, you are. The mindset of a winner is unbeatable.

I believe this approach equips you to be prepared in the wilderness, to be ready for "crunch time" and you release the arrow you've been envisioning time and time again at the animal of your dreams.

Training like this teaches you there are different degrees of being uncomfortable. The key is to grow accustomed to it through weight training and running. I'm uncomfortable, but I still feel at home. I'm out of my comfort zone, but I am still able to perform.

Emulating exhaustion and manufacturing misery allow me not to lose my head on a hunt. It reminds me that I've been here a million times and that I will be fine and that I will make good decisions and that I will do what I'm here to do.

Doing all of this for decade after decade after decade is why I get it done.

In the 2000s, there was a humorous TV advertising campaign featuring situations that always ended with the same catch phrase. One commercial featured an operating scene with a surgeon surrounded by nurses working on a patient.

"How's everything look?" the surgeon said.

"Looks good," the nurse replied. "Looks real good."

"What's his BP?" he asked.

"One twenty over eighty," another nurse said.

"Okay, folks, close him up," the surgeon ordered, taking off his surgical mask.

A nurse looked at him in surprise. "You're not Dr. Stewart."

"No," he said nonchalantly as he began to leave, then adding, "but I did stay at a Holiday Inn Express last night."

The commercials ended with the line "It won't make you smarter. But you'll feel smarter."

I think of those commercials when I've been asked specific questions about my workout or my diet or any specific thing related to my training. I feel like any advice I give needs to come with an asterisk, like I need to add, "No, I'm not a fitness expert, but I did stay at a Holiday Inn Express last night!"

That's why I don't give advice and I don't share some mythical blueprint.

I'm not a fitness expert.

I am not a bodybuilder and don't want to be. I lift to be a well-rounded hunting athlete.

I am not a powerlifter, although I respect guys in this discipline greatly . . . I learn so much from the guys at the local gyms here in town. I do my best and I am always learning, honing my craft, but I am not an authority on the subject of fitness.

I am not a doctor. Otherwise, I wouldn't do the stupid, jeopardizing, health hazardous stuff I do. Consult a doctor if you have questions on any of this before you try it.

All I am is a bowhunter who is trying to raise my game to the highest level I can. In that regard, I believe the only limits we have, both physically and mentally, are those in which we place on ourselves. Believe, and you will achieve.

My approach works for me, but that doesn't guarantee that it will work for anyone else.

I'm not even the best bow shot, but I want to be. There are guys at my hometown pro shop, the Bow Rack, that are better shots than me, but I do work very hard at it.

The key to my success is to throw hard work at everything I do. I can't scout elk every day, so I lift, run, and shoot.

No, I didn't stay at a Holiday Inn Express last night. I slept outdoors in the wild, waiting for all my work to pay off. I slept, knowing there was nothing more I could, should, or would have done differently.

Today I'm going to have to play the cards that will be dealt to me and see what happens, but whatever cards I hold, I'll use them to win the hand. This is the mindset I take to the mountains. To be aggressive, hunt smart, and come out of the hills loaded down with meat and antlers.

Know your worth.

I'm terrible at this typically, because I'd bowhunt for free. Truthfully, when money enters the equation, it seems to dilute the true impact bowhunting has made on my life as a man. But I can't be stupid and I know I have value, so that too deserves respect. My family depends on me to make good decisions because, I use those decisions to provide a better quality of life for them and for their future. I've used my value as a bowhunter to pay for private schools, college, cars, and houses all in the name of my family. As for me, I don't need anything. I'm completely happy and satisfied with a shit house, shit car, and the normal nine-to-five job I still have now; my wife and kids would also say they are happy. But I know if I can invest in education for them it will lead to more opportunities, or if I can pay off their car and truck loans, then they can be more focused on success instead of paying bills.

Keeping all of this in mind, I recently negotiated a new contract with one of my best sponsors, Hoyt, which is the brand of the bow I shoot. I was underpaid and knew it, but for years I wasn't worried about it because I'm not

What is your own personal rock that you can haul up the proverbial mountain every day? What atomic habit can you begin today that will help you achieve success? How hard will you work, day after day? Remember the love you have for your passion, your skill, your calling. Decide to finish that book or climb that peak. Work at it relentlessly, carry that rock, knowing it's work but realizing it's worth the sacrifice.

motivated by money. However, when the time came to sign a new contract, I decided to be more serious about my value, because if we aren't our own advocate, how can we expect someone else to be? I said I needed more money, as I knew I was underpaid for what I offered. They said they would double my current contract, and I said that was great but still not enough. So they offered to double it again, moving me into six figures annually to do something I'd do for free. But I needed to be smarter than to do it for free.

The other side of the equation here is I put in many years of good work for Hoyt and earned their trust. I'm fortunate to have a sponsor like them who, aside from money, has always believed and supported me. My goal is to still be their best value even at four times what they were paying me last year. My goal is to work so hard for the people that pay me, my regular job or my sponsors, that if times are tough, I'd be the very last person they'd let go.

Ten times a day I'm asked on social media the following questions:

"How can I become a pro bowhunter?"

"How can I get sponsored?"

"I want to do what you do . . . Can you help me?"

The answer is no, I can't help you. Only you can help you. Everyone wants to get noticed these days, it seems, so I will always ask the same question:

"What are you doing to set yourself apart?"

I'll meet kids who want to be featured in hunting magazines and have their names on a bow and want to have their own shoes, so they ask me how they can achieve that. They don't get it. It's hard to explain. All that stuff came after the journey took place. After all those long, solitary, unseen moments on my own trying to do this thing I love.

All I ever say to them is, "Do you love shooting your bow?"

"Yeah," they might say.

"Okay, then shoot your bow. A lot. Get good at shooting your bow. Worry about the other stuff later."

You can't design a hunting boot before you destroy your first few pairs.

I always say to make sure your journey is fueled by your passion. Don't set the goal to be a great marathon runner unless you really love to run. Unless your passion is there, it's just not going to work.

This even happens sometimes at my nine-to-five job. Guys will ask me, "How do I get your job?"

"Why do you want my job?" I ask them.

"Because you make good money," they say.

"Well, if your goal is to make good money, then it's not going to happen," I say.

That's not how it works. If your goal is you want to grow and you want to challenge yourself and you want to help people succeed, money will come. If your goal is the money, it's probably not going to work out for you.

It's easy to see the ads and the videos and the merchandise, and then for these young kids or writers to say, "I want to be a famous bowhunter."

That's not really a great goal. Do you want the fame, or do you want the bowhunting?

The goal should be to be the best bowhunter you can be. To figure out a way to sacrifice, to go on the best adventures, to experience life at the highest as a bowhunter.

If you want to hunt in the wilderness, even if you don't have the time or the resources, you will figure it out if it means that much to you.

I'll say it again: My path isn't the only path. It's just mine. Your path to success might be much different, but I'll bet it'll involve hard work and sacrifice. I promise you, anyone you look up to in any field works their butt off and has a positive, winning outlook.

An elite running athlete does what everyone hates, running intervals, pushing themselves, maybe even puking, eating perfect, and sees their vision as destiny.

An elite businessman outworks his colleagues, writing reports, crunching numbers, being a leader by expecting dedication.

An elite construction foreman sees the big picture, looks ahead, keeps his crew working and motivated.

These people don't complain or look for the easy way out of work. They challenge themselves and others by raising the bar.

If you want to make it in any field, including the hunting industry, get to work. And do it with a smile, because every day is a gift.

Honor that gift.

STAY ON THE PATH

There is no blueprint.

There is no book of instructions.

There is no recipe.

There is no right way.

There are, however, thousands of wrong ways.

I don't give advice.

I'm not speaking for anybody else.

I don't care what you do and I'm not looking for your approval.

This is my journey.

All that said, you're welcome to join me. And for those who already have, you're welcome to keep running with me.

I've never told anyone they need to do what I do, and I never will.

I don't want to discount or minimize anybody's effort because I know just trying your best every day is a huge deal. I know it's a hard path at times.

I'm not speaking for anybody else with my running and my training.

This is your journey.

We're all on different trajectories. I'm at this point and have been doing this now for decades. There are certain ways I prepare, and that's going to change and evolve. I'm going to continue to get better and I'm going to learn and grow.

All of us are evolving. It's just a process. A process that takes time.

Even if our goals are the same, our journeys will be different.

Know what your weaknesses are and don't play into them. Concentrate on your strengths. My strengths are: I'll put in the work every day and I won't quit. I do things that enhance my strengths. That's running. That's lifting. That's hunting.

My hope is that you have confidence in your ability, and that you stay on the path. I hope you see a destination and then work like hell to get there. How you arrive at that destination has nothing to do with me. But I believe in you and will always celebrate your success.

CHAPTER 13

HATING ME WON'T HELP YOU WIN

Your body gives what you ask of it. Don't ask much and it won't give you much. Ask a lot and it will give you a lot. I haven't found my limit yet, but I am trying.

The great UCLA basketball coach John Wooden once said, "You can't let praise or criticism get to you. It's a weakness to get caught up in either one."

Here's my take on praise and criticism. Kind and complimentary words from fans and followers are appreciated and acknowledged. But as for the hate?

I got that shit memorized.

"You don't have to run marathons to kill an elk."

When I was first making a name for myself, some hunters didn't like me and didn't appreciate my methods. They said running and lifting to prepare for bowhunting was stupid. They said I was wasting my time. They criticized me more than giving me credit for what I did.

Early on, I carried the criticism like a chip on my shoulder. I wouldn't judge guys who scoffed at my training, but I was never going to apologize or minimize the value of what I did. Whether someone loved my approach or hated it, I kept plugging away. I had found a formula that worked for me, and I intended to ride it as long as I could. As I got in better shape physically and mentally, I killed more animals and achieved more of my hunting goals.

Our body and mind are tools to use in the woods. Training hones those tools, simple as that. The better the tools you haul into the mountains, the more success you'll have.

Over time, as I saw people being inspired by what I did, I ignored the haters. A decade ago, it was thousands of emails pouring in; these days it's tens of thousands of comments posted online. I love hearing how people have reinvented themselves for the better in the name of fit hunting. I discovered I could deal with legions of naysayers if the trade-off was helping even one person enhance their quality of life.

Years ago, I remember hearing the following quote: "They don't make statues of critics." Those words are powerful to me. To me it means that it's easy for people who aren't taking chances, sharing their passion, or exposing themselves through their words or actions to sit back and criticize those who are. Nobody likes to be judged, including me, but I've come to terms with it because I put myself out there—and in doing so, I know dealing with critics is part of the deal.

If you have a burning passion for something that moves you, never be afraid to share it. When you do, you're making a positive difference and inspiring others.

The critics, no one will remember them.

"Yeah, sure he killed that bull. He shot it with a rifle then stuck his arrow in the hole."

Some people just couldn't accept my success in bowhunting. I killed bulls every year from season number one on, including some near the small town where I lived. Guys talking shit about me simply served as a microcosm of the internet. Some people can't accept others' victories and won't allow you to feel good.

When I started bowhunting, I wanted to dream big. I would look at hunting magazines and tell myself, *I can do this. I can do what these guys do.* But before I began to hear the praise and acceptance of others, I had to hear a lot more negativity. Nobody was there saying, "Yes, you can do it, Cam! You can do that!" There was Roy, but he was in Alaska, and back then we didn't have FaceTime or Zoom to keep in contact. We had plain old phones, so the times we connected weren't super frequent.

Dreams need to come with dividers, keeping out the doubters and demonizers. You will have to hear their comments, but they can't harm you or keep you from doing the work you need to do. The best ability you can learn is to not care what somebody else thinks. Chances are, they're probably jealous anyway.

Arnold Schwarzenegger said it best: "You have to remember something: Everybody pities the weak; jealousy you have to earn."

It has been written that, back in his heyday, when Arnold Schwarzenegger was in the gym, the overall temperature of the place rose dramatically. *Everyone* trained harder. But that being said, very few could keep Arnold's grueling pace. That is the type of influence I aspire to. I am not comparing myself to Arnold, just admiring his work ethic. I never want to be "outworked" by anyone. Like Arnold in the gym, my goal is to set the pace.

> **"Learn to love the hate. Embrace it. Enjoy it. You earned it. Everyone is entitled to their own opinion and everyone should have one about you. Haters are a good problem to have. Nobody hates the good ones. They hate the great ones."**
> **—Kobe Bryant**

While jealous people can be a pain in the ass to you, they are a torment to themselves. They are so wrapped up in envy that they can't truly appreciate their own accomplishments. When I see someone better than me or someone who's accomplished something that I'd love to achieve, I use them as motivation. I work harder and become more focused *because* of them.

If anyone is jealous of me, all I have said and will ever say is that if I've done it, anyone can. I believe with years (probably fewer than it took me) of hard work, sacrifice, and dedication, many can do any of the things I've done. The only reason for my success is because I've stuck with it . . . bowhunting, running, business, etc. I was either terrible or average at best at most of what I'm now considered "good" at. I've simply outworked my weaknesses and the other guys who were naturally better than me.

Do you have big dreams you're chasing? If you do, you will surely be judged and second-guessed like I have, not only by strangers but maybe even friends and family. Don't waver. Keep fighting, keep working, and stay strong in your convictions.

I say it all the time, but I'll say it again—dreams can come true. They have for me.

"What kind of perverted jerk are you? Killing for fun! I vomit on you!"
Signed, anti hunter

Is vomiting on people a thing? Didn't know that.

Let's forget the utter stupidity of this comment left for me online and address what they suggest.

While I enjoy the challenge of bowhunting and being an active, self-sufficient member of the circle of life, killing does not bring me enjoyment. I wouldn't call it fun.

> **"All men are the same except for their belief in their own selves, regardless of what others may think of them."**
> —Miyamoto Musashi, *The Book of Five Rings*

One quote I share often is from *Meditations on Hunting* by José Ortega y Gasset: "One does not hunt in order to kill; on the contrary, one kills in order to have hunted . . . If one were to present the sportsman with the death of the animal as a gift he would refuse it. What he is after is having to win it, to conquer the surly brute through his own effort and skill with all the extras that this carries with it: the immersion in the countryside, the healthfulness of the exercise, the distraction from his job . . ."

When I am successful, an animal dies, and I take responsibility for that. After which, I butcher that animal, and it feeds either my family, friends, or people in need of meat more than me. I see hunters as providers.

What I wish people knew was the utter joy that comes with a successful hunt. Taking a passion and a purpose, then pairing it up with precise timing and pinpoint accuracy, then feeling this overwhelming sense of respect and pride with the outcome.

Haters won't ever know the happiness that comes when you've made a picture-perfect fifty-five yard shot on a big ole' Roosevelt bull. When things couldn't have gone better. When you've been working your butt off walking and calling and trying to get bulls to be in rut even when they don't want to. Then to make a clean shot.

I have no patience for social-media keyboard cowboys. Those who leave mean, judgmental, or stupid comments are promptly blocked and gone forever from my page. I feel sad that they probably never have the moments of pure contentment I experience when I'm by myself, when I've killed an animal and I've got a lot of weight on my back carrying it out. Each slow, painfully hard step of getting that animal out—that's like the best feeling of satisfaction ever. It's a goal achieved. You've been rewarded for the grind. The sacrifice has paid off.

*"You kill animals just for taste and fun, trust me if somehow we meet, I'll kill you motherf*er. F* you."*

Imagine someone coming up to me and saying that? Instead, they are nameless, faceless trolls.

When do you suppose the last time was a hunter deliberately threatened the life of a non-hunter? Never. Know why? Because hunters have respect for life. And, because hunting takes skill, dedication, and hard work. And it teaches one how to deal with failure, as most days afield end with nothing more than a pure experience and appreciation for the beauty of the wild, hunters are repeatedly humbled. Being humble is good. To be clear, success—that is, a dead animal—is rare for most, so a hunter spends most days learning and becoming more well rounded.

I've said it before, but I need to remind people about something. It's tough bowhunting. One in ten bowhunters kill an elk. Another way to look at it is that you'll kill one elk every ten years.

That's a 10 percent success rate.

But I've always killed a bull every year. When everybody else is going out and killing one every ten years, they cannot stand the guy who kills one every year, so naturally they have to make up shit to say to justify their lack of success or reasons why or how I killed again and they didn't. So often the familiar refrain is: "This guy poached or cheated."

Who knows what they say and why they say it. That's just ego and pride, and all men have it. That's just the way it goes.

For those who don't know: For a hunter, the kill is not the true reward; it's the pursuit and the journey. If the hunter is blessed with success, the animal is cherished because it means meat in the freezer. Hunting also teaches honor. While conversely, making online death threats is cowardly. Either way, for me, messages like that are telling. When non-hunters live lives that offer no opportunity for honor, hard-earned success, or out-of-your-comfort-zone living that builds success when completed, one can get spoiled and soft. When people like that see something they don't understand, like, or agree with, they throw a tantrum and say things like, "I'll kill you . . . because you killed an innocent animal."

Why be negative and unhappy? Why not do something to change your life instead of pulling others down to wallow in your misery?

Look, I have my days. Days when I grow tired of the people lurking and lying in the shadows, waiting for me to fuck up and say something or maybe get irritated and lash out. They fucking wait and don't say shit until they can say, "Oh, gotcha."

Fucking pussies.

If people just now are figuring out I'm a little bit psycho about elk hunting,

"These 'can't catch a break' guys—get them the fuck away from me. I can't be around those guys. I don't want to hear that shit. I don't want to hear that shit. I don't buy it. 'Cause everybody has bad breaks. I've had a shit ton of bad breaks. But you know what I did? I stayed up and I fought through it and I figured out what the fuck I did wrong. And then I went back. It's like—I fucked up everything I've ever done a hundred times . . . There's no other way to do it. And I've had a bunch of shitty breaks. Everybody has. But you gotta realize when you have those shitty breaks what that is . . . And the people that look at those challenges and go, 'Why do I always have that's the way it goes. I'm not apologizing or changing. If you're not going to be able to handle it, fucking don't follow me! I don't give a shit who follows me. I'm not begging for followers. And don't use it like you got some power over me. If you aggravate me on social media, I will block you. I couldn't give two shits about you.

I don't know anybody who likes complete strangers giving them unsolicited advice and telling them what to do. I think everybody can agree with that.

The only blessing to find amid the haters and trolls is that I've found people like Goggins to connect with. People who have a similar mindset about everything, especially the haters out there. Goggins refuses to let those haters impact him in any way, as he shared online in a favorite post of his.

"We live in a world full of haters and jealous people," Goggins wrote. "People so fucked up in their own lives that they can't move forward so they put their hate for themselves on you. This world is full of distractions—a lot of them are from other people, social media, some are self-imposed. In a world full of distractions, you must learn to live in it undistracted,

the challenges'—they're cancer. Those people are dangerous to be around. They will rob you of your enthusiasm. They don't give you any fuel—they're the opposite of fuel . . . All the time you're complaining, you could be instead hustling. You could be instead chasing your dream. You could be instead figuring out what you're doing wrong, trying to improve certain aspects of your life, getting your shit together, reading a book, meditating—something! Fucking something. But this 'I can't catch a break' shit is not helping anybody and it pushes everybody away from you."

—Joe Rogan

unphased. Never let the weakness of this world infiltrate your mind! To do that you must truly know yourself! Don't allow people to puppet master you from being fucking great!"

"IDIOT I HOPE YOU DIE SOON!!! THEN WE ALL HAVE A PARTY F*ING YOUR DEAD BODY!!!"

Sounds like a really fun party, right?

Okay, okay . . . Enough with these hater comments. All of these were real, all coming from crazy people. This one came after I posted a photo of the brown bear I killed last year in an area of Alaska that has so many brown bears, non-residents can kill two annually in an effort to help the moose population. It's called wildlife management. When I saw the post, I was in Los Angeles and I hadn't seen one brown bear, yet that didn't mean they were extinct. It seems some people struggle with logic when it comes to the role hunters play in conservation. And, instead of trying to understand, they spew bile.

Social media can be so strange as it gives people an opportunity to sit and judge pretty much 24-7. I don't really get that part of it. I've never found myself wanting to criticize someone doing their best, chasing a dream. Nobody likes reading negativity, especially the sort I've shared here from haters. When you work really hard at something, you don't want to be criticized or second-guessed. Maybe some people don't believe me when I say I'm not that talented. It's like, no, I'm just working harder than you. That's all there is to it. Maybe you're better than me, but you're not sacrificing. That's how I've always felt.

I've never felt like I'm better, but I just give more.

I don't expect anyone to understand my obsession or mindset for fitness and challenge. I can try to explain it, but I know full well we are all different, and I respect that. I don't look down on anyone who has a different motivation or a different approach to earning physical and mental confidence in themselves. I've been critiqued and judged for years, so just know, you won't get that from me. I've never told anyone, "You need to do what I do if you want success." Truthfully, I don't want anyone to do what I do. Running 100-mile races is hard on your body. I want you to do what's in your heart and do it to the best of your ability.

I'm never going to make everybody happy. If I did, that would mean I stood for nothing, and what's the point in that? Online, I share my life. That is what I do. That is what I think. And that's just how it goes. I don't care what people think. I don't care if my sponsors have a problem with it. I don't need everyone to agree with what I say or post; differing opinions are fine. All I ask is that you're respectful to others and if you can't handle that, you're not welcome here. There's nothing I love more than blocking rude, hateful, weak haters.

My goal is to build others up and make a positive difference.

"I signed up for my first half-marathon about two months ago and found you on Instagram. It's been motivating to watch you . . ."

These are the comments that drown out the noise. I am motivated at least ten times as much by the positive energy I receive from others over the criticism I receive. I'm inspired daily to hear about the successful journeys people have embarked on because they've been motivated by my story. I can't tell you how much I enjoy getting messages and comments from people who talk about how they just ran their first ultra or marathon or half-marathon. The distance doesn't matter. I love hearing about someone's first 10K or even mile!

> **"You can't make people joyous just by being joyous yourself. Joy has to be generated by oneself: It is or it isn't. Joy is founded on something too profound to be understood and communicated. To be joyous is to be a madman in a world of sad ghosts."**
> **—Henry Miller, *Sexus***

I get many of these every day. The energy and the love and the accomplishments put a smile on my face and put humility in my heart. I get people saying how they look up to me. They say thank you for the motivation. Thank you for the inspiration. It's so powerful to me to see this.

Then there are those messages that go beyond simple praise. Ones like this:

This past weekend I had the pleasure to meet the legendary Cameron Hanes! I've looked up to him for a long time and meeting him was something I never thought I'd be able to do. Last year, from my hospital bed I would watch videos of him hunting deer and elk, I'd also watch videos of him running in marathons and ultramarathons. He even ran with Lance Armstrong in Boston and he's one of the biggest names in bow hunting and conservation. He takes every chance he can get to inspire others and that's why I bought one of his "Keep Hammering" hats before my first round of chemo. His motivation and his hard-working mindset helped me stay positive throughout the 12 treatments. After my 6th round of chemo I was able to take my first coues deer with a bow and right after my 11th round I was able to take my first elk with a bow. I have many people to thank for all of the help I've received this past year, and I'm still shocked that I was able to thank him in person for helping me out!

I wonder what that unhappy, little kid from a broken home, on his paper route would have thought about reading the words "legendary Cameron Hanes."

I wonder how that lonely teen would have reacted to hearing that someone dreamt of meeting him?

I wonder if that loser jumping off the top of his truck into the swimming hole could have dreamt that one day he would be doing anything more exciting than that?

It's good to ignore the haters, and I would include those who doubted what I was doing in the first place. The ones who said nobody in the hunting industry cared about all the running and exercise that I did. I remember specifically what one person in the industry told me.

"The average person doesn't need to be inspired or motivated. That gets old. If that's all you offer, you won't be around long."

Is thirty-plus years long enough for you?

More than thirty years of hearing the same old shit.

You don't need to run every day to bowhunt.

You don't need to lift weights to bowhunt.

You lift wrong.

For all the lifting you do, you're actually weak.

You shoot your bow wrong.

You don't need to shoot that high a poundage.

You're a sellout.

Why do you cut the sleeves off your shirts?

Why do you hunt?

Why would you kill a bear?

All noise in the background.

I remember being told once by a longtime industry person, "Cameron, no one cares about your running."

I'll be honest, that one statement had me clenching my jaw and biting my tongue. It also motivated me for many years. I knew they were wrong, and I love proving people wrong.

I also love providing a light in a dark world. There's enough negativity going on. I just want to be a guy who can inspire others.

Inspiring others is a wonderful thing, but I also believe families need strong men who protect, love, and keep order. Our communities need the same. Coincidentally enough, it's sometimes while I'm training that I've been called upon to help.

One time a few years back the opportunity was especially important as I was with my son Truett running a hill on the outskirts of Eugene, called Spencer's Butte. As fathers, our behaviors are studied and modeled by our children. We all know that, or we should. During one afternoon run in the rain, Truett and I were making our way up the trail when I heard someone yell. I stopped and asked Truett, "Did you hear that?" He had. We heard a cry for help from up the butte where the terrain was very steep.

As we made our way up, the screams for help got more intense. I told Truett when we were about 100 yards away from the woman calling out that in situations like this, one needs to be aware. I said that there have been times when people feigned injury or need in order to lure someone into a trap; and before they knew what happened, the savior became the victim. So never assume you know what's happening and charge into a trap. Always be on guard.

When the woman was in sight, I surveyed the situation and believed she genuinely needed help. She was clutching on to a tree on a nearly vertical section of the mountain and I could see cuts on her legs and abrasions on her arms.

After making our way to her, I told her I was there to help her get off the mountain. She wasn't badly injured but was scared of falling again. I had her get on my back and holding on like a child might with her arms around my

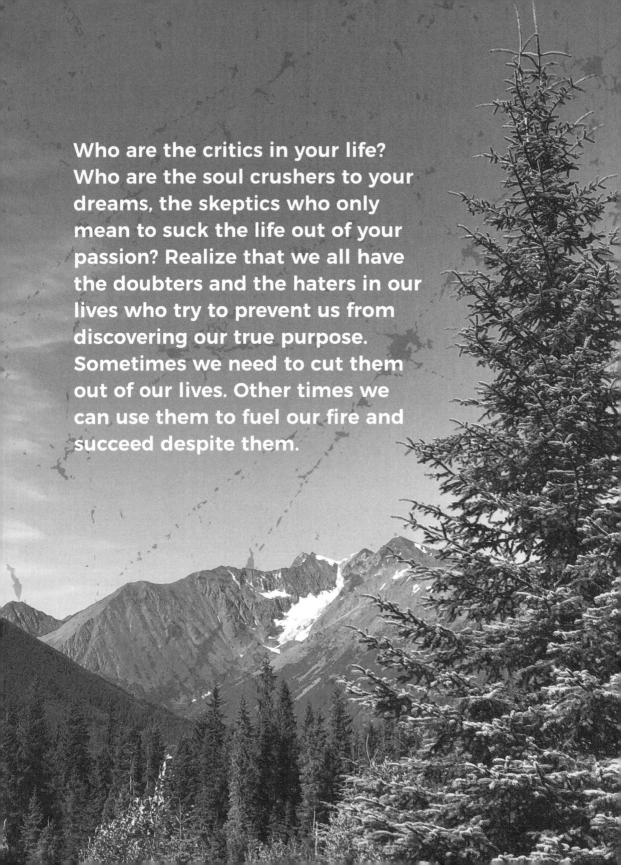

Who are the critics in your life? Who are the soul crushers to your dreams, the skeptics who only mean to suck the life out of your passion? Realize that we all have the doubters and the haters in our lives who try to prevent us from discovering our true purpose. Sometimes we need to cut them out of our lives. Other times we can use them to fuel our fire and succeed despite them.

shoulders and neck and her legs around my waist. Slowly and with great effort, I got her off the hill to safety.

This is what we're here to do above all else, I told Truett. To help those in need.

Another example of this was one afternoon a few years back, when I was on my daily lunch run. Once again, I was called upon to help a college-aged woman who was being attacked.

It was an overcast day, a perfect day for running, so I headed down the bike path that parallels the Willamette River near the UO campus. I was about five miles into my run, closing in on the Autzen Footbridge, when I saw a man grab a young woman off her bike. I closed in fast as he pulled her by the waist, and she screamed, trying to get away. I grabbed him and threw him down on the pavement as she scrambled away crying. She picked up her bike and walked toward the bridge, where others came to her aid.

I kept my left knee on the side of his head and held his right arm across his chest with my right hand while I called 911. He fought back, but I was able to keep him down as I told the 911 operator what happened. It took nearly ten minutes for the police to get there while he went through bouts of fighting and thrashing, saying I was hurting him. I just kept telling him to quit fighting and I'd let up a little.

Eventually the police showed up, and after they talked to me and the girl, I resumed my run back to work to finish my day.

A couple days later, I looked online at the Eugene police bookings and saw the attacker had been charged with six crimes from that day, including possession, assault, and resisting arrest.

I feel a pressure to not let down an important group of people that follow me. Not to the haters, but to those who follow me and respect me. There are so many good-hearted people out there—guys and gals who are thankful for another day of work, fitness, family, and chasing their dreams. What happens if I quit a race or mess up like humans mess up? Am I going to let all these people down? I want to say the right thing and don't want to overreact to something online. I don't want to let people down.

But this is what I signed up for. This is the road I'm traveling down. This worries me sometimes because I'm far from perfect.

While there are people I look up to, I don't compare myself to any man. I don't need to prove myself and I'm not driven to "win" a competition of followers or "likes." Remember, if you live for the praise and acceptance of others, you will conversely die by their criticism. Don't give them that power.

My purpose is greater than competing. I am dedicated to one mission: to be at my best in the mountains on the hunt. Therefore, my loyalty is to the animals I pursue. I am motivated to be the most lethal, compassionate, respectful, and merciful hunter I can be.

If you're obsessed with achieving an "unrealistic" goal or chasing a life-defining dream, don't let anyone try to put limits on you. They don't know what drives you. They don't know your heart and spirit. If they are the type to interject negativity into another's life, they likely aren't as unrelenting and focused on success as you are.

Listen.

Acknowledge.

Then prove them wrong.

Dream bigger.

Achieve more.

You alone determine your worth!

Imagine if you were blind. Ask yourself how badly you'd like to see. If pushing yourself to your limits could give you sight, would you do it? If there was a cure, would you let anything stand in your way? Would you risk the haters and the critics to see again?

Be blind as you chase your goals.

LISTEN TO THE HATE

Why all the hate, some ask me.
Why all the criticism, some post.
Why all the judgment, some say.
I don't know.
I don't care.
I use the slams—the shaming—
the spite—the bullshit—I use all of it as fuel.
It motivates me.
Where would I be without the doubters?
What would my life look like without all the disdain?
I hope I never find out.
Since day one, thirty-three years ago when I first picked up a bow,
the disrespect has come. Men and women, vegans and comedians,
even bowhunters . . . All have talked shit and still do.
Not only have I fed off the hate and have never faltered, but it's also
made me more focused, hungrier, and less satisfied.
There will always be those who want to see someone who's
motivated fail, because the effort of others reminds the weak
of their lack of passion and purpose.
There will always be those who want to feel that passion and
purpose too, but it's hard. The grind hurts sometimes.
So all they can do is hate and detract.
They don't realize that apathy is death.
They don't know that the approval of others doesn't make a
difference to the driven.
Hatred only provides fuel.
So please . . . I'm begging you.
Keep the vitriol coming.

CHAPTER 14

THE FICKLE WINDS OF FATE

Do I deserve to be here?

I had dreamt of hunting the San Carlos Apache Indian Reservation for decades. Located in southeast Arizona and encompassing 1.8 million acres of land, San Carlos produces what I believe are the most amazing elk in the world.

As a lifelong-obsessed elk hunter, it was a blessing and a dream come true to carry my bow in search of the country's biggest bulls in these magical mountains.

The surreal experience was one I never anticipated as a young bowhunter from Oregon more than thirty years earlier when I had so little money. Back then I didn't even entertain the notion of an out-of-state elk hunt.

The reservation allocates only a handful of tags each year because the densities are low and they manage this country for trophy bulls. This means to hunt there is very expensive. Altogether a hunt like that costs upward of $70,000, which is more than I've made annually for nearly all of my life. Compare that to the tag for my first out-of-state elk in Wyoming, which cost $1,100!

The hunt for a giant bull and adventure in legendary land was my driver, but the money weighed on me. I remembered years ago when this first became an additional stressor. In 2005, when I was editor of *Eastmans' Bowhunting Journal,* Eastmans' sent me on a premium Colorado elk hunt, which they filmed for the TV show. The hunt came with a $10,000 price tag. I had a hard time getting the cost out of my head and staying focused on releasing a perfect arrow. On a hunt like that, if you make a poor shot and draw blood, even if the shot isn't fatal, that's your animal. I agonized over the possibility that I'd screw up, botch the shot, and Eastmans' would have to write a check for $10K and we'd have nothing to show for it.

I ended up making a perfect shot on the biggest bull I'd ever killed, a 350-inch six-by-six. He went fifty yards and piled up dead in seconds after I placed an arrow through his lungs. I've always put an immense amount of pressure on myself to make a clean kill, but the money riding on me performing in crunch time ramped the intensity up another level.

Nowadays some of the best elk hunts can be four times that $10,000 Colorado elk hunt. I learned quickly that hunting premium country is a business. The animals are valuable to outfitters, so when going on a hunt like that, you sign a "wounding policy." As I mentioned above, this written agreement is if you draw blood on an animal, it's yours. Doesn't matter if it's a fatal hit or if you simply graze the animal and he runs off never to be seen again. If one drop of blood hits the ground, you own it.

> **By my honorable conduct as a hunter let me give a good example and teach new hunters principles of honor, so that each new generation can show respect for God, other hunters, and the animals, and enjoy the dignity of the hunt.**
>
> **—Novena prayer to Saint Hubert, patron saint of hunters**

Bowhunting wild animals is very difficult, but compound that with making the shot with thousands of dollars on the line, with an animal's life at stake and years of dreams and savings all hanging in the balance. The fact is, I'm not wealthy; I have a regular nine-to-five job and a family depending on me. But I'm a born-and-bred hunter and live for adventure. When I go on an expensive hunt, I feel extra pressure to not let down those who rely on me.

The San Carlos $70,000 was divided between the cost of a tag ($40,000), an outfitter's fee ($18,000), and a tip for the guide ($12,000).

Nobody wants to have to write a check that big and have nothing to show for it, so there was a lot riding on my making a perfect shot. Bowhunting the biggest, most coveted elk in the world adds to this pressure. You can't stop thinking about all you've sacrificed, and the years worked to pay for this opportunity. To me that money essentially could affect the quality of life I provided for my family.

All of this stuff starts weighing on you. That was why I kept wondering whether I deserved the honor to be at San Carlos. On many of the incredible hunting opportunities I've been blessed with over the years, I have felt like I didn't belong or really deserve the chance. I'm not sure why this is, but I know this perspective keeps me focused on capitalizing on and being appreciative of the experience.

My goal was to live up to the expectations of being a respectful bowhunter and celebrating these special elk mountains appropriately. Two words that come to mind are the ones Maximus says at the start of the battle in *Gladiator*.

"Strength and honor."

Bowhunters need to be strong, mentally and physically, but they also need to show honor. Honor is, to me, the attribute that makes bowhunting special.

To the bowhunter, the animal is held in highest of regard. And when a bowhunter is successful, the animal's death is but a part of the journey. I prepare for my hunts all year, as I feel I will best honor the life of the animal if I am highly proficient with my bow and can release a precise arrow that will kill quickly. I want nothing more than to be a merciful hunter. The meat yielded from each kill becomes a cherished staple for months, and the hide, antlers, or skull are displayed in my home to serve as visual reminders as, to me, this is showing respect for the animal's life.

Train. Hunt. Provide. Honor.

That is why I take those four words so seriously. I release arrow after arrow, day after day, month after month for one reason—to be a merciful hunter. I hunt with purpose and, when in bow range of the hunted, I ease my weapon back to full draw and focus with calm intent as my tunnel-visioned goal is to release a perfect arrow, killing the animal quickly. When this happens, I am relieved and satisfied that my hard-earned precision has justly honored the animal's life with a quick, compassionate death.

I am proud to be a respectful hunter and, as such, I have tremendous reverence for the animals I pursue, kill, and provide to my friends and family to eat. I would love nothing more than for non-hunters to understand what I've described, but I've learned that really, only a hunter can truly know how a true hunter feels. I'm not talking about those who pile into their trucks, head out to hunting country with a bow in one hand and a beer in another, shooting animals without any thought or regard. I'm talking about the hunters who care about the animals they hunt and love the country the animals call home.

That is why I prepare for the hunt even more seriously than a pro athlete prepares for a game. If I am going to take the life of one of those animals, I need to be my best, and I want it to be an ethical kill. Killing an animal is a big deal; it's not like buying a steak at the grocery store. There is so much reverence in that moment. There's a life at stake, and if I'm not at my best, I'll feel like I'm not honoring that life.

Prior to hunting San Carlos for the first time, I knew for a fact I'd never seen a ten-by-nine bull before in my life. I didn't even know that was a thing. And a 400-inch bull—never had I laid eyes on one in the wild. To hunt a bull of that world-class caliber? It wasn't even a realistic dream for me. When I got to camp, our guide, Chris Goode, showed me a video of the bull. All I could say was "Incredible." Chris had taken this video through his spotting scope recently and said the ten-by-nine was living in steep, rugged country. He thought it might be perfect for me to spot and stalk this bull. This is how I've killed 90 percent of my bulls.

Kip Fulks, one of the original founders of Under Armour and a good friend of mine, was there with me, and he was the one who had given me this opportunity at San Carlos. As I headed out into the best elk country in the world for two solid weeks if need be, I was confident, but to think I'd even get a chance at a once-in-lifetime bull like this seemed completely far-fetched. I honestly didn't even spend much time envisioning the possibility. Instead, I told myself that if I could arrow a 380-inch bull, even that would be more than I deserved. Such an animal would be slightly more fitting for someone like me.

Chris had other plans in mind. A 400-inch bull was his goal for us. Truth be told, a 400 bull is always the goal in that country. That's their benchmark. I called the ten-by-nine beast the "Tight Bull" because he was narrow. What were the odds of finding him? After all, the reservation was 1.8 million acres, it was big country, and the rut was going, so the bulls could be on the move and on a hot cow anywhere.

After a few days of elk hunting that included about ten miles a day of hiking, calling, glassing, stalking bulls, and so on, we had some close encounters but no can't-miss opportunities. One memorable evening, as we made our way up a hill through a burn, we heard what sounded like a good bull bugling, answering Chris's cow calls.

The wind was quartering up the hill from left to right so I knew we needed to get at least even, or slightly above, where the bull would pop out of the timber at the edge of the burn. Kip, Chris, and I hustled as fast as we could straight up through the burn. When we were about fifty yards above the bull, we set up.

I leaned on the shadow side of a big burnt tree while scanning the tree line intently. Chris and Kip were behind me, over a little spine ridge about forty yards away.

All good so far.

The still-unseen bull screamed a bugle. He was close. I estimated where he'd come out of the timber and looked for shooting lanes. It was a mess. The burn had burnt trees and brush everywhere. I got nervous that once he entered the burn, I wouldn't have a clear shot. I had seconds to make a decision.

I believe this photo captures precisely what I am best suited to do in this life. This is me carrying an elk quarter after a successful bowhunt in logging country of the Oregon coast range. Western Oregon is where I learned to bowhunt and I'm drawn back to these elk woods each September.

At the moment of truth, a bowhunter makes certain decisions that impact success or failure. The line between the two is razor thin.

I glanced at the tree I was leaning against and noticed some good limbs to climb. I quickly surmised that I'd increase my potential shot opportunities if I climbed up the tree. Since I had been set up on the shady side of the tree, my movement would be much less noticeable in the shadows. Scaling the tree as quickly as I could, I climbed ten to fifteen feet up and set up to shoot. This elevated position opened up my shooting lanes greatly.

Seconds after getting set in the tree, the bull ripped a bugle, answering Chris and exposing himself. It was the Tight Bull thirty yards away!

While we were in his country, we had no idea he was the bull coming in. I took one quick look at his 400+-inch, ten-by-nine rack, recognized what bull he was, and directed my focus on getting a good arrow in him.

Chris cow-called and Tight Bull closed in, heading straight toward me and ultimately stopped directly underneath me. I slowly eased my bow back. The bull noticed movement or sensed or heard me—probably thinking "mountain lion" if you could have asked him—and he became spooked, running back toward the timber. He stopped at just under thirty yards, quartering away as I frantically tried to get positioned to shoot while balancing on a burnt tree limb fifteen feet up an old burnt snag.

The Tight Bull stood, staring back at me, trying to piece together what was happening. I had to act fast. My sight was set on thirty yards, which

On the hunt for a big bull in Utah. I often hunt with an arrow nocked as it is here, meaning I am ready to react quickly if an opportunity arises.

would work, so I quickly readjusted while trying to stay calm. I settled my sight pin on his vitals, but there was one small limb covering his chest, so I raised up on to my tiptoes in the tree and picked a spot.

It was crunch time.

For a bowhunter, this is the most critical moment to master, as adrenaline speeds through your body and your heart races. If you can't remain under control, success will be tough. If you can, releasing a perfect arrow is just another part of the process. If you've put in the work, you'll crave crunch time because it's your chance to shine. Bend that bow back, anchor in, pick a spot, and send a razor-sharp broadhead on its way. The arrow flashes toward the bull and lands home, as you knew it would, because you've worked too hard to fail. After following a short blood trail, you find your bull and respectfully kneel by the amazing animal that gave its life to you. The bull's memory would be celebrated when his antlers eventually adorned your wall and his flesh nourished you.

I quickly let an arrow go toward the biggest bull I'd ever seen. I felt confident in the shot on release, confident about the work I'd put in, confident the arrow would strike where I'd visualized it would. Perfect . . . but that's not what happened.

The arrow flew off the mark, hitting the bull high and to the right, striking the top of his shoulder blade. A high, too-far-forward shot is about the worst shot you can make on a big bull since it's high and forward of the lungs, which is where you want the arrow to hit. The bull is protected by heavy muscle and bone, so an arrow that strikes here will typically only wound the bull and not cause death.

I felt sick to my stomach as he ran over the ridge with what looked like half my arrow sticking out of his shoulder. How did I blow an opportunity I'd worked my entire adult life preparing for? My dream became a nightmare in the fraction of a second it took my arrow to leave my bow and hit the bull.

For me a hunt is filled with a multitude of emotions, including gratitude, as I'm immersed in the beauty of nature, and respect, as on some hunts I move among predators and through terrain that can snatch a man's life in the blink of an eye. It's a reminder to all who are paying attention that death favors no man.

There is also a heightened sense of awareness once the heavy senses-muting cloak of the civilized world is shrugged from the shoulders. Then finally hunting instinct can take over. For me, this instinct comes back quicker each season as years in the mountains have now turned to decades.

Killing with what is essentially a sharp stick is still never a given, though. Man is very much a visitor to the wild, so in one respect the animals have the upper hand in the backcountry. But we have reason and an intelligence advantage that helps us get within bow range if we hunt well and the wind holds. If our aim is steady and our timing precise, that "sharp stick" will make a fatal strike on our quarry. He will run a short distance and find his last bed.

We try our best to honor this experience with words and photos from the great challenge we overcame in unforgiving country. We talk about respect, we give reverence to the animal that fell to our arrow and yes, there are bittersweet feelings when you've achieved your hunting goal while an animal lies dead at your feet. We accept that death is part of life, and hunters take ownership of the fact that, for us to live, animals will die.

Honestly, I don't care about how big antlers are, which a lot of guys do. They say that's trophy hunting. I'm not so concerned with the size of the trophy, but I want an old animal. I want an animal like the Tight Bull that's served its purpose, that's bred, that's done its job to facilitate survival of the herd, and is essentially now past its prime. That's what I want to kill.

This is where those months of training and running and lifting pay off. I have confidence in my abilities and my equipment to be precise and focused. My number one concern is to do everything I can to make a perfect shot that kills the animal quickly. There is a huge relief when I do. If I cause an animal to suffer, I then suffer in my mind many times over, for years.

I understand that hunting and the death of an animal are hard to understand for some. Even for me, after hunting for many decades, the actual death of an animal is not something I enjoy. Achieving my goal and life's purpose? Yes, that is fulfilling, and I accept the fact that, as a bowhunter, success for me means the animal dies. The blood is on my hands, and I'll deal with it, because it means elk meat will be nourishing me, my friends, and my family for months. As we know, nothing lives forever. An old bull might make it to ten or twelve years old. The oldest I've killed has been fifteen. But even so, if not for a perfect arrow, death in the wild will be much more drawn out and painful. I take solace, even with its emotional baggage, when I can deliver, via a perfect arrow, a beautiful death of an animal I respect like no other.

I grew up loving horses and have parlayed that love into helping me hunt remote country. This photo was captured on a backcountry hunt in Nevada.

The Tight Bull was a regal animal I respected greatly, but I failed to deliver that perfect shot.

I fucked up the shot from less than thirty yards.

I climbed down the burnt tree and slipped off my boots. With just socks on my feet, and not hard-soled boots, I could feel the ground better, which would allow me to sneak forward silently and see I what kind of blood I had to track. As I followed the sparse blood trail, my fears were confirmed. The bull didn't bleed much at all, a few drops, which was what you'd expect given that shitty shot. Eventually, the light blood trail stopped altogether. I continued on, following just the bull's tracks. The weight of his big body caused his hooves to scar the ground, allowing me to follow his progress down the hill to where I found half my broken arrow about 150 yards from where I shot the bull. I inspected what was left of my arrow and read the blood on the shaft. Shaking my head at what I saw, I silently backed out, so as not to spook the wounded bull in the event he was close by, bedded down because of the injury my arrow caused.

Sometimes if you do it right and hit them good, they will go down and will be dead in seconds. But they're tough animals, and if you don't hit them perfectly, something like this happens.

I was devastated.

Not only did I let myself down and my family and friends and followers, but I felt like I let the Apache tribe down as well. This bull was so unique and so incredible, and I had made a poor shot on him. He deserved better.

Now I had to go and tell the head of hunting for the tribe that I had made a poor shot. Kip, Chris, and I hiked miles back to the truck. The rugged road back to camp caused the truck to bounce and rattle and, while the vehicle made noise, creaking and thumping at it moved over rocks, the three of us didn't speak a word. It was a somber drive back in silence as each of us wondered about the fate of the Tight Bull.

Maybe the Tight Bull was hurt more than I thought, I suggested when I spoke to tribal members at camp, but I didn't really know for sure. I showed my broken arrow, and it didn't give us a good feeling. These bulls are huge, their shoulders are very muscular, and the bones are heavy, especially the shoulder blade where I hit. The campfire crackled and popped, the light from its flame pushing back the inky blackness of night. Nobody said much. I shook my head and stared at the ground, a pit in my stomach.

There are 10,000 Apache who live on the San Carlos reservation. This was the first time I ever set foot there; they didn't know who I was. I worried that to them I was just another rich white guy coming to pretend to be a bowhunter. Truth was, I was neither rich nor was I pretending. But either way, I knew I needed to earn their respect. But now I had done the very opposite of that. My heart felt heavy. The wind moaned through the trees.

Before going to bed that night, Kip and I talked about the Tight Bull.

"What do you think the odds are that we're going to get him?" Kip asked.

"Twenty percent," I said. "It's not good. A high shoulder shot on a big bull like that. I fucked up."

"Well shit," he muttered.

Kip told me later that he was so upset that night, knowing how much this bull meant to me and to our trip, that he cried before falling asleep. And keep in mind, he's one of the toughest guys I've ever met.

This was something that people who vilify hunters will never understand. The journey as a hunter is complicated and rife with challenge. It can take its toll on a man but also it can mold you into something more. Something deeper and more meaningful in a world seemingly defined by superficial fluff.

Respecting the life of the animals we hunt is *the* most important part of the hunter's creed.

I had a hard time sleeping even for a second that night, and it wasn't the first time I've had heartbreak in the mountains. I remember more than once blowing it on a big bull, times when I should have gotten a kill and screwed it up. And it has haunted me. Crushed me. I've joked that I probably needed counseling, but I'm sure I actually did. That was how much bowhunting and achieving my goals means to me. Each time something like that happens, I tell myself I never want to feel like that ever again. Each time I was crushed, I told myself I simply needed to work harder and push myself even more. My reasoning was, I failed because I hadn't sacrificed enough.

The animals I hunt and ultimately kill have my respect. As a hunter I take ownership over the fact that for me to survive, animals die. Life eats life.

The next morning, we got up and headed out at first light to where I hit the Tight Bull. Mark and Dan Stevens, Chris's uncle and cousin, joined us to lend a hand if need be. We all walked to a ridge a mile or more away from where I had shot the bull. As I scanned across the canyon with my optics, I spotted something but couldn't make it out.

"What am I looking at?" I asked the guys. "By those three yellow quaking aspens. To the bottom left of them. What am I seeing?"

"That's your bull," Chris said.

He was bedded. I studied intently through my binos and didn't see him move.

"Is he dead?" I asked.

Chris cow-called, and right when he did, the bull moved his head.

Fuck...

He's not dead but he's hurt.

"All right," I told them. "Let me go down and get this mess cleaned up."

As they stayed there, I made a big circle around to the other side of the canyon, where the Tight Bull was bedded. It took me over an hour, maybe even two hours, as I wasn't taking any chances with the wind and went very wide.

When I was a couple hundred yards from the three quakies, which were my landmarks, I slipped off my boots and continued on slowly and silently in just my socks.

As I neared where the Tight Bull should be, I looked through my binoculars over to Kip, Mark, Dan, and Chris and saw them motioning with their hands. With hand signals from a mile away, they were telling me the bull was going up the hill. When I neared the quakies, I spotted him slowly making his way up the hill. He was stoved up, but I needed to get another arrow in him or risk losing him.

It was going to take a very long bow shot to make that happen, but I got a good range on him and knew the distance exactly. I already had an arrow nocked, so I quickly dialed in my sight and drew back my bowstring. Settling my pin on his ribs as he quartered away. He would take a couple steps and stop, regather himself and take another couple of steps. I waited at full draw for him to stop. By this time I was completely relaxed and felt rock steady, pulling my bow hard against the back wall of my draw. I cheated the pin up a couple inches on his body as he'd moved a yard or two farther up the hill from when I ranged him, and slowly squeezed the trigger of my release.

The arrow arced high, covering the long distance before dropping home, sinking into his ribs as it angled toward the bull's lungs. This time my shot was perfect. I hustled up the mountain as fast as I could in my socks, nocking an arrow as I went. He hadn't gone far from where I hit him and, though still on his feet, now his head was down. It was quite a poke, ninety-two yards, but I was in kill mode as I came to full draw and released. Again, the second long bow shot also hit him perfectly. The bull went down and, after a few kicks, died quickly. A wave of relief washed over me.

When I reached the Tight Bull, I saw that my first arrow from the evening before had penetrated about thirteen inches, through the top of his shoulder blade, and had hit the bull hard enough to cause massive damage. I didn't get into his vitals as it was too high, but the near shoulder blade was broken where my arrow had penetrated and the broadhead was lodged in the offside shoulder blade. His shoulders were almost pinned together which is why he wasn't moving fast. However, once he got going and adrenaline kicked in, if I hadn't killed him with those additional shots, he likely could have gone for miles.

Keep in mind, I shoot a high-poundage bow set at a level 95 percent of bowhunters would say was dumb and unnecessary, mostly because they aren't strong enough to pull it back. They could if they trained, but not many train for bowhunting. That said, at a ninety-pound draw, I shoot a hard-hitting arrow, which allowed my first shot to punch through that old warrior's shoulder blade. Even though the bull hadn't bled, he had been wounded enough for me to track him down and eventually get him killed. With a less powerful bow, this bull wouldn't have been recovered. I have no doubt about that. The first arrow wouldn't have punched through the shoulder blade, it would've stopped after going in two inches, and the arrow would have fallen out when the bull ran off, never to be seen again.

Sitting beside the dead Tight Bull was a bittersweet moment of relief. My mind was conflicted; I had succeeded in achieving my goal, but knowing I ended the life of a truly majestic animal to do so brings a hint of melancholy. There was also a solemn sense of pride that comes with knowing once the bull hit the ground, the ending of his life would help sustain me and my family for months.

I took a moment to give reverence for the life of the animal I killed.

Thanks for the nourishment, beast. Your flesh will fuel me and your antlers on my wall will ensure your life is honored as long as I live.

I have a lot to be thankful for, but near the top of that list is having the ability and opportunity to be a provider. Going into the mountains with bow in hand and coming out with meat on my back, which makes its way to my freezer and then the dinner table of family, friends, or those in need is why I hunt. If you don't hunt, you'll have a hard time understanding the connection and respect hunters have with the animals we pursue. The entire journey of self-sufficiency or the honor of giving is why we do it, not just the kill. Hunters take pride in their craft, while, in my experience, many non-hunters criticize what they don't understand.

Here is the bare-bones, raw part of hunting that, looking from the outside in, probably seems like savagery but is simply something that must be done.

The animal is then skinned, and butchered. At some point the animal's head will be removed and packed out as well. The animal is cared for and meat is placed in the cooler and ready for the trip home or to the butcher for further processing.

I bring back home all the meat from my kills, as that's what helps fuel me all year and that's what I've been doing for almost forty years now. The meat is not wasted. Many times during September I'm traveling from hunt to hunt, so I have the meat cut and wrapped by a processor local to the area I'm hunting. They then freeze all the packaged meat and send it to me. Personally, I don't care how much it costs. If a bull falls to my arrow, I want the meat, and either my family will eat it or I will share it as I see fit from my house to those who need or want meat. I love sharing the meat from my kills, as that's what I think a hunter should do . . . We are providers.

The blood on our hands as hunters might be symbolic, but to a hunter there is honor in doing the "dirty work." Where I grew up, and traditionally, great hunters were respected and admired because they were keeping their community alive. I believe this is how it still should be.

All humans have blood on their hands, proverbial or otherwise. Hunters aren't ashamed of the fact that for us to live, animals die. Some anti-hunters with their backward logic have threatened my life because I am a provider and am self-sufficient, which means I hunt, kill, and eat. They cuss and spew hatred while standing on their holier-than-thou soapboxes, yet their fridges, freezers, and plates are full of meat that someone else has raised and killed for them—frequently in not-so-nice ways. Do hunters judge them for their choices? Far less often than they get judged. Ethical hunters are respectful.

To the vegans who want to clamor on about not eating meat, guess what? Animals died for you to live. If you drive a car, animals were displaced and killed to make room for the roads you drive. Furthermore, the wood to build your dwelling was made from trees that were cut down, killing woodland animals such as bears, large cats, wolves, amphibians, birds, and reptiles. If you're living in that house, you're responsible for the lives lost. The wheat field where your bread comes from . . . animals died during the growth and harvest of that grain. If you're eating the bread, you're responsible for that too. Rabbits, deer, mice—they all die by the truckload on agricultural land during harvest time. Don't feel guilty, though . . . it's the circle of life, and you're part of it, regardless of how detached you are from that reality.

Hunters don't have blinders on, pretending Disney is real life and that everyone lives until they're old, man and animal alike, dying peacefully in their sleep.

Humans *can't* exist without causing death . . . life eats life.

There are hunters you can vilify for good reason if you choose; however, ethical hunters should be in the group of people you respect. Man has been hunting since the beginning of time. It's our true calling and the natural order.

The comments I hear from the anti-hunting meat eaters are claims like, "Hunting is barbaric, cruel, and not something evolved people need to be doing today. We can buy meat instead of killing beautiful animals." When typical anti-hunting meat eaters are in the mood to grill a steak, their money goes to the supermarket where, typically, they buy the meat in a tidy Styrofoam container covered with plastic wrap. The store pays a middleman, a food distributor, who then pays the rancher. In the end, an animal was killed by a supermarket hit man for the anti-hunter with little reverence for the animal's life, because that consumer is very, very far removed from the kill. The "circle of life" may as well be a fairy tale. The animal killed probably had a shitty life living in confinement, not free like an elk in the mountains that is as "free-range" as one can get. The supermarket hit man is going to get his kills for sure, and on cattle it'll happen generally at eighteen months. A life much shorter than that of an old mountain-savvy bull elk.

> **"Death by violence, death by cold, death by starvation—they are the normal endings of the stately creatures of the wilderness. The sentimentalists who prattle about the peaceful life of nature do not realize its utter mercilessness."**
> **—Theodore Roosevelt, *African Game Trails***

Many times the hate I hear from the extreme, anti-hunting activist non-meat eaters includes their denials at being responsible for animals dying. They believe that not only is hunting unnecessary but also that cattle ranching isn't required for meat.

If few people ate meat, farmland and habitats would quickly be overrun by too many animals. Too many cattle, for instance, hammer habitats, fields, water sources, and so on, and eventually that would lead to diseased, starving animals and a weakened gene pool.

Same goes for hunting. Without hunting, the numbers of wild game would rise above what the habitat (which is shrinking as human encroachment expands) could sustain, and vehicle-animal conflicts would increase. Eventually, starving animals would be wandering around, weakened and diseased, and if not taken down by predators, eaten alive, or hit by cars, hopefully not causing a human fatality in the process. Wounded animals would ultimately have to be put down by government hunters instead of licensed hunters paying for the right to harvest. Taxpayers would be funding the government shooters. This is by far the worst-case scenario. Some people believe zero hunting and zero beef consumption is a good thing, which couldn't be further from the truth.

As a lifelong hunter, I can speak for all ethical hunters when I tell you our number one goal is a quick, merciful kill. Conversely, wildlife feels no sympathy. When death comes calling, the best option for a game animal is that a hunter takes its life and cherishes the meat from the kill for sustenance. Activists forget or ignore the fact that animals in the wild just don't die of old age in a nursing home with their family gathered around, mourning. It's brutal and unforgiving in the mountains. They get singled out by a predator or group of predators and run to exhaustion, then are eaten alive. Or they get old, weak, and can't find enough food, can't run, and get eaten alive by predators. Or winter hits hard and fast and they can't find good food, so they get weak, can't run, and get eaten alive by a bear, lion, coyotes, or wolves. That's pretty much it. If you love animals like elk, moose, and deer, death by a hunter is about the best they are going to get.

Man has compassion, animals don't.

Among the Plains Indians of North America, "counting coup" is the warrior tradition of winning prestige against an enemy in battle. It is one of the traditional ways of showing bravery in the face of an enemy.

Historically, any blow struck against the enemy counted as a coup, but the most prestigious acts included touching an enemy warrior with a hand, bow, or coup stick and escaping unharmed and without harming the enemy, except for the enemy's wounded pride. Touching the first enemy to die in battle or touching the enemy's defensive works has also been considered counting coup, as has, in some nations, simply riding up to an enemy, touching him with a short stick, and riding away unscathed. Counting coup has at times also involved stealing an enemy's weapons or horses tied up to his lodge in camp. Risk of injury or death is traditionally required to count coup. Escaping unharmed while counting coup has traditionally been considered a higher honor than being wounded in the attempt.

Those last two sentences are meaningful to me, and I've developed my own loose translation of counting coup when I'm bear hunting. After putting an arrow through an animal, but before it dies, I like to touch my quarry—a big black bear for instance, as it can inflict deadly injury which is paramount to counting coup. To me, being there with the bear as its life and spirit passes takes on great meaning.

A number of times I've hunted with John Rivet in Alberta, Canada, and I've put an arrow through the bear I've chosen to kill and ran to it before it died. To get there in time to touch it and tell it, "Thank you for offering me your life" has been powerful to both me as the hunter and to John the times he's been with me, moving him to tears more than once. That's how much these animals, hunting and taking the life of something we love and respect, means to us. Hunting is more than killing, and to me, my version of counting coup drives that into my soul.

There is nothing quite like venturing into the wild with bow in hand and coming out with a buck draped over your shoulders.

I have video of a couple of my counting coups. Actually, one time I posted video of a powerful experience but took it down after about thirty minutes as I could tell by the feedback and comments that the general public didn't understand my perspective. I guess I can't expect anyone to understand how much being a bowhunter means to me and the connection I have with the animals I kill. Knowing this, I probably shouldn't have posted it in the first place. It took a call from my friend Wayne Endicott to convince me to take it down, as after talking to him I was concerned that it could be used to hurt hunting, even though to me it illustrates the emotional link and conflicted nature of hunter and hunted. It's a bit of a paradox.

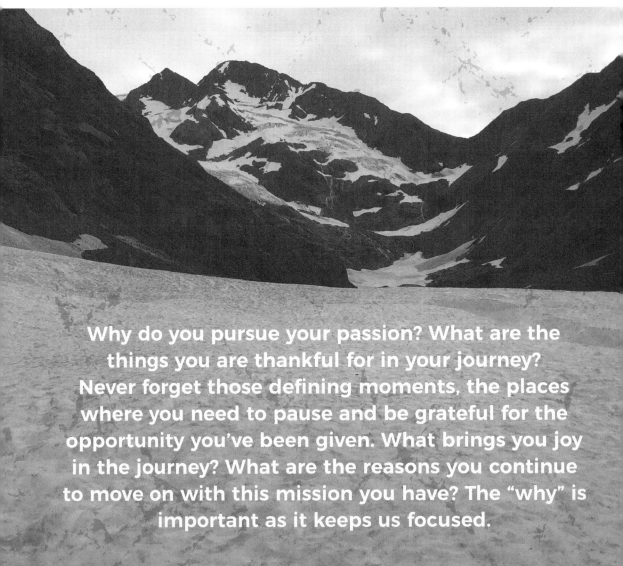

Why do you pursue your passion? What are the things you are thankful for in your journey? Never forget those defining moments, the places where you need to pause and be grateful for the opportunity you've been given. What brings you joy in the journey? What are the reasons you continue to move on with this mission you have? The "why" is important as it keeps us focused.

I've also counted coup hunting bear in Alaska (not grizzly yet) with my late friend Roy Roth. And of course I had to touch my Dall sheep before it fell off a cliff as it was dying—I grabbed its horns to pull it onto a small rock ledge while it was kicking in its death throes. But I don't consider the sheep as counting coup because there isn't a risk of it killing me as there is with a bear. And that risk is a key element in the original definition of counting coup.

I'm not worried about getting injured or killed when counting coup because, to me, risk is part of the deal. I'm trying to kill the bear, and if in turn it kills me, then fair play.

This is why I'm proud to be a hunter.

Hunters love and appreciate being immersed in our craft. We welcome the work it takes to provide meat for our families, and we accept that there will be sacrifices made to be at our best in the mountains. It's all part of the hunter's journey.

The things I love about bowhunting are the history, tradition, honor, challenge, respect, legends of the past, and the stories.

I respect the animals I pursue, the wild country where they live, and my craft. I am self-sufficient, accept responsibility for the animals that die so that I might live, and respect others who choose not to hunt.

Hunting the San Carlos Apache Reservation has been really good for me, because I respect the Apache tribe, love the culture and traditions, and enjoy its land and the animals.

Here is what I've learned and know. The very best hunters I know are hard-working, respectful, loving, loyal, and honorable community leaders. They are the type of self-sufficient people who are called upon when someone needs help. In other words, the men and women who make up the hunting community are protectors and providers who others can count on.

THERE'S ENOUGH CAKE FOR EVERYONE

"If it wasn't for you, I wouldn't even be doing this."

There's nothing I love to hear more than when someone tells me this. It could be about running an ultramarathon or a 10K or about starting to work out, but I especially love to hear it about bowhunting. In a perfect world, I'd personally introduce one person per day to the empowering world of archery.

Joe Rogan said those magical words to me back in 2017 as we were talking while glassing (using binoculars to locate game) during a Utah elk hunt. For a word that's used a little loosely, I can definitely say the results of that hunt were *epic*. We both killed great bulls and created the type of mountain memories that bond men together forever.

I've been friends with Joe since going on his show in 2014. I had heard he was talking about me carrying my rock up the mountain, so I made a Facebook post along the lines of this:

"Anyone on here know Joe Rogan personally? If so, tell him I'd love to come on his show and talk about pretty much the only two things I'm good at. Bowhunting and suffering."

Rogan had me on his show and has had me back many times. The exposure from the most powerful podcast in the world has truly changed the trajectory of my life. It's put me and my bow in front of millions of people that otherwise wouldn't know a thing about me. That first podcast started a friendship that sparked and has now been forged in the hunting woods. I took him on his first-ever bowhunt in 2014, and he killed a bear. I preached respect for the hunt and honoring the animals we pursue on his show. Joe gets it and wholeheartedly emulates that creed. And now, considering his gigantic platform, he is one of hunting's best-known advocates.

One thing I appreciate about Joe is his attitude. During that 2017 elk hunt, Joe kept grinding it out, despite the challenge that is bowhunting, with an awesome outlook. In reflecting on the experience, he said, "It can be kind of frustrating . . . I didn't feel frustrated like I wanted to quit. I felt frustrated, like I wanted to press on and I wanted to be successful."

What I've learned about Joe Rogan over the years is that he is hands down one of the most generous people I've ever been around. Not just with his money but with his praise. In the very competitive world of hunting, where really only a few people make money, there are lots of big egos and competition. Some people resort to shit-talking in an attempt to elevate themselves by diminishing another's accomplishments. Joe isn't like that. He's always complimentary. He's like, "Listen, just because I have cake doesn't mean you can't have cake. Everybody can have cake. There's enough cake for everyone."

Joe sees the best in people, and it's helped me develop the same perspective. It's great to start wanting other people to be successful, and then what's even better than that is to actually help them be successful. Bringing him into the world of bowhunting and seeing him flourish has been incredible. I never tire of his unbridled passion for archery and his student-of-the-game mindset. I remember wanting to see Joe succeed, much more than I wanted to succeed myself, and when he did I couldn't have been happier.

I remember on the first show I did with him, I shared how, to the right person, bowhunting can give one's life purpose, and how it can be life-changing to those who need something that could help define them or motivate them. Now I was seeing the impact it had on Joe.

"It's amazing," Rogan said. "You got me into bowhunting, man . . . It changed my life."

And you've changed mine, my friend.

CHAPTER 15

LEGENDS NEVER DIE

"*The mountains never lie.*"
I posted this quote on Instagram on September 30, 2015, showing a photo from my recent Alaska moose hunt and talking about how even though people lie and we even deceive ourselves, the mountains never lie.

If I head out on a hunt like my Alaska moose hunt last week and I'm not in shape and mentally prepared for a tough grind, I don't kill.

There was a lot to overcome on that hunt, tough weather, grizzly running off bulls, impenetrable fog that had visibility down to nothing for most the hunt . . . just the typical backcountry hunting challenges that one faces in the mountains of Alaska. But, when you're beat down, cold, low on food, and can't see, it doesn't take much to push you off the mountain and back down to the comforts of town licking your wounds.

It's times like this that the mountain tells you how strong and prepared you really are. Because the mountains never lie.

Personally, I live for the tough love the mountains dole out.

Four days after sharing those thoughts online, the mountains would ask me how strong and prepared I was to face the harsh wounds life could bring. They would dole out that tough love, making me discover an awful truth . . . that my spirit was weak, my heart could break, and my faith could disappear.

The confidence I had spent so many years building didn't just crack. It crumbled.

Some bonds built in the mountains are so strong that when broken, it feels like a piece of you is gone.

"What's up?"

Roy was calling to check in with me at work.

"Oh, you know, just in my cubicle," I said. "It's *crazy* in here. So freakin' exciting, doing purchase orders. Ten times better than being on the mountain, arrowing bulls or bears, and packing meat. *Way* better!"

"Oh, really sounds fun," Roy said.

"What about you? You living on the edge today?"

"Well, I went to Home Depot and got some light bulbs."

"Seriously?" I said with feigned excitement. "That sounds insane."

"Yeah, but wait till you hear this. I had to go back because I got the wrong ones. So that was pretty intense."

We laughed together at our pathetically boring day. Not only did I get to share so many awesome hunts with Big Roy, but I also enjoyed those dumb conversations. They were always a way to check in with each other, to banter and reconnect, to talk about recent hunts, and sometimes to talk about nothing except to remind ourselves that we were still there for each other. Always.

Our last hunt together only a week earlier had been a hell of a tough moose hunt in Alaska. I had to make a ninety-yard bow shot and then we had to pack all the moose quarters four miles out from deep in the mountains. Like all the other tough hunts we'd experienced, we surely grew from that tough test—as bowhunters and men. It was one of the most memorable backcountry hunts we had shared.

The moose hunt had come right on the heels of an epic bear hunt, which was also a hunt we didn't think we'd ever top. I arrowed two big wild country brown bears—one of which was a nine-foot six-inch monster boar, the other a seven-foot boar and a good-looking black bear—for camp meat. We were living high on the hog.

In another week Roy would be heading to the Dall sheep mountains while I was traveling to Colorado to chase rutting deer. Roy had asked if I wanted to go with him to hunt sheep and film, but I already had my deer hunt set up. We figured on staying in contact with nightly phone calls when reception allowed.

I couldn't wait to get back in the wilderness with Roy. Our last two hunts had been awesome. On each one, Roy had shown his toughness and strength and his belief that we would be successful. I had asked him before our mountain moose hunt in-country that was actually a rifle-hunting area where success was far from guaranteed—how long he thought it would take me to get a good bull killed with my bow.

"What do you think, three days?" I asked.

"Yeah, if that," Roy said with full confidence.

Sure enough, on the third day and on my first real stalk of the hunt, we were closing in on a bull I had bedded down earlier that day.

A couple hundred yards out, with a million things that could go wrong to sabotage a tough bowhunt, in nasty conditions with swirling winds, Roy looked at me and said, "Dude, it's gonna happen." I replied, "I know, buddy." And it did.

Roy's confidence didn't just come from believing in what was possible, but it also stared in the face of danger and didn't blink. This happened during the brown bear hunt we had gone on earlier in July that year. We'd had a big sow brown bear that turned into a problem. She saw us from about 130 yards away and started running full speed right at us. Roy readied

Me and "Big Roy," also known as The Guru, Gazelle Roy, and Roy Boy. A bond that will never be broken. I will see you again my friend.

his .375 that he'd brought as backup, and I nocked an arrow. Not sure what an arrow would do to a charging brown bear, but it's all I had. Roy said, "If she gets to our side of the creek, I'm going to have to shoot her."

She crossed the creek without hesitation and ran toward us. At about twenty yards she stopped and stood up aggressively, huffing and staring us down, head rocking side to side. We were standing in the wide open, in knee-high grass, so there was no mistaking we were humans. We were giving her a chance to make a better decision since we didn't want to kill her unless we absolutely had to.

"Get out of here," we hollered.

It didn't matter. The brown bear dropped down and, with deadly intentions and ears pinned back, she charged. Roy fired one shot and stoned her at close range. Mere feet from us. I couldn't help uttering a loud and inappropriate cuss word.

"Fuck."

I was mad that we had to kill another bear. I had killed a nice boar already,

Roy Roth and I shared so many hunts together over the years and we were so similar in archery technique that I could pick up his bow and hunt with it and likewise, he could pick up my bow and kill. And we did just that a number of times. On this trip, a river float trip for moose, he used my bow to kill a bull moose. On another hunt I used his bow to kill a big black bear on Prince of Wales Island. "Bowhunting Brothers" defined.

and we were on a high after that awesome success and sweet footage of my perfect bow shot. Now we had another killed, which we didn't want.

Despite the fact that we were in grave danger, that aspect never even entered our minds. After I cussed, mad, shaking my head, Roy said matter-of-factly, "Dude, I had to." I replied, "I know, it just sucks."

A typical response might have been, "Oh my God, we could have been killed, are you okay? I'm shaking." But I knew the partner I had in Roy. He shared the same type of confidence I had. He was never rattled and was always in control.

I knew, in ten lifetimes, I'd never find another partner like Roy.

Where does your strength come from? The only way muscles are built is by doing something that breaks them down, then they repair themselves to answer a test and you repeat the process over and over. Bottom line: Your body gives you what you ask of it.

My regimen includes running Mount Pisgah, a local hill that offers me 1,100 feet of gain in 1.5 miles. I can do this multiple times per run and end up getting in great leg and cardio training. I also lift weights and spend time daily shooting a bow. You need to be disciplined to grow endurance, to become stronger.

Roy was pushed by something else. He once shared where his strength came from in a book he inscribed years ago to me.

Cam: Seasons come and go. This is the one consistent thing in my life.

Roy wrote this in a Bible he gave me. Over the decades I knew him, his faith never changed. While I had been all over the place, he always remained rock steady. He had one girlfriend, Jill, whom he loved and married. I followed a different path before settling down. He never said one cuss word his entire life; I said them too often. He never drank alcohol, while earlier in my life I drank enough for both of us. Despite being polar opposites on many things, our friendship never wavered, not even slightly. We were bound together by our love for bowhunting and by the strength we carried into the wilderness.

I was thankful not only that Roy was a great bowhunting buddy but even more so that he was always a man I could lean on in a time of need, someone I could tell anything to and never be judged. Even though he had always been a faithful Christian and I hadn't, he never "preached" to me. He modeled pure living, which I wanted to emulate, and always answered my questions on his beliefs.

Roy not only loved bowhunting, but he loved knowing that, through hunting, he was able to impact people whom he otherwise would never have met.

"I believe the hunting world is my mission's field," Roy once said. "I mean, you can't just come up to a lot of people and start saying, 'Hey, you know, this is what I believe. This is how I think maybe you should believe.' They have no respect for you. You've got to gain respect for people to listen to you, for you to have an impact on them. And the hunting world is a hard world that way. So if you can gain their respect through your hunting accomplishments, I believe that's why God gives you those talents."

A week later, now weeks after our moose hunt, I was in Colorado bowhunting with Kip Fulks and Marc Womack. As the sun set on the eastern plains, I spotted and stalked a big Colorado whitetail. He was in pre-rut and had just been watching another ten-point, so he was a little wound up. Marc and I were pinned down while Kip was hunting somewhere else.

"I'm just going to go for it, try to cut the distance down about 100 yards," I whispered to Marc, who was filming me.

I hustled toward the buck as quietly as possible. He saw something a few times, but I was staying pretty low, crawling mostly. We figured he thought I was that other buck, so while I closed in on him, he started coming my way. He came pretty fast, licking his lips, and even stopped to make a scrap in the sage brush. At sixty yards he started to skirt me a bit, so I figured it was time. The shot felt good, but it was a touch low and he was quartered to a tiny bit. I felt it was good enough to kill him, so Marc and I backed out, planning to come back at first light to recover him.

That night before bed, we reviewed the footage and concluded "dead buck." Looked like liver, but you never know. I climbed into my bed that night with excitement and belief that we would find the buck in the morning. Sleep wouldn't come, however. At 11:00 p.m., my cell phone rang. It was Trace.

"Roy's been in an accident," she told me.

She didn't know all the details about what had happened, so I knew I needed to call Jill, Roy's wife. I phoned her and asked what was going on.

After a long pause Jill said, "Cam, Roy's not coming home."

Jill's voice sounded soft and tired.

I asked, "What do you mean?"

She said, "He fell. He passed away."

My stomach dropped and the darkness of the old farmhouse kitchen I stood in, there in the middle of nowhere, Colorado, felt darker and lonely. I couldn't believe her words.

Right away I thought of their children: Taylor and Justin and Ellen.

Roy had fallen 700 feet from a cliff in the nasty country we hunted sheep in. He was on Pioneer Peak, the exact same mountain where I had killed my ram in 2008 and where Roy had killed rams since. Now in 2015, the mountain had won.

He lost his footing doing something we'd done many times over the years, in the type of country we loved to hunt. Tough, rugged, unforgiving. A fellow hunter named Colt Foster was with him and witnessed the tragedy. They eventually had to get a helicopter in there to retrieve Roy's body.

> **"The proper function of man is to live, not to exist. I shall not waste my days in trying to prolong them. I shall use my time."**
> **—Jack London**

Jill had lost her husband, their kids had lost their dad, and their business had lost its heart and soul. It was devastating.

I sat up all night heartbroken, mad, and confused how someone I thought was invincible in the mountains could have a life-ending accident. When the alarms finally went off and the others stirred, I filled them in on the news as we waited for the sun to rise. They sipped coffee, I sat and stared, tears welling in my bloodshot eyes and rolling slowly down my cheeks. When there was enough light to go look for my buck, we headed out.

That morning search for the buck was painful. I had a handful of good men helping me. After the initial futile effort, instead of hanging around the others, I wandered off by myself, scanning the ground while looking for blood through tears. I crossed paths with the other guys every so often, so I'd try to dry my eyes as we'd say to each other, "Anything?" Meaning any sign of blood.

"Nope" was the answer each time.

I wanted to find this buck so bad for Roy it hurt. But hunting can be an exercise in frustration at times. I knew the buck wasn't concerned about Roy and wouldn't be sacrificing himself to give me a sliver of something positive to offset the pain.

However, I knew Roy would have loved to see my buck and hear a good hunting story. I had to find the deer for Roy. We all vowed to look until we found him, because Roy and I had always been on the same page when it came to tough blood trails. If the animal died or was going to die, we'd get him. And we always did. However, no blood trail in this country meant it would be tough going.

I thought about Roy and how he had just gotten his outfitter's license. We had big plans. We had spent decades building a brotherhood, chasing Alaska's most epic bowhunting adventures, and things were finally starting to click. Roy's outfitting business was blowing up as everyone wanted to hunt with Big Roy. He was planning to do this great caribou and grizzly combo hunt. Becoming an outfitter was going to give him more opportunities to be exposed to true Alaskan adventure, so both of us were excited about the future. It had just seemed like it was all coming together for Roy.

Life is never going to be the same.

I thought about how Roy would have acted if he had heard this sort of news about me. I knew he would have remained tough. And conversely, I couldn't have felt weaker. I was mad that we would never be able to share another hunt together. I hurt because I would never again get to be miserable with him in the mountains, which was one of our favorite pastimes. My heart ached for his family.

Eventually Roy's inspiration, or maybe it was his guidance, led us in the right direction and the grid search paid off. We found what I've dubbed "Roy's buck" dead, after he went about a mile from where I'd hit him the night before. My GPS tracker showed I'd walked six miles that morning looking, and the other guys—Marc, Kip, Sean, and Tom—had done at least the same. I owed them all for staying so steadfast in the search for Roy's buck.

He was a beautiful animal, and the meat was still good, sweet smelling as ever. I was thankful for that. The Colorado whitetail I had killed would always be Roy's buck to me.

More tears flowed as I called Jill and told her it felt like Roy was there with us and helped me get my buck. We had stayed "Roy tough" and it had paid off.

Roy's service was beautiful, emotional, and empowering. I think many in attendance encountered God's love in the midst of the pain. Everything Roy loved was there: his family, Palmer High School (where his kids went and where he helped coach baseball and football), hundreds of friends and legions of tough Alaskan hunters just like he was. Roy set the standard that many of us strived to match. The respect for Roy in the community was made evident by the large crowd. He had made a difference. He made people want to do more, work harder, be better, and love deeper. I think that what Roy would have loved the most though was the strong presence of the Lord.

The pain from Roy dying was deep for everyone at his memorial service. What I planned on doing was being strong to help those who were hurting worse than me, like his wife, Jill; their kids; his mom and dad; sisters; and so on. As I stood behind the podium, however, I found that talking about Roy in the past tense was harder than I thought it would be. I didn't have notes and hadn't really made a plan for what I wanted to say. I just wanted to speak on what was in my heart. I did that. But there was still no way to truly express everything I felt.

How could I adequately sum up the story of how Roy first introduced me to my life's passion and then embarked on many adventures with me?

How could anybody know that, as a kid and young man navigating a broken home poisoned by alcoholism, I had finally found peace in archery and with Roy as my anchor and best friend?

How could I begin to explain Roy's unceasing belief in me and my dreams? Not just bowhunting dreams but writing dreams and business dreams.

No challenge was too big in Roy's mind. Nobody could ever understand this the way I did. We thought we could succeed with our bows in any situation and for almost 30 years, in some of the most rugged unforgiving, wild country, we did.

I felt like I failed while I was on-stage speaking at his service. Jill saw me in pain and felt inclined to come up and hug me as I spoke about what Roy meant to me. When I went and sat down after speaking, I was hard on myself.

Wow, way to screw that up.

While it would have been nice to

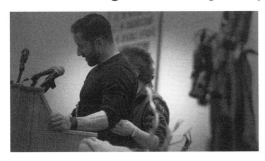

Speaking at Roy's funeral was one of the hardest things I've even done. I spoke at my dad's and grandma's services and was strong, doing what I needed to do and saying what I needed to say, but at Roy's, I couldn't. Jill Roth, Roy's wife, came up to offer support.

be a little more composed, I later felt that maybe I had achieved my goal of conveying the impact Roy had had on me after reading a message a gentleman sent me on Facebook.

Hi Cameron,

I wanted to tell you how much I valued what you had to say about your friend. Your words about friendship and love and faith and doubt were so raw, so real. I think we are all accustomed to pleasantries and platitudes, where emotion from the heart is watered down into trite phrases, but you offered only honesty. "I sure loved that man. I think he loved me, too . . . Some days I believe I'm going to see him again, but there are other days when I just don't know . . .

I was crying. I think everyone else was, too.

What really struck me from the service is how much Roy impacted those around him. I've gotten so used to hearing packaged sermons and haphazardly sprinkled Bible verses, but Roy was the gospel for the people in his path. The way he lived his life and chose to love those around him, including you, was an example for everyone who knew him of what a life in communion with God looks like.

I'll leave you with one more thought I've been dwelling on. All of the "Roy stories" I have heard over the years, including your words about your dear friend, tell of a big man who lived a big life. And now, partly because of Roy's impact on your life, you have chosen to share with people a glimpse into your faith. Maybe that means you are the gospel as well? Maybe I can be the gospel, too?

I couldn't answer that man's question, because I didn't know. It was just another chapter in the saga of my own meandering path through friendship and love and faith and doubt.

Roy Roth was the toughest person I've ever met. I sometimes find myself unfairly comparing others to him and then I remember: There will never be anyone like Roy. But the second-toughest person I've known might be his wife, Jill. She was strong at his service, and she has remained strong. Soon after Roy's passing, Jill set the goal of creating a room for Roy, which would include some of his mounts, mementos, photos, and so on . . . all things Roy. With the help of friends, family, and Roy and Jill's kids, Roy's Room was completed just as she envisioned, two years after his death.

To celebrate the unveiling, Jill organized a gathering held at their home, and it was amazing. Roy's Room was filled with so many good people, which included Roy's mom, dad, sisters, children, grandchildren, hunting buddies, fellow coaches, and friends from church to name a few. Stories flowed freely. It was just the type of crowd and conversation Roy loved and it all happened because of Jill and her loyalty to Roy.

I am honored to have known Roy and call him my best friend, and similarly I am honored to know, love, and respect Jill. She's not tough in the mountains like Roy was but she's just as tough in her own way. Her strength and poise in losing Roy has amazed me.

Just like Roy, Jill leads by example.

I could fill a book with stories to illustrate Roy's toughness and positive attitude, and maybe one day I will. One story that I will never forget is our Dall sheep hunt in 2008 on the beautiful and rugged Pioneer Peak, Alaska, that was wonderfully captured on film. The words I wrote in my article about the hunt seemed to foreshadow what happened to Roy in that same country, on the same type of bowhunt exactly seven years later.

The climb to sheep country is brutal and one I won't soon forget . . .

I'd been nervous about this hunt from the get-go. I knew full well that this could very well be the only sheep hunt I'd go on in my entire life . . .

Make no mistake, if you got in trouble on the mountain, there is nothing anyone in the valley could do for you. Alaska sheep country is as unforgiving a place as there is, regardless of the view.

As many have seen, on that sheep hunt I had a terrible hit on my ram. My arrow deflected off a rock I was attempting to squeeze the shot by, and it hit him in the ankle. Basically, it cut his wrist. He made it up and over the mountain as we glassed him the entire way. The sheep was bleeding, but that wasn't a shot anyone wanted on an animal. After watching him go over the top, I hiked up to where Roy had watched my stalk and the shot from. He too saw the blood on the ram's ankle as it limped up the mountain.

"Nice shot," Roy said sarcastically as I approached him.

I looked at the top of the rugged ridge the ram disappeared over. "Yeah, cool huh? I suck."

"We will get him. Might take a week, but we will get him."

"Yep," I said as I nodded.

That type of attitude and unwavering confidence was huge. In the end, we did get him, as those who have seen the video know. It was ugly: I had to grab the not-quite-dead-yet ram before he fell off a cliff and hold him there as he died, but we got him.

That hunt will always be a reminder that even though Roy was fearless, he always respected the danger of those mountains. The same country that ultimately took his life. I think it's important to share the advice Roy gave me as I headed down to finish off my sheep, because while he had hard-earned confidence, he also wasn't stupid and didn't take crazy risks. My ram was on the edge of a cliff in very steep country covered with ice and snow. Glassing the injured ram from the ridgetop, I said, "Well, I have to go get him."

Roy studied the cliff. "Cam, where he's at, I'm not sure if you can even get down there. And if you do, you might not be able to get back out."

Looking down at the weakened ram, I said, "Maybe so. I guess we are going to find out."

And off I went. Fate was on our side that day. I got to the ram, killed him, and we got him off the mountain. In the same situation now, I'd guess the outcome likely would be similar, but the victory wouldn't be as sweet as it was then, because then I shared it with Roy, the only person on this earth who could know what killing that ram meant to me and what it took to get it done.

I think he felt similar about me because when he did something "next level," I'd be his first call. When he stuck his head in the brown bear den and the ten-foot bear took a swipe at him as it boiled out, he called me minutes afterward from the mountain, excitedly telling me the story. When he killed a big Dall or giant grizzly, which is something he had done more than any other bowhunter in the world, I'm pretty sure, he'd call and his first words would be something like, "Too hard." This

Roy Roth and I in the rugged, unforgiving Chugach Mountains of Alaska with my first Dall sheep.

was "code" for us, so I'd jokingly feed into the game and say, "Well that's okay, it's good just to get out in nature. You don't have to kill to have a good time, Roy."

We'd laugh and I'd usually follow this up with something like, "So, now that we got the jokes out of the way, you get it done?" He'd invariably answer, "Cam, that's why I went."

Yep, Roy always got it done.

"When the chips are down, what gives you strength to keep pushing?"
I once asked Roy this, and the first thing he mentioned was his strong Christian faith. Just like on my Dall sheep hunt, he trusted everything would work out according to God's plan, and this gave him great confidence. He always kept a positive attitude and expected to achieve his goal on every single hunt. Roy believed God gave him the strength and the ability to be successful, which in turn would allow him to have a positive influence on others.

As for my faith . . . I still have a hard time.

When someone dies, everybody always says, "They're in a better place" and "We'll see him again." People talk about how glorious Heaven is going to be, and that all sounds good. It makes you feel good. But my faith isn't so much that it's unshakable. I do have faith, and some days I feel good and feel like I will see Roy again. Then some days I wonder.

We had such great hopes and big plans in 2015. We'd had two of our best hunts and were excited about Roy getting his outfitter's license. I knew Roy would make the best outfitter ever because of his likable personality, his knowledge of hunting, and his toughness. Things were happening, and

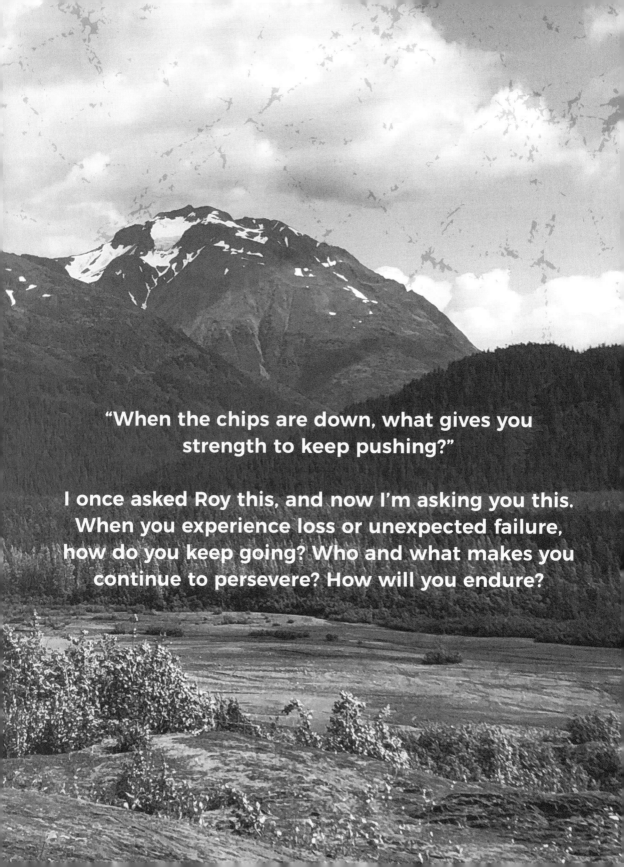

"When the chips are down, what gives you strength to keep pushing?"

I once asked Roy this, and now I'm asking you this. When you experience loss or unexpected failure, how do you keep going? Who and what makes you continue to persevere? How will you endure?

I'll be honest—I'm still mad that it happened. But I will never forget what Jill told me about the night Roy died. It gives me comfort the same way I'm sure it gives her comfort.

The night Jill learned Roy had fallen to his death, she understandably couldn't sleep after receiving the phone call. She was up at 1:00 a.m. and looking out the window. From their house you could see Pioneer Peak, so Jill stared up at the mountain Roy had died on when all of a sudden a glow came over the mountain. A bright light, as Jill remembers it.

Jill told me it was like the Lord was saying, "Don't you worry about Roy Boy. I am watching over him tonight."

She knew she wasn't sleeping and dreaming it. Jill told me that at this moment she knew things were going to be okay, that she felt a peace come over her.

Hearing that made me feel good. Sometimes I wish I could have seen that myself. I still don't feel a peace inside whenever I think about Roy. That's not what's inside my heart.

The rescue team couldn't get Roy off the mountain until the next morning after he fell because of weather and then they had only a little window of time before another storm came in. When Jill got the call from them saying that Roy's body was coming in on the helicopter, she and the kids went to the Palmer airport and waited for him to get there. Then, for Roy's family, the tragedy became real.

Whenever I have a good hunt or I've had a good year, I tell Roy. That's what we always talked about—our successes. My success was his success, and his success was my success. Roy cared about me and he loved what I loved: bowhunting, challenges, doing things no one else would do, and living on the edge.

I always admired Big Roy's unwavering faith and I long for the same peace he always had regarding eternal life after death. He was irreplaceable as a presence in my life, but I'll endure and keep hammering and do my very best to always honor the legend of Roy Roth.

LOVE ONE ANOTHER

Take time to think about what you're grateful for. I love doing this while I'm on my runs.

Pray for people going through hard times. Not just family and friends but also people you work with and encounter.

Be grateful to know the stories and the suffering others have to go through.

Think about those you've lost and honor their memory.

Make sure the people you love know that you love them.

If you love someone, tell them.

If you value someone's friendship, tell them.

If someone inspires you, tell them.

If you've hurt someone, tell them you're sorry.

Life is too short to be bitter, prideful, or vengeful. Tell them how you feel sooner rather than later as tomorrow isn't guaranteed.

And listen—I'm not perfect and I let people and myself down all the time, so this is a sobering reminder to me as well as any of you.

Love one another.

CHAPTER 16

THE INVINCIBLE IMPOSTER

Train Hard, Hunt Easy: This means to train so hard that even the most grueling hunts are easy in comparison. That's what I do and it allows me to be at my very best during the course of even long mountain hunts.

I'm invincible.

My alarm is set for 4:55 a.m. because getting up "in the fours" sounds better in my head than getting up in the fives, more committed, but I never make it to the alarm. I turn it off before it goes off.

I don't dread getting up; I love it.

It's another chance to hammer.

I've convinced myself that every day is a gift and I get to jump out of bed and go run. I'm usually out the door before 5:00 a.m. (in the fours) to start my fasted cardio run.

As I run down the empty streets and see the houses knowing everyone is asleep inside, in my head I kind of like it. I don't envy them, because I feel like each morning is another chance to sacrifice a little more. I turn it into a positive and just think how I'm out there working already. That makes me feel good.

The saying goes, the greater the sacrifice, the greater the reward.

Always has been true.

Always will be true.

You can second-guess, take shortcuts, and dismiss, but you'll never change the game. When you change the positive effort you put in, the odds tilt in your favor. That's a fact.

There is never a question in my mind asking if I'm going to run today. I'm going to run no matter what. If I'm sick, I'll still run. If I'm hurt, I'll go slower. I'll limp. Nothing will change. A lot of people look for ways or reasons not to run or exercise. Those things don't even come to my mind anymore.

If I think I'm tired, I remember moments when I'm running hundreds of miles in an ultramarathon and I'm getting an hour of sleep or less. *That's* when I should be tired. The other times means I'm just being weak.

Even though I've killed a number of bulls, upward of sixty now, over thirty-plus years of bowhunting them, and I've had more than my fair share of success, all of that means absolutely nothing this coming elk season. That's what keeps me grinding day after day.

I think about that a lot when spending time around others who are amazing in their field. Who succeed because they too work their assess off, but on top of it they have much more God-given talent than I to focus on their craft. They have Olympic-level ability, tunnel-visioned focus topped off by sacrifice or an inhuman level of toughness and mental strength. They will succeed because their ability and their work ethic are both extreme, which is what makes them living legends performing at a level that many have never seen.

I succeed only because I work more, because I'm up at this hour, every day, grinding it out.

This type of effort in training has given me supreme confidence in the mountains. The more I sacrifice and hurt but keep pushing toward my goal in training, the more deadly I feel with my bow. Is it overkill? Not for me. I've found that one can never really prepare too much.

You learn something every year, every hunt, every day, but you have to sacrifice to keep the education going. So you want to bowhunt? You want to run ultramarathons? That shit doesn't happen overnight. You have to keep at it every day. You have to keep sacrificing, sacrificing, sacrificing.

There'll be a payoff. But it's going to take a while.

Tomorrow's never guaranteed. I could have big goals and dreams down the road, but I could be dead tomorrow. So I pretty much take one day at a time. I give the best I can every day.

I'm an impostor.

Sometimes I look at my life and wonder what the hell happened and how did I get here? I remember where I came from and see what I've achieved and see so many things I don't deserve. I think about the hunts I get to do and the people I encounter and the lives I get to impact and I sometimes feel like somebody's going to come in my house and wake me back up to reality.

"What the fuck is going on here, Cam? What are you doing here? What do you think this is? Get back to your shitty little town and the shitty life that you deserve."

There are times when I feel like that is going to happen. I've mentioned that to Joe Rogan before, and he says he even feels like that at times because of where he came from. Here's this regular guy who signed a massive $200 million podcast deal and he feels what experts call the "impostor syndrome," feeling like a pretender in your life. I get that.

Even at work, I'm the superintendent, but I don't feel like I deserve to be there. The guys respect me and I'm good at managing men, but I don't know if I deserve to be superintendent. I don't have a degree. I never asked to be superintendent. I was the buyer and I was good at that. My buddy got promoted to director, and I knew he needed help with the field guys, so I said I'd do it. It's not like I ever dreamt of being a superintendent, especially with all this other stuff going on. So I didn't know then and I still don't know. Sure, I know I sacrifice a lot, but I know other people sacrifice a lot and don't get the rewards that I do.

When people leave comments saying how I changed their lives, I am humbled. I don't feel like I deserve that type of influence. I'm humbled that I have

There is no way I could be prouder of my kids. Tanner, Taryn, and Truett have filled my heart with love. I pushed them and, thankfully, Tracey offset my style with her beautiful motherly support.

it. To me, I feel unworthy as I think about all the people over the years I have let down, disappointed, and not shown compassion for when I should have, or the times I've been selfish when I should have given. It haunts me.

One day I was listening to this podcast when I was running, and people were saying, "Cam gets to go on some pretty sweet hunts" and, "I can't afford $70,000 for an elk hunt like he can." I'm thinking to myself, *What are you talking about? I can't afford it either, just like you can't!* I'm lumped in with the rich guys, but in my mind, I'm still thinking I'm just this warehouse worker because somebody's going to figure this charade out and that's where I'm going to be back. I'll be working back in the warehouse and be like, "Hey, can I get some overtime?" Because at overtime, I'd actually be making a decent amount of money. Because if you're making ten dollars, well now at time and a half you're making fifteen dollars. That adds up. That means something. That's still my mentality. I understand people who put me in some elevated category or preconceived box, but that's neither who I am nor how I feel.

Maybe that's one reason I never feel like I've done enough. Why I feel like I have to sacrifice more than anyone. Maybe it shows that, okay, this is why I have all of this, this is why I'm blessed. It's because I'm giving more.

I think I'll die before I will ever feel like I've made it, like I've arrived and I can take a break now. The downside, if there is one, is honestly, I think what I do isn't a recipe for a long life.

I'm obsessed.

Be obsessed or be average, I say. Sometimes it takes obsession to succeed at difficult tasks.

When I first started bowhunting, I was so obsessed with tagging a bull with my bow that I didn't go to any college classes, missing the first two full weeks of school, until I arrowed that bull toward the middle of September. If I hadn't gotten him, I would have missed an entire month with no regret. It meant that much and still does.

I get obsessed with things. But as I always say, if you're not obsessed, you're going to be mediocre. I don't care what it is. If you have a healthy, balanced relationship with whatever dream you have, then nobody will ever know your name. That's the cold, hard truth. Sure, there are those born with the physical capabilities to play in the NBA, but I'm sure LeBron James would say he's been obsessed with basketball his whole life.

The great Wayne Gretzky once said that parents always come up to him and ask if he could tell their sons how many hours a day he used to practice playing hockey.

"I say, I didn't," Gretzky said. "It was a passion. I would be out there all day long 'cause I loved it."

If you want to excel, you've got to think about it, obsess about it, and sacrifice, or it's never going to happen. That's all there is to it. I became obsessed with bowhunting. End of story.

Actually, it's not the end of the story. The story continues each and every day through hard work. Through obsession.

San Francisco 49er Jerry Rice, one of the greatest players to ever compete in the NFL, used to run a hill. In fact, it's nicknamed "The Hill." The steep incline was 2.5 miles up, and Rice ran it every day when the season was over.

"It taught me endurance," Rice said. "Being able to function when you're really tired.

"When there's nothing else, somehow you find a way to dig a little deeper. So that last 800 meters, it made a lot of guys cry. It made a lot of guys throw up. That was part of my regimen during off season."

Jerry ran The Hill to achieve dreams and get his Super Bowl rings. Some players probably told him that running hills had nothing to do with football, that it didn't help a man become better at catching footballs. They said this mostly because they didn't want to run hills, as it's hard, so by discounting Jerry's approach, they created a way out for themselves. Jerry believed otherwise, so he did it religiously. He outworked the competition and by running hills he earned three Super Bowl rings. Did running hills help him? Sure seemed to. He is the GOAT of NFL receivers.

His former teammates would vouch for his obsession when talking about Jerry Rice.

"I don't think I've come across anyone in life who has a greater obsession with being perfect than Jerry," former 49ers tight end Brent Jones recalled. "He wanted to be perfect in every single aspect of the game. It really drove him."

That's the mindset I carry into the wilderness. I obsess about the thought of not being successful on a hunt. That's the reason I run my own hill. I run because I believe it's helped me achieve my dreams. And, like Jerry's naysayers, plenty of people have taken shots at me for thirty years now and discount my training. They say running to prepare for bow season is a waste of time, yet I find success each year. For some weak souls who don't have what it takes to work and sacrifice, or those who don't prioritize hunting the

My greatest achievement is the success of my children. They are better in virtually every single way than I was at their age. I am so proud to be their dad. A great deal of credit goes to Tracey. She's been the one that always showed them love and support when I was too hard on them.

way I do, it very well might be a waste of time.

You have to work hard and sacrifice. You have to stand out to succeed. You have to pick and choose what you're going to be, what you're going to excel at. You can't excel at 100 different things, because you have to be obsessive to excel. So if you're obsessive about business, you're probably not going to have time to be obsessive about archery. Because that's what it takes. Obsession to be the best at that one thing.

I'm an example.

As parents, we have high hopes and expectations for our kids. The biggest thing for me is that I've always wanted to be a good example to my kids and to show them what hard work can mean. I've told them repeatedly that I'm nothing, that I'm not special. I've told Tanner and Truett that they're more athletic than me. I've told Taryn she's way smarter than I was. They are all way better people than I was at their age. So if I've achieved what I've achieved, I'd said to them, you can achieve more. I want to show my kids what giving your best can equate to.

Going back to the subject of obsession, if you're going to be great at one thing, you're probably not going to be great at other things. The way I've looked at it, I know I definitely have been short in some areas because I've been obsessive about other things. I know I probably wasn't the best dad, the best husband, the best whatever, because I've been obsessed about bowhunting. For example, spending $3,000 to go on an out-of state hunt when you don't have the money and have a newborn baby at home . . . yeah, that's probably not a good decision. That's not being the best provider you can be, because I put *my* dream ahead of being a provider for my family, for the people who rely on me. If you're being honest with yourself, and I have been honest with myself, I know I've fallen short. That's not justifying it at all, that's just being real.

Oftentimes what we expect of our kids isn't necessarily in line with what we expect of ourselves. We push them and say things like, "You don't have to be *the* best; just give *your* best," while many of us are simply going through the motions at work and life. But I've always committed to giving more and working harder than others, and I've tried to explain that mindset to my kids.

"Listen, you guys aren't special," I always told them. "If you give what everybody else gives, you're not going to stand out. You're going to have to give more if you want to achieve anything. You have to give more than everybody."

-year-old Tanner Hanes loves the out-s. His dad, Cameron, took him on a ess archery hunt for Rocky Mountain Oregon. It was a weekend he will ber forever.
aturday afternoon, Tanner's dad shot lk. They waited 30 minutes and then ollowing the tracks. In bowhunting, f the work begins after the shot, er's dad showed him the different f sign found along the trail. Patches f red pointed to a solid hit, while the confirmed it. The elk's right front leg n slightly dragging — a sign of Seventy-five yards into the tracking, s fell and the hunters returned to [hey hoped the elk would lie down to cefully in a short distance.
next morning, on the trail Tanner he arrow that had fallen out of the nething they had missed at twilight. d dried blood were on it. Then the

After the hunt, lugs an elk shoul hoof back to c

Tanner, when he was seven years old, helping me pack out an elk.

That's always been my mindset, but as a parent, sometimes I've second-guessed this. When my boys were young, they would go and spend the night with their friends, and they came home telling stories about the other dads. I would say, "Well, he's teaching his son to be a pussy, basically." I wanted my kids to be prepared for the shit we go through in life, because life is a competition. If you want to excel, you're going to have to sacrifice. So maybe I didn't teach them certain things, but I taught them how to be tough. I was always hard on them, especially the boys. I loved them and they knew I loved them, but I wouldn't ever cut them slack.

As I've become older, I've sec-ond-guessed how I raised them and the things I said. *Ugh, did I screw up these kids?*

Tanner is like me in many ways, which caused us to butt heads when he was a young man. Being his dad has taught me a lot. He'll never know how much he changed me.

I remember when Tanner came and told us he was going to go to Army basic training because he wanted to be an Army Ranger. I had a terrible thought. ***Did I mess this kid up by my weird excessive approach to life?*** Tanner was at the time a sheriff's deputy in our town, which is a good job. He was making $70,000 a year, and more than that, it is a respectful, important field and could be a rewarding career. I was fine with his job as a deputy *and very proud of him*. But I had also told them growing up, "If you're average, then you're a failure!" I had come clean and told them that I never should have said that having an ordinary job and an ordinary life meant you were a failure. I was wrong. There's nothing wrong with that. We need people to count on for jobs like that. Deep down, regret whispered in my ear.

Did I fuck up my boys?

Tanner gave me some reassurance when I spoke with him before he left for basic training. "No, Dad. It's just I feel like I have more to offer this world than just working at the jail for the next twenty-five years."

He's right: Being a Ranger is tough. Rangers are elite soldiers, but he's great at it and he's a freakin' beast.

Sometimes the biggest thing in parenting my kids was trying to give life to this mindset of mine.

I've spoken to myself, "God, life is hard. Why does it feel unfair and defeating?"

I've learned firsthand, the hard way, that if you're weak of body and spirit, life is going to be that much harder. Knowing this meant I had to show them tough love.

Recently when Tanner was home on leave, he was watching some of the videos from when he played basketball in high school.

"Dad, you were right! I was so lazy."

"No shit," I told him.

"I never played defense."

"No kidding!"

He's twenty-seven and can see that now, but back then, we used to have the biggest arguments about effort. I was always like, "You get on that ball. Be ready!" But he didn't want to do it. On offense he was great; one time he scored thirty-two points in a half and earned All-State as a senior. So in my mind, I wondered what he could have done if he worked harder? Yet even so, I would sometimes second-guess myself. *Am I a psycho, or is he actually trying his best?*

I live every day feeling like if you're not giving all you got, then you're not really honoring the gift of life. I don't want to just get by. But at the same time, I don't want to discount those out there who give their all in different ways, like moms who are giving it all they got and being the best to them means being the most nurturing and loving mom for their kids. With the boys, I was focused more on giving all you got from a physical standpoint, but now with Taryn, I've had to adjust. For her, it means striving to achieve greatness from an educational and intellectual standpoint since that's where she excels. She is brilliant, actually, so to stay true to my recalibrated expectations I'm trying to get her to apply to Oxford University or another renowned institution of higher learning. She's got the ability.

Recently, Truett finished his first 100-mile endurance foot race. Last year he exceeded David Goggins's 24-hour pull-up record of 4,030 by doing 4,100. Accomplishments like this cause me to reflect on how being a dad to my three amazing kids has so enriched my life. I've failed as a parent many times and maybe been too hard on my kids, thinking I'm "preparing them" for the challenges life is sure to throw their way. These misgivings have been mitigated for a couple of reasons that have little to do with me. One, Tracey has offered unwavering motherly love and support when I've been too hard or demanding, and two, our kids (not really kids anymore; men and a perfect young lady) are tough, smart, and much more capable than most. It is because of these reasons my errors as a dad aren't as noticeable to others. To me they're glaring.

All that said, what I've always tried to do in regard to "expectations" is, while yes I expect a lot of them, it's not more than I expect of myself.

No excuses, give your all, show up when you're supposed to, speak your mind, own your mistakes, think with perspective, and live a life worth remembering.

My middle child, Truett, gets a lot of attention on social media for his accomplishments: breaking David Goggins's world record mark in pull-ups, running 100-mile ultramarathons, and so on. He deserves the accolades as those feats are impressive, but my other kids, while not celebrated in public, shine as well. Tanner, my oldest, is an Army Ranger, a special operations unit, and has deployed as such. My daughter, Taryn, is brilliant and kindhearted. Each of them is unique in their own right but regardless of their chosen interests or craft, they excel. That's all I've expected of them. I often said, I don't care if you're THE best, just give it YOUR best. And they have.

When typing those last few sentences just now, something occurred to me. My kids might reflect these attributes better than I do? Maybe the teacher has become the student?

I endure.

Everyone has strengths—my strength is the ability to endure in the mountains. To endure the pain, the pace, the frustration, all of it. If I keep pushing, eventually I will outlast whatever roadblock is stopping me from reaching my goal.

That makes me feel invincible. That lessens my feeling like an impostor. This explains why I'm obsessed. Maybe this shows why I am an example to others?

Many years ago, I decided I was going to work hard every day on being the very best bowhunter I could be. Along with taking care of my family, that is my purpose in life. Everything I do is prioritized around this drive and this dream.

I start at 5:00 a.m. and finish at 8:00 p.m. every day.

I give it my best.

I have gratitude for the gifts and opportunities I am given.

I enjoy the journey.

Steve Prefontaine was right. "To give anything less than your best is to sacrifice the gift."

That's exactly how I look at it.

Bowhunting can be a struggle. It's hard, and very competitive. It can be very cutthroat. But so can life.

The steeper, more rugged it gets, the more the climb asks of my legs, the harder my heart and lungs work moving blood and oxygen to fuel my quick and aggressive ascent to the summit . . . the happier I am.

Start early, train more, work hard, excel, and, over time, you create separation.

Our passions and hopes and dreams in life can resemble that Dall sheep I arrowed in Alaska with Roy. Sometimes those dreams lie bleeding at the edge of a cliff, clinging to life.

Life can be tough and can beat us down. We experience loss. A loved one or family member, a job or a dream. We battle our own demons and dependencies. We all take hits and get beaten down.

That's when we have choices to make.

Only you can choose not to hesitate.

Only you can keep moving.

Only you can climb over snow and ice and tough footing and steep, rugged country.

You're the only one ultimately able to grab onto those horns and see if there's any life left.

You're going to fight for it. You're going to get kicked. Clasping on to hope can be hard. It's easy just to give up.

Will your dream get pulled over that cliff?

Are you going to be able to survive?

Can you find the strength to endure?

When I grabbed onto the horns of that Dall sheep, time stood still for a moment. My life flashed before me. I thought of all those who were important to me.

Is this it?

There I was, holding on to a 250-pound wild animal that with one false move could pull me over that cliff. Ultimately, I dragged him up onto that small ledge, tied him off, and held him there.

I breathed in and stared down the mountain.

I survived. I'm going to make it home from this.

I thanked God for one more day to see those whom I love. I made it off that mountain with a trophy on my back.

Looking back, it was no doubt a highly questionable decision to try to hold him inches, so close to certain death, but this was *my* sheep. I had waited a lifetime for that moment. I held a dream in my hands and I wasn't going to let it go for anything.

What cliff are you standing next to, and what will prevent you from falling down it?

What dream do you hold that you're not going to let go of?

My achievement on Pioneer Peak was one I never, ever thought I'd realize. It's also a reminder of what I repeatedly say . . .

If I can do it, anyone can. But you will have to earn it.

You will have to endure.

What are we doing? I often ponder what it is we are doing on this journey we call life. It can end in a blink of an eye and whether I'm here or gone, other than for my immediate family, not much would change. Thinking about what's important and what's not while balancing time and prioritizing obligations, sometimes I wonder.

Can I do everything I need to do to the level I want to do it, or is it too much of a burden that might not really matter in the grand scheme of things anyway?

What keeps me on track with all of this and drives home the answer to this question is *you*. Every person who's read one of my posts and who is reading this now.

Because you care, I care. I talk to you and listen because my life's focus is not on the haters of the hunting industry or my regular work, the naysayers or trolls, but instead on people who live with passion and love life. I look you in the eye with respect and connection because our journey is a shared one and, for whatever reason, your life has given my life a sense of purpose.

That said, I hope you find your passion, your true passion in life. Some people never do, and they die without ever really knowing what lay dormant inside of their soul. That's where I feel lucky; I found something that motivates me.

RELENTLESS

Every epic adventure concludes with a return home. Rocky lasts in the ring with Apollo Creed; and while he doesn't win the fight, he wins back his confidence and Adrian's love. Luke Skywalker and Han Solo receive medals for helping the Rebellion blow up the Death Star in *Star Wars*. Maximus defeats Commodus in *Gladiator* but dies in the process, being reunited with his family in the afterlife. The hero always comes home, but he is a different person from when he first left. The journey has changed him. He's wiser and tougher, and he carries a few more scars.

We all love stories. Dramatic and epic tales of heroes and their journeys. Especially when they're about real people. But I like what Joe Rogan said best.

"I love a success story, but even more than that, I like a dude who fucks his life up and gets his life together again story."

Joe's quote hits home. I've earned some success but not after many F-ups. That's probably the story of most people. People love hearing about the success and the rewards, but they often ignore the decades of work and dismiss the grind. That's one reason I created an instant bond with David Goggins. He too overcame hellish odds, much greater than mine, to get to the mountaintop. We still love the grind as much as ever.

There's a great line Goggins shares about both our journeys: "It's about what we do with opportunities revoked or presented to us that determines how a story ends."

Our lives can be similar to a bowhunt. Sometimes on a hard hunt, it might all come down to one opportunity that I must take advantage of.

When will your opportunity come? What will it look like?

Hard to say. All you can do is be ready for it.

In some ways, I have come back home. Well, to a home of sorts. It's May 2021, and I'm back in Alaska. It's the first time I've returned to hunt Alaska since the moose hunt with Roy in 2015. Shortly before his death.

I don't think about tomorrow and I usually don't think about yesterday. But today I'm looking back, thinking about Roy.

Memories flood me. I think back on our first out-of-state bowhunt back in 1990. Roy and I drove from our hometown of Marcola to northern California to arrow wild boars and bring bacon back home.

Packing those pigs out of steep canyons by slinging them over our shoulders made us a bloody mess. Picture two young men—just kids—loving

life and beginning to live out their dreams. God only knew what adventures and journeys they were about to take.

We shared over thirty hunts in Alaska, from Kodiak Island to Prince of Wales, to as far north as you can go after moose, caribou, sheep, deer, black bear, grizzly . . . we lived for the biggest, most epic experiences. We lived for the journey, not just the reward. Roy and I didn't go to the movies, bowling, shopping mall, or tavern together like some guys do with their friends. Ours was a friendship forged exclusively during years of hard, remote, challenging bowhunting endeavors. Tests that had us beat down, weakened, questioning our toughness, spirit, and manhood only for us to rise up, endure, and overcome it all many times on the way to against-all-odds success.

People who have shared intense, difficult experiences with others know how fast a bond can form. I've seen one tough mountain hunt turn a regular friendship into a brotherhood. Well, Roy and I experienced hard, challenging hunts together probably 100 times over for almost three decades. The bond we had was powerful.

It hurts the same every time I think about Roy, and I don't know if that's ever going to really change. I miss the hunts, the talks, the gas station junk food on the way to bowhunting in the mountains, and carrying the last load out after all the meat has been hauled off the mountain. I miss him badly as my irreplaceable hunting partner, but as my friend, I'm afraid that's a hole that will never be filled.

I miss you, Big Roy, but I understand your work here was done.

Our greatest successes are the most meaningful because of who we share them with. If someone is important to you and has helped you out along the way, tell them you appreciate them.

That's a good segue into my saying thanks to you. So many people have shared their passions and their pursuits with me, and I've been inspired to hear their stories of victory and failure and personal growth and overcoming. I'm driven by comments from those who have been motivated by something I've said or done.

I'll say it again: With hard work, you can do incredible and amazing things. I'm here because of my consistent work, not my incredible talent. You can achieve greatness. I'm here standing on the sidelines believing in you.

What's cool is you don't need anyone to believe in you. Not even Cam Hanes. You just need to believe in yourself.

A famous bowhunter named Bobby Fromme helped come up with the phrase "Keep Hammering." He's a stud—he owns a pro shop in San Diego called Performance Archers and has killed all twenty-nine big game animals in North America. He used to call me Cam the Hammer. Inspired by that, a gym I trained at in Eugene called Forever Strong put "Keep Hammerin'" on a T-shirt with my name on it for me. I decided I liked it.

As Joe Rogan joked in an impromptu skit we did while on a Utah elk hunt, "It's catchy. I feel like you should make some shirts or something."

"With 'Keep Hammering'?"

"Yeah."

So I guess I'll just go ahead and give Joe all the credit.

There's an incredible quote that inspires the San Antonio Spurs that is a beautiful summary of the "Keep Hammering" mindset. I love the Spurs and their approach to professional basketball. They are always focused on how they do things, not the reward for what they do. They care about the process, not the result. In 2018, NBA star and former Spur George Hill told me about the words of twentieth-century poet Jacob A. Riis that hangs in the Spurs' locker room:

"When nothing seems to help, I go and look at a stonecutter hammering away at his rock perhaps a hundred times without as much as a crack showing in it. Yet at the hundred-and-first blow it will split in two, and I know it was not that blow that did it—but all that had gone before."

George said that keephammering reminded him of what the Spurs coach Gregg Popovich always preached: Work hard, do it right, and you'll earn those just rewards.

I couldn't say it any better, George. Thanks for sharing this quote with me, and now with the rest of the world.

The journey is everything. And as I said at the start of this book, all I'm asking is that you get up and go.

Begin a journey. Take that first step.

I've shared some of those steps in these pages. I look back and clearly remember my first buck, bull, mule deer with a bow, water buffalo, big bear, Cape buffalo, 100-mile run, 200-mile run . . . There was even my first hunt without Roy, the day after he fell.

Without "firsts" there is no progression. As painful as it is sometimes, live, learn, and enjoy the journey. You never know when it's going to end.

That's why you have to start.

This journey as a hunter, you can't shortcut it. You have to learn those tough lessons, you have to know what success is, and you have to fail. And I think a lot of people, they want a shortcut. They want to get to the top of the mountain without ever being at the bottom. That slow journey up is what makes it special. It's the reason why I am who I am today.

Do you have a passion? Have you found your tunnel-visioned driven purpose? If not, then go looking for it. And if you have found it, then cling to it. Inspiration is a beautiful and powerful thing to discover. When you find something that lights you up, hold on to it. You might just need it when the dark days of life come rolling in. And they will.

Life has a way of squelching dreams.

Anyone else in love with hard work . . . the struggle . . . chasing unrealistic dreams like I'm guilty of? I'm here for you. We can be dream-chasing buddies.

My mindset doesn't cost you anything.

You don't need a break to get it.

It's not about who you know or how rich you are.

Over the years I've seen plenty of people who are jealous when others are successful. They make excuses as to why they themselves haven't experienced similar success.

Truth is, each one of us can attain even the loftiest of goals by simply being relentless, every second, every minute, every day. Keep grinding, working, get knocked down, then get back up, let people talk shit and smile, because if you're focused and driven, no one has the power to stop you. Down the road they will still be talking shit and you'll be reaping the rewards of all your tenacity.

The journey is the reward.

The Greek philosopher Heraclitus said, "No man ever steps in the same river twice, for it's not the same river and he's not the same man."

A river never stops moving. It's always flowing, always changing, just like we are.

I've spent fifty-three years, moving and flowing and changing.

Whatever path you choose, own it, be the best you can be, and don't apologize.

Just keep hammering!

In my heart the legend will live on forever

My entire life I was obsessed with finding the hardest men that walked this planet Earth. I sought them in the most difficult jobs in the military and the endurance events in which I participated. I had no idea I would come across such a savage due to a chance encounter.

I have trained with many of the toughest and hardest men on the planet and only one stands out. That one is Cameron Hanes. Now if any of you know who I am, I am not saying this for a passage in his book, I am saying it because it is truth.

He embodies what it means to push beyond human capabilities on a daily basis. That is what separates him. On a day in and day out basis, he tests and pushes his limits. In doing so, he has inspired millions and continues to do so. As we are pushing 6-minute miles on a 20-mile training run, he is encouraging every runner and cyclist who crosses our path with his famous tagline "Keep Hammering."

His mindset is one where he doesn't just want to be a hunter. He doesn't just want to be a runner. He doesn't just want to lift weights. He wants to do it all at the highest level possible and continually seeks out the best so that he can better himself.

It's very easy to misunderstand this guy. When someone is so driven to be the very best, they can often be misunderstood because he makes you look at yourself. Because of how hard he works, he forces you to look at yourself to see what you could be doing. He exhausts himself on a daily basis to show others what is possible.

Cameron is an old school leader who doesn't lead by running his mouth, he leads by example. That is very obvious by how amazing his family is. His children exemplify a work ethic and discipline that is rare these days all of which was learned by watching their father extract every last bit of his soul to be his best.

I used to think I was out here alone, never thinking someone was out here working as hard as I was. I now know there is another.

When I get with Cameron Hanes, we don't talk about it, but I know that we are both trying to break the other one. In January 2021, Cameron spot-checked me. If you don't know what a spot-check is, it is basically when a buddy of yours calls you out of nowhere and tells you he/she is coming into town. The idea is to catch you slipping. Being that I know that there is a Cameron Hanes out there that exists and has my number, I can't ever slip.

So when Cam called me and said he was coming to town and wanted to know if I wanted to go for an "easy, light run" and lift some weights, I knew exactly what that meant. It meant a long hard run and a brutal ass weight workout. Me knowing that, it was my time to break Cam, so I thought. See he was coming to my home turf. I knew the course, I knew the distance, all of the variables as well as the pace. So we met up at the M Hotel in Las Vegas and I took him on one of my standard runs. My girl was with me so I think he thought that we would just be going out for an easy one. Little did he know, my girl can also throw down.

We get about 7 miles into the run and my girlfriend was only going to do 14 miles so she turned around and we continued on. This is where my plan was going to come into effect. The idea was to take Cameron out three more miles to give us 10 miles before turning around.

You can't feel the downhill as you head out which I know but Cam doesn't. My idea was to try to break him going back the 10 miles going uphill. At the turnaround, I started at a 6:30/mile pace. I could tell the uphill was hurting him as he started to fade ever so slightly off my left shoulder and he stopped talking. We had nine miles to go, all of it was uphill. As we got to mile 15, I could tell he was extremely tired and so was I. My plan of trying to break Cameron Hanes was starting to fall apart. The more I tried to break him, the better he started to run. Before I knew it, Cam was no longer a step behind, he was now a step in front. I was now being paced by Cameron. The tables had turned.

– David Goggins
June 2021

AFTERWORD

I'm an example of how your passion can change your life, even if that passion is something as obscure as bowhunting.

I went from an insecure, 15-year-old pictured here standing by the meat pole at hunting camp after killing my first deer to speaking to huge groups of people and impacting many daily.

I went from driving a wrecked Toyota 2-wheel-drive pick-up to go hunting to flying private to out-of-states hunts.

My life changed not because I'm special but because I chased my passion and wouldn't accept defeat. I became obsessed and realized that if not obsessed, I'd be average. Bowhunting changed my life. Your passion, whatever that may be, can change yours

"You don't need
anyone's permission
to chase your dreams."